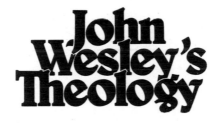

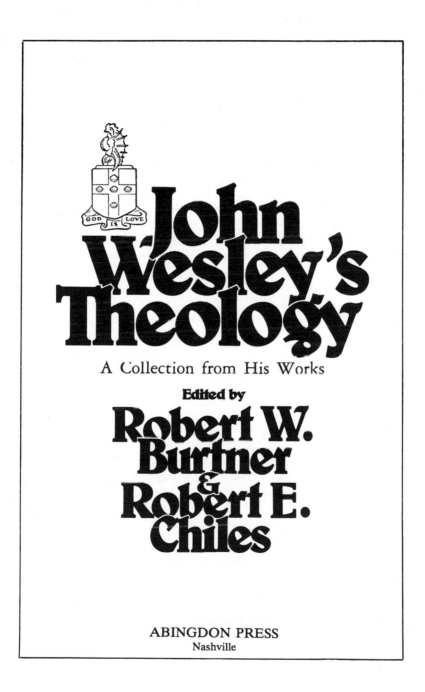

John Wesley's Theology

A Collection from His Works

Edited by

Robert W. Burtner
&
Robert E. Chiles

ABINGDON PRESS
Nashville

JOHN WESLEY'S THEOLOGY: A COLLECTION FROM HIS WORKS

Library of Congress Cataloging in Publication Data

WESLEY, JOHN, 1703-1791
    John Wesley's theology.
    Originally published: A compend of Wesley's theology.
    Nashville: Abingdon Press, [1954]
    Bibliography: p.
    Includes indexes.
    1. Theology, Doctrinal.   2. Methodist Church—
Doctrinal and controversial works.   I. Burtner, Robert Wallace.
II. Chiles, Robert Eugene.   III. Title.
BX8217.W54B82   1982   230'.7   82-6735   AACR2

ISBN 0-687-20529-8 (pbk.)

MANUFACTURED BY THE PARTHENON PRESS AT
NASHVILLE, TENNESSEE, UNITED STATES OF AMERICA

In Memory of
DAVID C. SHIPLEY
Christian Scholar, Teacher, and Friend

PREFACE

JOHN WESLEY is widely recognized as the leader of a great eighteenth-century religious revival and as a man of unflagging zeal and varied and unusual talents. This book grew out of a conviction that his greatness must be measured also in the field of theology. When it first appeared thirty years ago, this assertion seemed a bit strange. In the intervening years, however, Wesley's theology has received considerable attention in publications, classrooms, and local congregations. We are pleased that our volume is again available to this continuing conversation.

Our earlier text is reprinted without change. The original selections and arrangements, of course, were unavoidably arbitrary; changes made now would be inescapably arbitrary as well. Further, it is our conviction that Wesley's words have not lost their power and that, despite the shortcomings of our collection, it will much more assist than impede the study of his theology.

The systematic arrangement of select passages from his theological writings can assist those studying Wesley's theology in several ways. The first is based on the fact that Wesley's collected works total well over thirty volumes in the editions used here and that some of these are not easily available or are out of print. Again, the number and variety of these different publications form a bulk of material that is not easily surmountable. To some extent a compend meets these difficulties by making available in a single volume some of the valuable theological writings of the numerous volumes and by providing references to more. Further, by its very nature this collection is an index to Wesley's thought, as the reference to each passage makes readily accessible the context from which it was taken. The subject index is an additional guide providing cross references for material within the book.

Wesley was not a systematic theologian as, for example, was Calvin. In his busy life he rarely pursued his study of a doctrine long enough to work all the subtle details into adequate systematic form. In this respect he is not unlike Luther. Perhaps the most rewarding sources of Wesley's theology are his sermons, which were preached to the plainest of folk. Though they are logical and succinct and carry doctrinal analysis to surprising lengths, their nature precludes their being short theological treatises. This work seeks to place in small compass, systematically formulated, the central doctrines of Wesley's thought. This systematic formulation, though not present in explicit detail, is nevertheless everywhere presupposed in his writings.

Such an undertaking involves several difficulties. The material used must be extracted in most cases from its context. This demands somewhat arbitrary decisions as to the beginning and ending of passages, and necessitates the elimination of very helpful commentary. Again, problems continually arise concerning the arrangement and division of doctrines and the apportionment of space, to say nothing of the problem of gaining much needed continuity. Further, any attempt to consider separately various aspects of doctrine tends to be unnatural, as can be seen with respect to Wesley's doctrine of humanity, for example. It is hoped that recognition of these difficulties and certain steps of precaution may give positive worth to this book. If it succeeds in selecting and arranging the best of Wesley's thought in such fashion that it will reach a larger circle of readers, it will have achieved its purpose.

All of Wesley's major collected writings have been surveyed in an effort to produce a work representative of his total theology. In general we have aimed at breadth of selection, representing subjects under consideration from a variety of sources. In a further effort to make the selections representative, secondary works on Wesley's thought have been examined. Their outlines of his theology have been studied and frequently referred to in the organization of the selections. In addition, the material quoted in these secondary sources has been checked in the original and examined for possible inclusion. Consequently, more material has been extracted, considered, and finally excluded than now makes up the volume.

Nearly all the selections have come from writings after the Aldersgate experience of 1738. Special emphasis has been placed also on the doctrinal standards of historic Methodism. Wesley drew up and printed in the *Minutes* of the conference of 1763 (and continued to reprint) a Model Deed that was to be followed in matters pertaining to the ownership and use of Methodist chapels. Among other things it provided that the

> trustees of the said premises shall permit such persons as shall be appointed at the yearly conference of the people called *Methodists* . . . and no others, to have and to enjoy the said premises, for the purpose aforesaid: Provided always, that the persons preach no other doctrine than is contained in Mr. Wesley's "Notes upon the New Testament," and four volumes of "Sermons." (*Works:* VIII, 330-31)

Subsequent publication of additional sermons and the rearrangement of sermons in later editions led to uncertainty as to the exact sermons referred to in the Model Deed. However, this uncertainty has been resolved in favor of the view that those intended were the forty-four sermons in the first four volumes of the eight-volume edition of Wesley's *Sermons*, published in 1787–88. These and the disputed sermons, together with a history of the dispute, are contained in Sugden's edition of the *Standard Sermons*. With the *Notes* these form the doctrinal standards appointed by Wesley and enjoined upon his followers in the Model Deed. Therefore, in keeping with Wesley's express wish, materials from the "standards" have been given priority and have been regarded as normative in the compilation and arrangement of this collection.

In the arrangement of the book simplicity, readability, and conformity with Wesley's own disposition and desire have been the criteria. We have made every effort to permit Wesley to speak for himself. Where they occur, contradictions and omissions have been permitted to stand. We have tried not to distort Wesley by forcing an appearance of exactness and comprehensiveness where in fact such does not exist. It may be believed that a man who made "extracts from and abridgments of the choicest pieces of Practical Divinity which have been published in the English tongue" in his *Christian Library* would approve this venture designed to initiate and stimulate acquaintance with theological ideas he thought of greatest worth.

Chapter introductions give some indication of the peculiarities and the problems of each particular theme and suggest its relationship to the whole of Wesley's theology. Chapter bibliographies for each topic refer to additional material in Wesley's writings. The verses at the close of each chapter illustrating the various doctrines are taken, as nearly as can be determined, from the poetic writings of John, rather than Charles, Wesley. An annotated bibliography of secondary works indicates further avenues for investigation.[1]

[1]From among some of the many volumes on Wesley's theology published since this bibliography was compiled, a few might well be noted. Ole E. Borgen's *John Wesley on the Sacraments* (Nashville: Abingdon Press, 1972) is a careful description of the meaning and importance of baptism and the Lord's Supper in Wesley. John Deschner's *Wesley's Christology* (Dallas: Southern Methodist University Press, 1960) based on Wesley's *Notes* adds new dimensions to the place and importance of Wesley's Christology. In *Christianity According to the Wesleys* (London: The Epworth Press, 1956) Franz Hildebrandt demonstrates the essential continuity between Reformation and Wesleyan theology with emphasis on the Wesleyan hymns. Albert Outler's *John Wesley* (New York: Oxford University Press, 1964), a contribution to A Library of Protestant Thought, reproduces a number of key Wesleyan writings together with illuminating commentary and careful notes. Two smaller works by Outler, *Evangelism in the Wesleyan Spirit* and *Theology in the Wesleyan Spirit* (Nashville: Tidings, 1971 and 1975) present insightful and accessible interpretations. Martin Schmidt has written a two-volume

To facilitate reading we have taken the liberty of inserting or omitting words or phrases at the beginning of passages where such is required for more exact meanings. In all cases the paragraph numbering has been taken out of the text but retained in the identifying reference. These references occur in somewhat abbreviated form. Roman numerals indicate the part, and Arabic numerals the section, of the work cited. Within parentheses exact volume and page numbers are given for the editions that have been used. Sermon entries have an "S" for Sugden's edition of the *Standard Sermons,* and "J" for Jackson's listing of the remaining sermons. The editions quoted are those most widely accepted and used. They are listed in the bibliography with the general nature of their contents noted. References throughout the book are to these editions. In most instances, however, the information given is sufficient to locate passages in any complete edition.

The development of this book had the benefit of a number of suggestions from Wesley scholars and students. The late Edwin Lewis read the manuscript and offered helpful suggestions. Albert C. Outler and the late Arthur W. Nagler, along with several former faculty members at both Garrett-Evangelical Theological Seminary and Union Theological Seminary (New York), were most gracious in reading and commenting on various parts of the manuscript. Bishops G. Bromley Oxnam, Gerald Kennedy, and Hazen G. Werner—all of whom were active during the compilation of the book—lent encouragement along the way to publication. To all these persons we are grateful.

To David C. Shipley, however, more than to any other person, this work owes its origin and reality. It was under his inspiration that the work was conceived and begun; his continuing concern and counsel helped carry it through to completion. We are indebted to him beyond measure. He was as generous with us as with a host of students in the course of his unstinting life.

ROBERT W. BURTNER
ROBERT E. CHILES
Aldersgate, 1982

---

theological biography, *John Wesley* (Nashville: Abingdon Press, 1962), relating Wesley's life to his theological convictions. Lycurgus M. Starkey, Jr., helpfully explicates a central Wesleyan doctrine in *The Work of the Holy Spirit: A Study in Wesleyan Theology* (Nashville: Abingdon Press, 1962). Colin Williams' *John Wesley's Theology Today* (Nashville: Abingdon Press, 1960) is a balanced, judicious presentation that relates Wesleyan theology to ecumenical interests. Finally, the new edition of Wesley's collected works under the editorial direction of Frank Baker has begun to appear and provides the original Wesleyan material together with valuable historical and interpretive notes.

CONTENTS

11

CONTENTS

CONTENTS

I

RELIGIOUS
KNOWLEDGE
AND
AUTHORITY

I. RELIGIOUS KNOWLEDGE AND AUTHORITY

THE BIBLE is Wesley's constant and ultimate source of knowledge and authority. His credo, "I am a man of one Book," is manifest throughout his sermons and works. In general Wesley is free from a binding literalism, as his Notes suggest, yet he frequently makes polemic statements in his effort to establish the infallibility of the Bible. Vigorously denying that Methodists renounce the criterion of reason, Wesley prescribes for all the same mental discipline which characterizes his own life. His distinctive doctrine of religious experience is used as a further testing ground for religious ideas. It consists of two elements: a direct inner experience of God's love, and an appeal to the community of believers for the confirmation of conduct and doctrine. Essentially this may be called an empirical theology; there is nothing abstract or theoretical about it. "Scripture, reason, and experience"—Wesley repeatedly cites these three in confirmation of his religious judgments. Two further sources of religious knowledge and authority are indicated: Christian tradition, which reflects Wesley's background in the Church of England and includes the writings of the early church fathers, the ecumenical creeds, and the Anglican Book of Common Prayer; and the natural creation, which suggests his deep interest in the physical world.

1. The Bible

To candid, reasonable men, I am not afraid to lay open what have been the inmost thoughts of my heart. I have thought, I am a creature of a day, passing through life as an arrow through the air. I am a spirit come from God, and returning to God: just hovering over the great gulf; till, a few moments hence, I am no more seen; I drop into an unchangeable eternity! I want to know one thing—the way to heaven; how to land safe on that happy shore. God Himself has condescended to teach the way; for this very end He came from heaven. He hath written it down in a book. O give me that book! At any price, give me the book of God! I have it: here is knowledge enough for me. Let me be *homo unius libri*. Here then I am, far from the busy ways of men. I sit down alone: only God is here. In His presence I open, I read His book; for this end, to find the way to heaven. Is there a doubt concerning the meaning of what I read? Does anything appear dark or intricate? I lift up my heart to the Father of Lights: "Lord, is it not Thy word, 'If any man lack wisdom, let him ask of God'? Thou 'givest liberally, and upbraidest not.' Thou hast said, 'If any be willing to do Thy will, he shall know.' I am willing to do, let me know, Thy will." I then search after and consider parallel passages of Scripture, "comparing spiritual things with spiritual." I meditate thereon with all the attention and earnestness of which my mind is capable. If any doubt still remains, I consult those who are experienced in the things of God; and then the writings whereby, being dead, they yet speak. And what I thus learn, that I teach.

Sermons: "Preface to the Sermons," 5 (S, I, 31-32).

JW

Concerning the Scriptures in general, it may be observed, the word of the living God, which directed the first patriarchs also, was, in the time of *Moses,* committed to writing. To this were added, in several succeeding generations, the inspired writings of the other prophets. Afterward, what the Son of God preached, and the Holy Ghost spake by the apostles, the apostles and evangelists wrote.—This is what we now style the *Holy Scripture:* this is that *word of God which remaineth for ever:* of which, though *heaven and earth pass away, one jot or tittle shall not pass away.* The Scripture therefore of the *Old and New Testament,* is a most solid and precious system of divine truth. Every part thereof is worthy of God; and all together are one entire body, wherein is no defect, no excess. It is the fountain of heavenly wisdom, which they who are able to taste, prefer to all writings of men, however wise, or learned, or holy.

An exact knowledge of the truth was accompanied in the inspired writers with an exactly regular series of arguments, a precise expression of their meaning, and a genuine vigour of suitable affections. The chain of argument in each book is briefly exhibited in the table prefixed to it, which contains also the sum thereof, and may be of more use than prefixing the argument to each chapter; the division of the *New Testament* into chapters having been made in the dark ages, and very incorrectly; often separating things that are closely joined, and joining those that are entirely distinct from each other.

In the language of the Sacred Writings, we may observe the utmost depth, together with the utmost ease. All the elegancies of human composures sink into nothing before it: God speaks not as man, but as God. His thoughts are very deep: and thence his words are of inexhaustible virtue. And the language of his messengers also is exact in the highest degree: for the words which were given them, accurately answered the impression made upon their minds: and hence *Luther* says, "Divinity is nothing but a grammar of the language of the Holy Ghost." To understand this thoroughly, we should observe the *emphasis* which lies on every word; the holy *affections* expressed thereby, and the *tempers* shown by every writer. But how little are these, the latter especially, regarded? Though they are wonderfully diffused through the whole *New Testament,* and are in truth a continued commendation of him who acts, or speaks, or writes.

Notes: "Preface," 10-12 (v-vi).

JW

There are four grand and powerful arguments which strongly induce us to believe that the Bible must be from God, viz., miracles, prophecies, the goodness of the doctrine, and the moral character of the penmen. All the miracles flow from divine power; all the prophecies, from divine understanding; the goodness of the doctrine, from divine goodness; and the moral character of the penmen, from divine holiness.

Thus Christianity is built upon four grand pillars, viz., the power, understanding, goodness, and holiness of God. Divine power is the source of all the miracles; divine understanding, of all the prophecies; divine goodness, of the goodness of the doctrine; and divine holiness, of the moral character of the penmen.

I beg leave to propose a short, clear, and strong argument to prove the divine inspiration of the holy Scriptures.

The Bible must be the invention either of good men or angels, bad men or devils, or of God.

1. It could not be the invention of good men or angels; for they neither would nor could make a book, and tell lies all the time they were writing it, saying, "Thus saith the Lord," when it was their own invention.

2. It could not be the invention of bad men or devils; for they would not make a book which commands all duty, forbids all sin, and condemns their souls to hell to all eternity.

3. Therefore, I draw this conclusion, that the Bible must be given by divine inspiration.

Works: "A Clear and Concise Demonstration of the Divine Inspiration of the Holy Scriptures" (XI, 478-79).

JW

The general rule of interpreting Scripture is this: the literal sense of every text is to be taken, if it be not contrary to some other texts; but in that case the obscure text is to be interpreted by those which speak more plainly. If any desires you to walk faster than your strength will allow, you have no leave from God to comply with it. If any desires you to go farther when you are already tired, you must desire him either to let you ride or to go on foot with you.

Letters: "To Samuel Furly" (III, 129).

JW

My ground is the Bible. Yea, I am a Bible-bigot. I follow it in all things, both great and small.

Journal: Thur. 5 June, 1766 (V, 169).

In matters of religion I regard no writings but the inspired. Tauler, Behmen, and an whole army of Mystic authors are with me nothing to St. Paul. In every point I appeal "to the law and the testimony," and value no authority but this.

At a time when I was in great danger of not valuing this authority enough, you made that important observation: "I see where your mistake lies. You would have a philosophical religion; but there can be no such thing. Religion is the most plain, simple thing in the world. It is only, 'We love Him because He first loved us.' So far as you add philosophy to religion, just so far you spoil it." This remark I have never forgotten since; and I trust in God I never shall.

Letters: "To the Reverand Mr. Law" (III, 332).

The Christian rule of right and wrong is the Word of God, the writings of the Old and New Testament; all that the prophets and "holy men of old" wrote "as they were moved by the Holy Ghost"; all that Scripture which was "given by inspiration of God," and which is indeed "profitable for doctrine," or teaching the whole will of God; "for reproof" of what is contrary thereto; for "correction" of error; and "for instruction," or training us up, "in righteousness" (2 Tim. iii. 16).

This is a lantern unto a Christian's feet, and a light in all his paths. This alone he receives as his rule of right or wrong, of whatever is really good or evil. He esteems nothing good, but what is here enjoined, either directly or by plain consequence; he accounts nothing evil but what is here forbidden, either in terms, or by undeniable inference. Whatever the Scripture neither forbids nor enjoins, either directly or by plain consequence, he believes to be of an indifferent nature; to be in itself neither good nor evil; this being the whole and sole outward rule whereby his conscience is to be directed in all things.

Sermons: "The Witness of Our Own Spirit," 6 (S, I, 225-26).

All Scripture is inspired of God—The Spirit of God, not only once inspired those who wrote it, but continually inspires, supernaturally assists those that read it with earnest prayer. Hence it is so profitable for doctrine, for instruction of the ignorant, for the reproof or conviction of them that are in error or sin; for the correction or amendment of whatever is amiss, and for instructing or training up the children of God in all righteousness.

Notes: II Timothy 3:16.

JW

This is the way to understand the things of God: "Meditate thereon day and night"; so shall you attain the best knowledge, even to "know the only true God, and Jesus Christ whom he hath sent." And this knowledge will lead you "to love him, because he hath first loved us"; yea, "to love the Lord your God with all your heart, and with all your soul, and with all your mind, and with all your strength." Will there not then be all "that mind in you which was also in Christ Jesus"? And in consequence of this, while you joyfully experience all the holy tempers described in this book, you will likewise be outwardly "holy as He that hath called you is holy, in all manner of conversation."

If you desire to read the Scriptures in such a manner as may most effectually answer this end, would it not be advisable, (1) To set apart a little time, if you can, every morning and evening for that purpose? (2) At each time, if you have leisure, to read a chapter out of the Old, and one out of the New Testament; if you cannot do this, to take a single chapter, or a part of one? (3) To read this with a single eye, to know the whole will of God, and a fixed resolution to do it? In order to know his will, you should, (4) Have a constant eye to the analogy of faith, the connexion and harmony there is between those grand, fundamental doctrines, original sin, justification by faith, the new birth, inward and outward holiness: (5) Serious and earnest prayer should be constantly used before we consult the oracles of God; seeing "Scripture can only be understood through the same Spirit whereby it was given." Our reading should likewise be closed with prayer, that what we read may be written in our hearts: (6) It might also be of use, if, while we read, we were frequently to pause, and examine ourselves by what we read, both with regard to our hearts and lives. This would furnish us with matter of praise, where we found God had enabled us to conform to his blessed will, and matter of humiliation and prayer, where we were conscious of having fallen short. And whatever light you then receive should be used to the uttermost, and that immediately. Let there be no delay. Whatever you resolve, begin to execute the first moment you can. So shall you find this word to be indeed the power of God unto present and eternal salvation.

Works: "Preface to Explanatory Notes upon the Old Testament," 17-18 (XIV, 267-68).

2. *Revelation and Reason*

As to Divine information or revelation, reason, knowing it to be Divine, is already convinced that it exceeds all human certainty. The only thing, therefore, which is to be convinced of here, is,

That the revelation is divine, or that the scripture is of Divine authority. In order to this, we may observe,

First, that, as God has made men the immediate instruments of all those revelations, so evangelical faith must be partly founded on human testimony. By men were both the Old and New Testament wrote; and if we consider them abstracted from their Divine authority, they must be allowed to be of equal credibility, at least, with all other ancient writings. Though we should suppose them to be upon the foot of mere human testimony, yet would our knowledge of them be, at least, of equal certainty, with that founded on any profane history. Now, if to this human, we add such Divine testimony, as cannot be pretended for any other writings in the world, as the miracles of Christ and his apostles: the concurrent completion of all the prophecies, from the beginning of the world, in him alone; the scriptures being the only book in the world, that gives us any account of the whole series of God's dispensations towards man, from the creation for four thousand years; the great exaltation of natural religion, visible in every part of it; and, lastly, the providential care so manifest in every age, for transmitting down several books, written at such great distances of time one from another, and all of them from us; their being at this day so void of any material error, that in the infinite various readings, which have been carefully collected, there cannot be found one contrariety in any fundamental point of faith or practice: if these things, I say, are thoroughly considered, they give the scriptures such a certainty, as no writing merely human can have, and are the greatest evidence for the truth of them which they are capable of receiving, with a continued, daily repetition of miracles. We may observe,

Secondly, that, as God has made men the immediate instruments of all his revelations, so he hath condescended to make use of human language, as well as of our natural ideas and conceptions, for the clear and easy representation of things supernatural, and otherwise incomprehensible. . . .

Nothing therefore is more absurd, than the objections of unbelievers against the Christian mysteries, as unintelligible; since Christianity requires our assent to nothing, but what is plain and intelligible in every proposition. Let every man first have a full conviction of the truth of each proposition in the gospel, as far only as it is plain and intelligible, and let him believe as far as he understands. Let him firmly believe, there is but one God, the object of any Divine worship whatever; and think and speak of him under that plain, scriptural distinction, of Father, Son, and Holy Ghost; leaving the incomprehensible nature of that union and distinction, to the great Author of our faith himself. Let him believe Christ to be the only begotten Son of God, in the obvious import of these words, and leave the manner of that inconceivable generation to the veracity of God. Let him believe, that Christ did as truly make an atonement to God for us, as one man atones for another to a third person; and leave the unintelligible part of that Divine operation, for the subject of future praise and contemplation. Let men, I say, believe as far as they thus clearly understand, without perplexing themselves or others with what is incomprehensible; and then they fulfil the whole purpose of God in all his revelations.

A Compendium of Natural Philosophy (II, 447-49).

JW

The Son of God begins his work in man by enabling us to believe in him. He both opens and enlightens the eyes of our understanding. Out of darkness he commands light to shine, and takes away the veil which the "god of this world" had spread over our hearts. And we then see not by a chain of *reasoning,* but by a kind of *intuition,* by a direct view, that "God was in Christ reconciling the world to himself, not imputing to them their former trespasses"; not imputing them to me.

Sermons: "The End of Christ's Coming," III, 1 (J, VI, 274-75).

JW

We see, when God opens our eyes, that we were before ἄθεοι ἐν τῷ κόσμῳ—*without God,* or rather, *Atheists in the world.* We had, by nature, no knowledge of God, no acquaintance with Him. It is true, as soon as we came to the use of reason, we learned "the invisible things of God, even His eternal power and Godhead, from the things that are made." From the things that are seen we inferred the existence of an eternal, powerful Being, that is not seen. But still, although we acknowledged His being, we had no acquaintance with Him. As we know there is an Emperor of China, whom yet we do not know; so we knew there was a King of all the earth, yet we knew Him not. Indeed we could not by any of our natural faculties. By none of these could we attain the knowledge of God. We could no more perceive Him by our natural understanding, than we could see Him with our eyes. For "no one knoweth the Father but the Son, and he to whom the Son willeth to reveal Him. And no one knoweth the Son but the Father, and he to whom the Father revealeth Him."

Sermons: "Original Sin," II, 3 (S, II, 216).

The more I converse with this people the more I am amazed. That God hath wrought a great work among them is manifest; and yet the main of them, believers and unbelievers, are not able to give a rational account of the plainest principles of religion. It is plain God begins His work at the heart; then "the inspiration of the Highest giveth understanding."

Journal: "Mon. 22 May 1749" (III, 401).

JW

You go on: "It is a fundamental principle in the Methodist school that all who come into it must renounce their reason." Sir, are you awake? Unless you are talking in your sleep, how can you utter so gross an untruth? It is a fundamental principle with us that to renounce reason is to renounce religion, that religion and reason go hand in hand, and that all irrational religion is false religion.

Letters: "To Dr. Rutherforth" (V, 364).

JW

The desire of knowledge is an universal principle in man, fixed in his inmost nature. It is not variable, but constant in every rational creature, unless while it is suspended by some stronger desire. And it is insatiable: "The eye is not satisfied with seeing, nor the ear with hearing"; neither the mind with any degree of knowledge which can be conveyed into it. And it is planted in every human soul for excellent purposes. It is intended to hinder our taking up our rest in anything here below; to raise our thoughts to higher and higher objects, more and more worthy of our consideration, till we ascend to the source of all knowledge and all excellence, the all-wise and all-gracious Creator.

But although our desire of knowledge has no bounds, yet our knowledge itself has. It is, indeed, confined within very narrow bounds; abundantly narrower than common people imagine, or men of learning are willing to acknowledge: A strong intimation, (since the great Creator doeth nothing in vain,) that there will be some future state of being, wherein that now insatiable desire will be satisfied, and there will be no longer so immense a distance between the appetite and the object of it.

The present knowledge of man is exactly adapted to his present wants. It is sufficient to warn us of, and to preserve us from, most of the evils to which we are now exposed; and to procure us whatever is necessary for us in this our infant state of existence. We know enough of the nature and sensible qualities of the things that are round about us, so far as they are subservient to the health and strength of our bodies; we know how to procure and prepare our food; we know what raiment is fit to cover us; we know how to build our houses, and to furnish them with all necessaries and conveniences; we know just as much as is conducive to our living comfortably in this world: But of innumerable things above, below, and round about us, we know little more than that they exist. And in this our deep ignorance is seen the goodness as well as the wisdom of God, in cutting short his knowledge on every side, on purpose to "hide pride from man."

Therefore it is, that by the very constitution of their nature, the wisest of men "know" but "in part." And how amazingly small a part do they know, either of the Creator, or of his works! This is a very needful, but a very unpleasing theme; for "vain man would be wise." Let us reflect upon it for awhile. And may the God of wisdom and love open our eyes to discern our own ignorance!

Sermons: "The Imperfection of Human Knowledge," Introduction, 1-4 (J, VI, 337-38).

JW

Let reason do all that reason can: Employ it as far as it will go. But, at the same time, acknowledge it is utterly incapable of giving either faith, or hope, or love; and, consequently, of producing either real virtue, or substantial happiness. Expect these from a higher source, even from the Father of the spirits of all flesh. Seek and receive them, not as your own acquisition; but as the gift of God. Lift up your hearts to Him who "giveth to all men liberally, and unbraideth not." He alone can give that faith which is "the evidence" and conviction "of things not seen." He alone can "beget you unto a lively hope" of an inheritance eternal in the heavens; and He alone can "shed his love abroad in your heart by the Holy Ghost given unto you."

Sermons: "The Case of Reason Impartially Considered," II, 10 (J, VI, 360).

JW

Is it not reason (assisted by the Holy Ghost) which enables us to understand what the Holy Scriptures declare concerning the being and attributes of God?—concerning his eternity and immensity; his power, wisdom, and holiness? It is by reason that God enables us in some measure to comprehend his method of dealing with the children of men; the nature of his various dispensations, of the old and new covenant, of the law and the gospel. It is by this we understand (his Spirit opening and enlightening the eyes of our understanding) what that repentance is, not to be repented of; what is that faith whereby we are saved; what is the nature and the condition of justification; what are the immediate and what the subsequent fruits of it. By reason we learn what is that new birth, without which we cannot enter into the kingdom of heaven; and what that holiness is without which no man shall see the Lord. By the due use of reason we come to know what are the tempers implied in inward holiness; and what it is to be outwardly holy,—holy in all manner of conversation: In other words, what is the mind that was in Christ; and what it is to walk as Christ walked.

Sermons: "The Case of Reason Impartially Considered," I, 6 (J, VI, 354-55).

3. Religious Experience

How does it appear, that we do love God and our neighbour, and that we keep His commandments? Observe, that the meaning of the question is, How does it appear to *ourselves,* and not to *others?* I would ask him, then, that proposes this question, How does it appear to you, that you are alive, and that you are now in ease, and not in pain? Are you not immediately conscious of it? By the same immediate consciousness, you will know if your soul is alive to God; if you are saved from the pain of proud wrath, and have the ease of a meek and quiet spirit. By the same means you cannot but perceive if you love, rejoice, and delight in God. By the same you must be directly assured if you love your neighbour as yourself; if you are kindly affectioned to all mankind, and full of gentleness and long-suffering. And with regard to the outward mark of the children of God, which is, according to St. John, the keeping His commandments, you undoubtedly know in your own breast, if, by the grace of God, it belongs to you. Your conscience informs you from day to day, if you do not take the name of God within your lips, unless with seriousness and devotion, with reverence and godly fear; if you remember the Sabbath-day to keep it holy; if you honour your father and mother; if you do to all as you would they should do unto you; if you possess your body in santification and honour; and if, whether you eat or drink, you are temperate therein, and do all to the glory of God.

Now this is properly the testimony of our own spirit; even the testimony of our own conscience, that God hath given us to be holy of heart, and holy in outward conversation. It is a consciousness of our having received, in and by the Spirit of adoption, the tempers mentioned in the Word of God, as belonging to His adopted children; even a loving heart toward God, and toward all mankind; hanging with child-like confidence on God our Father, desiring nothing but Him, casting all our care upon Him, and embracing every child of man with earnest, tender affection, [so as to be ready to lay down our life for our brother, as Christ laid down His life for us,—] a consciousness that we are inwardly conformed, by the Spirit of God, to the image of His Son, and that we walk before Him in justice, mercy, and truth, doing the things which are pleasing in His sight.

But what is that testimony of God's Spirit, which is superadded to, and conjoined with, this? How does He "bear witness with our spirit that we are children of God"? It is hard to find words in the language of men to explain "the deep things of God." Indeed, there are none that will adequately express what the children of God experience. But perhaps one might say (desiring any who are taught of God to correct, to soften, or strengthen the expression), the testimony of the

Spirit is an inward impression on the soul, whereby the Spirit of God directly witnesses to my spirit, that I am a child of God; that Jesus Christ hath loved me, and given Himself for me; and that all my sins are blotted out, and I, even I, am reconciled to God.

Sermons: "The Witness of the Spirit: I," I, 5-7 (S, I, 206-8).

JW

What Christianity (considered as a doctrine) promised is accomplished in my soul. And Christianity, considered as an inward principle, is the completion of all those promises. It is holiness and happiness, the image of God impressed on a created spirit, a fountain of peace and love springing up into everlasting life.

And this I conceive to be the strongest evidence of the truth of Christianity. I do not undervalue traditional evidence. Let it have its place and its due honour. It is highly serviceable in its kind and in its degree. And yet I cannot set it on a level with this.

It is generally supposed that traditional evidence is weakened by length of time, as it must necessarily pass through so many hands in a continued succession of ages. But no length of time can possibly affect the strength of this internal evidence. It is equally strong, equally new, through the course of seventeen hundred years. It passes now, even as it has done from the beginning, directly from God into the believing soul. Do you suppose time will ever dry up this stream? Oh no! It shall never be cut off.

Letters: "To Dr. Conyers Middleton" (II, 383-84).

JW

When Peter Böhler, whom God prepared for me as soon as I came to London, affirmed of true faith in Christ (which is but one) that it had those two fruits inseparably attending it, "dominion over sin and constant peace from a sense of forgiveness," I was quite amazed, and looked upon it as a new gospel. . . . Besides, I well saw no one could, in the nature of things, have such a sense of forgiveness, and not feel it. But I felt it not. If, then, there was no faith without this, all my pretensions to faith dropped at once.

When I met Peter Böhler again, he consented to put the dispute upon the issue which I desired, namely, Scripture and experience. I first consulted the Scripture. But when I set aside the glosses of men, and simply considered the words of God, comparing them together, endeavouring to illustrate the obscure by the plainer passages, I found they all made against me, and was forced to retreat to my last hold, "that experience would never agree with the *literal interpretation* of those scriptures. Nor could I therefore allow it to be true, till I found some living witnesses of it." He replied, he could show me such at any time; if I desired it, the next day. And accordingly the next day he came again with three others, all of whom testified, of their own personal experience, that a true living faith in Christ is inseparable from a sense of pardon for all past and freedom from all present sins. They added with one mouth that this faith was the gift, the free gift of God; and that He would surely bestow it upon every soul who earnestly and perseveringly sought it.

Journal: "May 24, 1738," 11-12 (I, 471-72).

JW

In my way to Luton I read Mr. Hutcheson's *Essay on the Passions.* He is a beautiful writer, but his scheme cannot stand unless the Bible falls. I know both from Scripture, reason, and experience that his picture of man is not drawn from life. It is not true that no man is capable of malice, or delight in giving pain; much less that every man is virtuous, and remains so as long as he lives; nor does the Scripture allow that any action is good which is done without any design to please God.

Journal: "Thur. 17 Dec. 1772" (V, 492).

JW

"But have any that had fallen from sanctifying grace been restored to the blessing they had lost?" This also is a point of experience and we have had the opportunity of repeating our observations during a considerable course of years, and from the one end of the kingdom to the other.

Sermons: "A Call to Backsliders," V, 6 (J, VI, 525).

JW

But it is certain I can trust none of my senses, if I am a mere machine. For I have the testimony of all my outward and all my inward senses, that I am a free agent. If therefore I cannot trust them in this, I can trust them in nothing. Do not tell me there are sun, moon, and stars, or that there are men, beasts, or birds, in the world. I cannot believe one tittle of it, if I cannot believe what I feel in myself, namely, that it depends on me, and no other being, whether I shall now open or shut my eyes, move my head hither and thither, or stretch my hand or my foot. If I am necessitated to do all this, contrary to the whole both of my inward and outward senses, I can believe nothing else, but must necessarily sink into universal scepticism.

Works: "Thoughts upon Necessity," IV, 3 (X, 471-72).

JW

How is a sober Christian to make this inquiry? to know what is the will of God? Not by waiting for supernatural dreams; not by expecting God to reveal it in visions; not by looking for any *particular impressions* or sudden impulses on his mind: no; but by consulting the oracles of God. "To the law and to the testimony!" This is the general method of knowing what is "the holy and acceptable will of God." ...

Suppose, for instance, it were proposed to a reasonable man to marry, or to enter into a new business: in order to know whether this is the will of God, being assured, "It is the will of God concerning me, that I should be as holy and do as much good as I can," he has only to inquire, "In which of these states can I be most holy, and do the most good?" And this is to be determined, partly by reason, and partly

32

by experience. Experience tells him what advantages he has in his present state, either for being or doing good; and reason is to show, what he certainly or probably will have in the state proposed. By comparing these, he is to judge which of the two may most conduce to his being and doing good: and as far as he knows this, so far he is certain what is the will of God.

Sermons: "The Nature of Enthusiasm," 22, 24 (S, II, 96, 98).

4. Christian Tradition

Traditional evidence is of an extremely complicated nature, necessarily including so many and so various considerations, that only men of a strong and clear understanding can be sensible of its full force. On the contrary, how plain and simple is this! and how level to the lowest capacity! Is not this the sum—"One thing I know; I was blind, but now I see"? An argument so plain, that a peasant, a woman, a child may feel all its force.

The traditional evidence of Christianity stands, as it were, a great way off; and therefore, although it speaks loud and clear, yet makes a less lively impression. It gives us an account of what was transacted long ago, in far distant times as well as places. Whereas the inward evidence is intimately present to all persons at all times and in all places. It is nigh thee, in thy mouth, and in thy heart, if thou believest in the Lord Jesus Christ. "This," then, "is the record," this is the evidence, emphatically so called, "that God hath given unto us eternal life; and this life is in His Son."

If, then, it were possible (which I conceive it is not) to shake the traditional evidence of Christianity, still he that has the internal evidence (and every true believer hath the witness or evidence in himself) would stand firm and unshaken. Still he could say to those who were striking at the external evidence, "Beat on the sack of Anaxagoras." But you can no more hurt my evidence of Christianity than the tyrant could hurt the spirit of that wise man.

I have sometimes been almost inclined to believe that the wisdom of God has, in most later ages permitted the external evidence of Christianity to be more or less clogged and encumbered for this very end, that men (of reflection especially) might not altogether rest there, but be constrained to look into themselves also and attend to the light shining in their hearts.

Nay, it seems (if it may be allowed for us to pry so far into the reasons of the divine dispensations) that, particularly in this age, God suffers all kind of objections to be raised against the traditional evidence of Christianity, that men of understanding, though unwilling to give it up, yet, at the same time they defend this evidence, may not rest the whole strength of their cause thereon, but seek a deeper and firmer support for it.

Without this I cannot but doubt, whether they can long maintain their cause; whether, if they do not obey the loud call of God, and lay far more stress than they have hitherto done on this internal evidence of Christianity, they will not one after another give up the external, and (in heart at least) go over to those whom they are now contending with; so that in a century or two the people of England will be fairly divided into real Deists and real Christians.

And I apprehend this would be no loss at all, but rather an advantage to the Christian cause; nay, perhaps it would be the speediest, yea the only effectual, way of bringing all reasonable Deists to be Christians. . . .

Clemens Romanus, Ignatius, Polycarp, Justin Martyr, Irenaeus, Origen, Clemens Alexandrinus, Cyprian; to whom I would add Macarius and Ephraim Syrus.

I allow that some of these had not strong natural sense, that few of them had much learning, and none the assistances which our age enjoys in some respects above all that went before.

Hence I doubt not but whoever will be at the pains of reading over their writings for that poor end will find many mistakes, many weak suppositions, and many ill-drawn conclusions.

And yet I exceedingly reverence them as well as their writings, and esteem them very highly in love. I reverence them, because they were Christians, such Christians as are above described. And I reverence their writings, because they describe true, genuine Christianity, and direct us to the strongest evidence of the Christian doctrine.

Indeed, in addressing the heathens of those times, they intermix other arguments; particularly that drawn from the numerous miracles which were then performed in the Church, which they needed only to open their eyes and see daily wrought in the face of the sun.

But still they never relinquish this: "What the Scripture promises, I enjoy. Come and see what Christianity has done here, and acknowledge it is of God."

I reverence these ancient Christians (with all their failings) the more, because I see so few Christians now; because I read so little in the writings of later times and hear so little of genuine Christianity; and because most of the modern Christians (so called), not content with being wholly ignorant of it, are deeply prejudiced against it, calling it "enthusiasm" and I know not what.

Letters: "To Dr. Conyers Middleton" (II, 384-85, 387-88).

JW

Not only that [the fathers] were not mistaken in their interpretations of the gospel of Christ; but that, in all the necessary parts of it, they were so assisted by the Holy Ghost, as to be scarce capable of mistaking. Consequently, we are to look on their writings, though not of equal authority with the Holy Scriptures, (because neither were the authors of them called in so extraordinary a way to the writing them, nor indued with so large a portion of the blessed Spirit), yet as worthy of a much greater respect than any composures which have been made since; however men have afterwards written with more art, and a greater stock of human learning, than is to be found not only in the following pieces, but even in the New Testament itself.

Indeed the manner in which they are written, the true primitive simplicity which appears in all the parts of them, is no just objection to them, but rather a strong recommendation to all considering men. They knew the excellency of their doctrine, and the importance of the revelations which it made of the future state; and therefore they contented themselves to declare these things in a plain and simple manner; and yet with such efficacy and power as surpassed all the rhetoric in the world.

Works: "Preface to the Epistles of the Apostolical Fathers," 11, 12 (XIV, 240-41).

5. *The Natural Creation*

The world around us is the mighty volume wherein God hath declared himself. Human languages and characters are different in different nations. And those of one nation are not understood by the rest. But the book of nature is written in an universal character, which every man may read in his own language. It consists not of words, but things which picture out the Divine perfections. The firmament every where expanded, with all its starry host, declares the immensity and magnificence, the power and wisdom of its Creator. Thunder, lightning, storms, earthquakes and volcanos, shew the terror of his wrath. Seasonable rains, sunshine and harvest, denote his bounty and goodness, and demonstrate how he opens his hand, and fills all living things with plenteousness. The constantly succeeding generations of plants and animals, imply the eternity of their first cause. Life subsisting in millions of different forms, shews the vast diffusion of this animating power, and death the infinite disproportion between him and every living thing.

Even the actions of animals are an eloquent and a pathetic language. Those that want the help of man, have a thousand engaging ways, which, like the voice of God speaking to his heart, command him to preserve and cherish them. In the mean time, the motions or looks of those which might do him harm, strike him with terror, and warn him, either to fly from or arm himself against them. Thus it is, that every part of nature directs us to nature's God.

A Compendium of Natural Philosophy (I, 313).

In contemplating even the things that surround him, that thought strikes warmly upon [man's] heart—"These are Thy glorious works, Parent of good"; while he takes knowledge of the invisible things of God, even His eternal power and wisdom in the things that are seen —the heavens, the earth, the fowls of the air, the lilies of the field. How much more while, rejoicing in the constant care which He still takes of the work of His own hand, he breaks out in a transport of love and praise, "O Lord our Governor, how excellent are Thy ways in all the earth! Thou that hast set Thy glory above the heavens!" While he, as it were, sees the Lord sitting upon His throne, and ruling all things well; while he observes the general providence of God co-extended with His whole creation, and surveys all the effects of it in the heavens and earth, as a well-pleased spectator; while he sees the wisdom and goodness of His general government descending to every particular, so presiding over the whole universe as over a single person, so watching over every single person as if he were the whole universe; —how does he exult when he reviews the various traces of the Almighty goodness, in what has befallen himself in the several circumstances and changes of his own life! all which he now sees have been allotted to him, and dealt out in number, weight, and measure. With what triumph of soul, in surveying either the general or particular providence of God, does he observe every line pointing out an hereafter, every scene opening into eternity!

Letters: "To Dr. Conyers Middleton" (II, 379).

JW

The whole progress of nature is so gradual, that the entire chasm from a plant to man, is filled up with divers kinds of creatures, rising one above another, by so gentle an ascent, that the transitions from one species to another, are almost insensible. And the intermediate space is so well husbanded, that there is scarce a degree of perfection which does not appear in some. Now since the scale of being advances by such regular steps as high as man, is it not probable, that it still proceeds gradually upwards, through beings of a superior nature? As there is an infinitely greater space between the Supreme Being and man, than between man and the lowest insect.

A Compendium of Natural Philosophy (II, 184).

JW

How is it possible I should know God, unless he make himself known unto me? By analogy or proportion? Very good. But where is that proportion to be found? What proportion does a creature bear to its Creator? What is the proportion between finite and infinite?

I grant, the existence of the creatures demonstratively shows the existence of their Creator. The whole creation speaks that there is a God. But that is not the point in question. I know there is a God. Thus far is clear. But who will show me what that God is? The more I reflect the more convinced I am, that it is not possible for any or all the creatures to take off the veil which is on my heart, that I might discern this unknown God; to draw the curtain back which now hangs between, that I may see Him which is invisible.

This veil of flesh now hides him from my sight; and who is able to make it transparent? so that I may perceive, through this glass, God always before me, till I see him "face to face."

I want to know this great God who filleth heaven and earth; who is above, beneath, and on every side, in all places of his dominion; who just now besets me behind and before, and lays his hand upon me; and yet I am no more acquainted with him, than with one of the inhabitants of Jupiter or Saturn.

O my friend, how will you get one step farther, unless God reveal himself to your soul?

Works: "A Farther Appeal to Men of Reason and Religion: II," III, 21 (VIII, 197-98).

JW

> O that I, like *Timothy,*
>   Might the Holy Scriptures know,
> From mine earliest infancy,

Till for God mature I grow,
Made unto salvation wise,
Ready for the glorious prize.

Jesus, all-redeeming Lord,
Full of truth, and full of grace,
Make me understand Thy word,
Teach me in my youthful days
Wonders in Thy word to see,
Wise through faith which is in Thee.

Open now mine eyes of faith,
Open now the book of God,
Show me here the secret path,
Leading to Thy bless'd abode:
Wisdom from above impart,
Speak the meaning to my heart.

Poetics: "Before Reading the Scriptures," Hymn XXXI (VI, 398 99).

SUPPLEMENTARY REFERENCES

THE BIBLE—*Sermons:* "Preface to the Sermons" (S, I, 29-34); "On God's Vineyard," I, 1-4 (J, VII, 203-4). *Works:* "A Farther Appeal to Men of Reason and Religion" (VIII, 108 ff.); "Popery Calmly Considered" (X, 141 ff.). *Letters:* "To John Newton" (V, 8); "To Dean D" (VII, 250-52). *Journal:* "Wed. 28 Jan. 1741" (II, 419-20); "Mon. 31 Aug. 1758" (IV, 280). *Notes:* "Introduction"; "Introduction to Matthew."

REVELATION AND REASON—*Sermons:* "The Imperfection of Human Knowledge" (J, VI, 337 ff.); "The Case of Reason Impartially Considered" (J, VI, 350 ff.); "On the Discoveries of Faith," 1-12 (J, VII, 231-35); "On Faith," 15-18 (J, VII, 334-35). *Works:* "An Earnest Appeal to Men of Reason and Religion" (VIII, 3 ff.); "Thoughts on a Late Publication" (XIII, 374-75). *Letters:* "To Ann Ford" (IV, 265); "To Mary Bishop" (VI, 205-6). *Notes:* "Hebrews 1:1."

RELIGIOUS EXPERIENCE—*Sermons:* "Original Sin," II, 2 (S, II, 215); "The Witness of the Spirit: II," III, 6 (S, II, 349-50). *Letters:* "To Mrs. Pendarves" (I, 76); "To 'John Smith,'" entire series (II, 74 ff.); "To Brian Bury Collins" (VII, 46-47). *Journal:* "Mon. 12 July 1773" (V, 521).

CHRISTIAN TRADITION—*Works:* "Farther Thoughts on Separation from the Church," 1-2 (XIII, 239); "Preface to the Epistles of the Apostolical Fathers" (XIV,

238 ff.). *Letters:* "To Dr. Conyers Middleton" (II, 328 ff.); "To Richard Tompson (III, 137-38).

THE NATURAL CREATION—*Sermons:* "God's Approbation of His Works" (J, VI, 206 ff.); "The Wisdom of God's Counsels," 1-5 (J, VI, 325-27). *Letters:* "To Miss March" (IV, 90-91). See also *A Survey of the Wisdom of God in the Creation: or A Compendium of Natural Philosophy,* Vols. I, II.

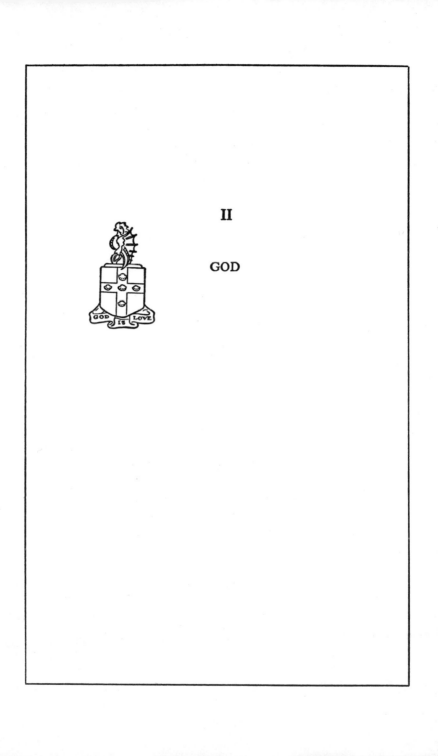

II

GOD

GOD IS LOVE

II. GOD

WESLEY ORIENTS his formulations of the doctrines of God, Christ, and the Holy Spirit about one central theme, the salvation of men's souls. Hence there is little philosophical speculation about the divine nature, while the love of God in saving grace is alluded to countless times. This love is basic to an understanding of the divine life; it is also the high calling of all men who are in Christ. It leads to a complete denial of the rigorous predestinarian doctrines of later scholastic Calvinism. God's love is poured out on all men who will be made whole by its power. Any conception that implicitly or explicitly denies this distorts Christianity. Salvation by grace through faith does not permit views of God's sovereignty and justice which are not consonant with his mercy and love. Thus Wesley attacks election most vehemently on the basis of a conception of God in which love is dominant and a despotic deity unthinkable. Wesley's preaching on the nature and activity of God has particular significance when seen against the prevailing deistic conception of God and his relation to the world. For Wesley, God is a personal being whose activity is manifest in his creation and preservation of the natural order, in his judgment of sinful men, and in his work through Christ for the redemption of the world.

1. God's Attributes

"There are three that bear record in heaven: And these three are one." I believe this *fact* also, (if I may use the expression,) that God is Three and One. But the *manner how* I do not comprehend; and I do not believe it. Now in this, in the *manner,* lies the mystery; and so it may; I have no concern with it: It is no object of my faith: I believe just so much as God has revealed, and no more. But this, the *manner,* he has not revealed; therefore, I believe nothing about it. But would it not be absurd in me to deny the fact, because I do not understand the manner? That is, to reject *what God has revealed,* because I do not comprehend *what he has not revealed.*

Sermons: "On the Trinity," 15 (J, VI, 204).

JW

The Lord of glory—The giving Christ this august title, peculiar to the great Jehovah, plainly shows him to be the supreme God. In like manner the Father is styled *the Father of glory,* (Eph. i, 17.) and the Holy Ghost, *the Spirit of glory,* (I Pet. iv, 14). The application of this title to all the three shows that the Father, Son, and Holy Ghost, are *the God of glory:* as the only true God is called, Psalm xxix. 3. and vii. 2.

Notes: "I Corinthians 2:8."

JW

Who can search out this God to perfection? None of the creatures that he has made. Only some of his attributes he hath been pleased to reveal to us in his word. Hence we learn that God is an eternal Being. "His goings forth are from everlasting," and will continue to everlasting. As he ever was, so he ever will be; as there was no beginning of his existence, so there will be no end. This is universally allowed to be contained in his very name, Jehovah; which the Apostle John accordingly renders, "He that was, and that is, and that is to come." Perhaps it would be as proper to say, "He is from everlasting to everlasting."

Nearly allied to the eternity of God, is his omnipresence. As he exists through infinite duration, so he cannot but exist through infinite space; according to his own question, equivalent to the strongest assertion,—"Do not I fill heaven and earth? saith the Lord"; (heaven and earth, in the Hebrew idiom, implying the whole universe;) which, therefore, according to his own declaration, is filled with his presence.

This one, eternal, omnipresent Being is likewise all-perfect. He has, from eternity to eternity, all the perfections and infinitely more than it ever did or ever can enter into the heart of man to conceive; yea, infinitely more than the angels in heaven can conceive: These perfections we usually term, the attributes of God.

And he is omnipotent, as well as omnipresent; there can be no more bounds to his power, than to his presence. He "hath a mighty arm; strong is his hand, and high is his right hand." He doeth whatsoever pleaseth him, in the heavens, the earth, the sea, and in all deep places. With men we know many things are impossible, but not with God: With him "all things are possible." Whensoever he willeth, to do is present with him.

The omniscience of God is a clear and necessary consequence of his omnipresence. If he is present in every part of the universe, he cannot but know whatever is, or is done there; according to the word of St. James, "Known unto God are all his works," and the works of every creature, "from the beginning" of the world; or rather, as the phrase literally implies, "from eternity." His eyes are not only "over all the earth, beholding the evil and the good"; but likewise over the whole creation, yea, and the paths of uncreated night. Is there any difference between his knowledge and his wisdom? If there be, is not his knowledge the more general term, (at least, according to our weak conceptions,) and his wisdom a particular branch of it; namely, the knowing the end of every thing that exists, and the means of applying it to that end.

Holiness is another of the attributes of the almighty, all-wise God. He is infinitely distant from every touch of evil. He "is light; and in him is no darkness at all." He is a God of unblemished justice and truth; but above all is his mercy. This we may easily learn from that beautiful passage in the thirty-third and fourth chapters of Exodus: "And Moses said, I beseech thee, show me thy glory. And the Lord descended in the cloud, and proclaimed the name of the Lord,—The Lord, The Lord God, merciful and gracious, longsuffering, and abundant in goodness and truth, keeping mercy for thousands, and forgiving iniquity and transgression and sin."

This God is a Spirit; not having such a body, such parts or passions, as men have. It was the opinion both of the ancient Jews and the ancient Christians, that He alone is a pure Spirit, totally separate from all matter; whereas they supposed all other spirits, even the highest angels, even cherubim and seraphim, to dwell in material vehicles, though of an exceeding light and subtile substance. At that point of duration which the infinite wisdom of God saw to be most proper, for reasons which lie hid in the abyss of his own understanding, not to be fathomed by any finite mind, God "called into being all that is"; created the heavens and the earth, together with all that they contain.

Sermons: "The Unity of the Divine Being," 2-8 (J, VII, 265-66).

JW

[The omnipresence of God] is far too vast to be comprehended by the narrow limits of human understanding. We can only say, The great God, the eternal, the almighty Spirit, is as unbounded in his presence, as in his duration and power. In condescension, indeed, to our weak understanding, he is said to dwell in heaven; but, strictly speaking, the heaven of heavens cannot contain him; but he is in every part of his dominion. . . .

If we may dare attempt the illustrating this a little farther: What is the space occupied by a grain of sand, compared to that space which is occupied by the starry heavens? It is as a cipher; it is nothing; it vanishes away in the comparison. What is it, then, to the whole expanse of space, to which the whole creation is infinitely less than a grain of sand? And yet this space, to which the whole creation bears no proportion at all, is infinitely less, in comparison of the great God, than a grain of sand, yea, a millionth part of it, bears to that whole space.

Sermons: "On the Omnipresence of God," I, 2-3 (J, VII, 239-40).

"How is it that [man] is not utterly lost in the immensity of God's works?" Is not the purport of the latter, "How can He that inhabiteth eternity stoop to regard the creature of a day,—one whose life passeth away like a shadow?" Is not this a thought which has struck many serious minds, as well as it did David's, and created a kind of fear lest they should be forgotten before Him who grasps all space and all eternity? But does not this fear arise from a kind of supposition that God is such an one as ourselves? If we consider boundless space, or boundless duration, we shrink into nothing before it. But God is not a man. A day, and millions of ages, are the same with Him. Therefore, there is the same disproportion between Him and any finite being, as between Him and the creature of a day. Therefore, whenever that thought recurs, whenever you are tempted to fear lest you should be forgotten before the immense, the eternal God, remember that nothing is little or great, that no duration is long or short, before Him.

Sermons: "On Eternity," 20 (J, VI, 198).

JW

The name of God is God Himself; the nature of God, so far as it can be discovered to man. It means therefore, together with His existence, all His attributes or perfections:—His Eternity, particularly signified by His great and incommunicable name, JEHOVAH, as the Apostle John translates it, Τὸ Α καὶ τὸ Ω, ἀρχὴ καὶ τέλος, ὁ ὢν καὶ ὁ ἦν καὶ ὁ ἐρχόμενος—"The Alpha and Omega, the beginning and the end; He which is, and which was, and which is to come";—His fullness of Being, denoted by His other great name, *I AM THAT I AM!*—His omnipresence:—His omnipotence; who is indeed the only Agent in the material world; all matter being essentially dull and inactive, and moving only as it is moved by the finger of God; and He is the spring of action in every creature, visible and invisible, which could neither act nor exist, without the continual influx and agency of His almighty power;—His wisdom, clearly deduced from the things that are seen, from the goodly order of the universe;—His Trinity in Unity, and Unity in Trinity, discovered to us in the very first line of His written Word; בָּרָא אֱלֹהִים,—literally, *the Gods created,* a plural noun joined with a verb of the singular member; as well as in every part of His subsequent revelations, given by the mouth of all His holy Prophets and Apostles;—His essential purity and holiness;—and, above all, His love, which is the very brightness of His glory.

Sermons: "Upon Our Lord's Sermon on the Mount—VI," III, 7 (S, I, 435-36).

2. *God's Character and Predestination*

Stand forth, then, free-will on the one side, and reprobation on the other; and let us see whether the one scheme, attended with the absurdity, as you think it, of free-will, or the other scheme, attended with the absurdity of reprobation, be the more defensible. Let us see (if it please the Father of Lights to open the eyes of our understanding) which of these is more for the glory of God, for the display of his glorious attributes, for the manifestation of his wisdom, justice, and mercy, to the sons of men.

First, his wisdom. If man be in some measure free; if, by that light which "lighteneth every man that comes into the world," there be "set before him life and death, good and evil"; then how gloriously does the manifold wisdom of God appear in the whole economy of man's salvation! Being willing that all men should be saved, yet not willing to force them thereto; willing that men should be saved, yet not as trees or stones, but as men, as reasonable creatures, endued with understanding to discern what is good, and liberty either to accept or refuse it; how does he suit the whole scheme of his dispensations to this his πρόθεσις, his plan, "the counsel of his will!" His first step is to enlighten the understanding by that general knowledge of good and evil. To this he adds many secret reproofs, if they act contrary to this light; many inward convictions, which there is not a man on earth who has not often felt. At other times he gently moves their wills, he draws and woos them, as it were, to walk in the light. He instills into their hearts good desires, though perhaps they know not from whence

48

they come. Thus far he proceeds with all the children of men, yea, even with those who have not the knowledge of his written word. But in this, what a field of wisdom is displayed, suppose man to be in some degree a free agent! How is every part of it suited to this end! to save man, as man; to set life and death before him, and then persuade (not force) him to choose life. . . .

We come next to his justice. Now, if man be capable of choosing good or evil, then he is a proper object of the justice of God, acquitting or condemning, rewarding or punishing. But otherwise he is not. A mere machine is not capable of being either acquitted or condemned. Justice cannot punish a stone for falling to the ground; nor, on your scheme, a man for falling into sin. For he can no more help it than the stone, if he be, in your sense, fore-ordained to this condemnation. . . . Shall this man, for not doing what he never could do, and for doing what he never could avoid, be sentenced to depart into everlasting fire, prepared for the devil and his angels? "Yes, because it is the sovereign will of God." Then "you have either found a new God, or made one!" This is not the God of the Christians. Our God is just in all his ways; he reapeth not where he hath not strewed. He requireth only according to what he hath given; and where he hath given little, little is required. The glory of his justice is this, to "reward every man according to his works." Hereby is that glorious attribute shown, evidently set forth before men and angels, in that it is accepted of every man according to that he hath, and not according to that he hath not. This is that just decree which cannot pass, either in time or in eternity. . . .

Just as gloriously does it display his love; supposing it to be fixed on one in ten of his creatures, (might I not rather say, on one in a hundred?) and to have no regard to the rest. Let the ninety-and-nine reprobates perish without mercy. It is enough for him, to love and save the one elect. But why will he have mercy on these alone, and leave all those to inevitable destruction? "He will—because he will!" O that God would give unto you who thus speak, meekness of wisdom! Then would I ask, What would the universal voice of mankind pronounce of the man that should act thus? that being able to deliver millions of men from death with a single breath of his mouth, should refuse to save any more than one in a hundred, and say, "I will not, because I will not!" How then do you exalt the mercy of God, when you ascribe such a proceeding to him? What a strange comment is this on his own word, that "his mercy is over all his work!" ...

The sovereignty of God appears, (1.) In fixing from eternity that decree touching the sons of men, "He that believeth shall be saved: He that believeth not shall be damned." (2.) In all the general circumstances of creation; in the time, and place, the manner of creating all things; in appointing the number and kinds of creatures, visible and invisible. (3.) In allotting the natural endowments of men, these to one, and those to another. (4.) In disposing the time, place, and other outward circumstances (as parents, relations) attending the birth of every one. (5.) In dispensing the various gifts of his Spirit, for the edification of his Church. (6.) In ordering all temporal things, as health, fortune, friends, everything short of eternity. But in disposing the eternal states of men ... it is clear, that not sovereignty alone, but justice, mercy, and truth hold the reins. The Governor of heaven and earth, the I AM, over all, God blessed for ever, takes no step here but as these direct, and prepare the way before his face.

Works: "Predestination Calmly Considered," 50-54 (X, 232-36).

JW

The almighty, all-wise God sees and knows, from everlasting to everlasting, all that is, that was, and that is to come, through one eternal *now*. With him nothing is either past or future, but all things equally present. He has, therefore, if we speak according to the truth of things, no foreknowledge, no afterknowledge. . . . Yet when he speaks to us, knowing whereof we are made, knowing the scantiness of our understanding, he lets himself down to our capacity, and speaks of himself after the manner of men. Thus, in condescension to our weakness, he speaks of his own purpose, counsel, plan, foreknowledge. Not that God has any need of counsel, of purpose, or of planning his work beforehand. Far be it from us to impute these to the Most High; to measure him by ourselves! It is merely in compassion to us that he speaks thus of himself, as foreknowing the things in heaven or earth, and as predestinating or fore-ordaining them.

Sermons: "On Predestination," 15 (J, VI, 230).

JW

If [election] be so, then is all preaching vain. It is needless to them that are elected; for they, whether with preaching or without, will infallibly be saved. Therefore, the end of preaching—to save souls— is void with regard to them; and it is useless to them that are not elected, for they cannot possibly be saved: They, whether with preaching or without, will infallibly be damned. . . .

This, then, is a plain proof that the doctrine of predestination is not a doctrine of God, because it makes void the ordinance of God; and God is not divided against himself. A Second is, that it directly tends to destroy that holiness which is the end of all the ordinances of God. I do not say, none who hold it are holy; (for God is of tender mercy to those who are unavoidably entangled in errors of any kind;) but that the doctrine itself,—that every man is either elected or not elected from eternity, and that the one must inevitably be saved, and the other inevitably damned,—has a manifest tendency to destroy holiness in general; for it wholly takes away those first motives to follow after it, so frequently proposed in Scripture, the hope of future reward and fear of punishment, the hope of heaven and fear of hell. . . .

Thirdly. This doctrine tends to destroy the comfort of religion, the happiness of Christianity. This is evident as to all those who believe themselves to be reprobated, or who only suspect or fear it. All the great and precious promises are lost to them; they afford them no ray of comfort: For they are not the elect of God; therefore they have neither lot nor portion in them. This is an effectual bar to their finding any comfort or happiness, even in that religion whose ways are designed to be "ways of pleasantness, and all her paths peace.". . .

Fourthly. This uncomfortable doctrine directly tends to destroy our zeal for good works. And this it does, First, as it naturally tends (according to what was observed before) to destroy our love to the greater part of mankind, namely, the evil and unthankful. For whatever lessens our love, must so far lessen our desire to do them good. This it does, Secondly, as it cuts off one of the strongest motives to all acts of bodily mercy, such as feeding the hungry, clothing the naked, and the like,—viz., the hope of saving their souls from death. For what avails it to relieve their temporal wants, who are just dropping into eternal fire? . . .

But, Fifthly, this doctrine not only tends to destroy Christian holiness, happiness, and good works, but hath also a direct and manifest tendency to overthrow the whole Christian Revelation. The point which the wisest of the modern unbelievers most industriously labour to prove, is, that the Christian Revelation is not necessary. They well know, could they once show this, the conclusion would be too plain to be denied, "If it be not necessary, it is not true." Now, this fundamental point you give up. For supposing that eternal, unchangeable decree, one part of mankind must be saved though the Christian Revelation were not in being, and the other part of mankind must be damned, notwithstanding that Revelation. And what would an infidel desire more? You allow him all he asks. In making the gospel thus unnecessary to all sorts of men; you give up the whole Christian cause. "O tell it not in Gath! Publish it not in the streets of Askelon! lest the daughters of the uncircumcised rejoice"; lest the sons of unbelief triumph!

And as this doctrine manifestly and directly tends to overthrow the whole Christian Revelation, so it does the same thing, by plain consequence, in making that Revelation contradict itself. For it is grounded on such an interpretation of some texts (more or fewer it matters not) as flatly contradicts all the other texts, and indeed the whole scope and tenor of Scripture. . . .

Seventhly, it is a doctrine full of blasphemy; of such blasphemy as I should dread to mention, but that the honour of our gracious God, and the cause of his truth, will not suffer me to be silent. In the cause of God, then, and from a sincere concern for the glory of his great name, I will mention a few of the horrible blasphemies contained in this horrible doctrine. . . .

This doctrine represents our blessed Lord, "Jesus Christ the righteous," "the only begotten Son of the Father, full of grace and truth," as an hypocrite, a deceiver of the people, a man void of common sincerity. For it cannot be denied, that he everywhere speaks as if he was willing that all men should be saved. Therefore, to say he was not willing that all men should be saved, is to represent him as a mere hypocrite and dissembler. . . .

Such blasphemy this, as one would think might make the ears of a Christian to tingle! But there is yet more behind; for just as it honours the Son, so doth this doctrine honour the Father. It destroys all his attributes at once: It overturns both his justice, mercy, and truth; yea, it represents the most holy God as worse than the devil, as both more false, more cruel, and more unjust. More *false;* because the devil, liar as he is, hath never said, "He willeth all men to be saved": More *unjust;* because the devil cannot, if he would, be guilty of such injustice as you ascribe to God, when you say that God condemned millions of souls to everlasting fire, prepared for the devil and his angels, for continuing in sin, which, for want of that grace *he will not* give them, they cannot avoid: And more *cruel;* because that unhappy spirit "seeketh rest and findeth none"; so that his own restless misery is a kind of temptation to him to tempt others. But God resteth in his high and holy place; so that to suppose him, of his own mere motion, of his pure will and pleasure, happy as he is, to doom his creatures, whether they will or no, to endless misery, is to impute such cruelty to him as we cannot impute even to the great enemy of God and man. It is to represent the most high God (he that hath ears to hear let him hear!) as more cruel, false, and unjust than the devil!

Sermons: "Free Grace," 10-11, 13, 18-20, 23-25 (J, VII, 376-83).

JW

Ah, poor predestinarian! If you are true to your doctrine, [election] this is no comfort to you! For perhaps you are not of the elect number: If so, you are in the whirlpool too. For what is your hope? Where is your help? There is no help for you in your God. *Your* God! No; he is not yours; he never was; he never will be. He that made you, He that called you into being, has no pity upon you! He made you for this very end—to damn you; to cast you headlong into a lake of fire burning with brimstone! This was prepared for you, or ever the world began! And for this you are now reserved in chains of darkness, till the decree brings forth; till, according to his eternal, unchangeable, irresistible will,

> You groan, you howl, you writhe in waves of fire,
> And pour forth blasphemies at his desire!

O God, how long shall this doctrine stand!

Works: "A Thought on Necessity," VI, 6 (X, 480).

JW

I believe [election] commonly means one of these two things: First, a divine appointment of some particular men, to do some particular work in the world. And this election I believe to be not only personal, but absolute and unconditional. Thus Cyrus was elected to rebuild the temple, and St. Paul, with the twelve, to preach the gospel. But I do not find this to have any necessary connexion with eternal happiness. Nay, it is plain it has not; for one who is elected in this sense may yet be lost eternally. "Have I not chosen" (elected) "you twelve?" saith our Lord; "yet one of you hath a devil." Judas, you see, was elected as well as the rest; yet is his lot with the devil and his angels.

I believe election means, Secondly, a divine appointment of some men to eternal happiness. But I believe this election to be conditional, as well as the reprobation opposite thereto. I believe the eternal decree concerning both is expressed in those words: "He that believeth shall be saved; he that believeth not shall be damned." And this decree, without doubt, God will not change, and man cannot resist. According to this, all true believers are in Scripture termed elect, as all who continue in unbelief are so long properly reprobates, that is, unapproved of God, and without discernment touching the things of the Spirit.

Works: "Predestination Calmly Considered," 16-17 (X, 209-10).

3. God's Activity as Creator

The eternal, almighty, all-wise, all-gracious God is the Creator of heaven and earth. He called out of nothing, by his all-powerful word, the whole universe, all that is. "Thus the heavens and the earth were created, and all the hosts of them." And after he had set all things else in array, the plants after their kinds, fish and fowl, beasts and reptiles, after their kinds, "He created man after his own image." And the Lord saw that every distinct part of the universe was good. But when he saw everything he had made, all in connexion with each other, "behold, it was very good."

Sermons: "On Divine Providence," 8 (J, VI, 315).

JW

[A Christian] is happy in knowing there is a God, an intelligent Cause and Lord of all, and that he is not the produce either of blind chance or inexorable necessity. He is happy in the full assurance he has that this Creator and End of all things is a Being of boundless wisdom, of infinite power to execute all the designs of His wisdom, and of no less infinite goodness to direct all His power to the advantage of all His creatures. Nay, even the consideration of His immutable justice, rendering to all their due, of His unspotted holiness, of His all-sufficiency in Himself, and of that immense ocean of all perfections which centre in God from eternity to eternity, is a continual addition to the happiness of a Christian.

Letters: "To Dr. Conyers Middleton" (II, 379).

JW

God reveals himself under a two-fold character; as a Creator, and as Governor. These are no way inconsistent with each other; but they are totally different.

As a Creator, he has acted, in all things, according to his own sovereign will. Justice has not, cannot have, any place here; for nothing is due to what has no being. Here, therefore, he may, in the most absolute sense, do what he will with his own. Accordingly, he created the heavens and the earth, and all things that are therein, in every conceivable respect, "according to his own good pleasure." 1. He began his creation at what time, or rather, at what part of eternity, it seemed him good. Had it pleased him, it might have been millions of years sooner, or millions of ages later. 2. He determined, by his sovereign will, the duration of the universe; whether it should last seven thousand, or seven hundred thousand, or numberless millions of years. 3. By the same, he appointed the place of the universe, in the immensity of space. 4. Of his sovereign will he determined the number of the stars, of all the component parts of the universe, and the magnitude of every atom, of every fixed star, every planet, and every comet. 5. As Sovereign, he created the earth, with all the furniture of it, whether animate or inanimate; and gave to each such a nature, with such properties. 6. Of his own good pleasure, he made such a creature as man, an embodied spirit, and, in consequence of his spiritual nature, endued with understanding, will, and liberty. 7. He hath determined the times for every nation to come into being, with the bounds of their habitation. 8. He has allotted the time, the place, the circumstances, for the birth of each individual:—

> If of parents I came
> That honour'd thy name,
> 'Twas thy goodness appointed it so.

9. He has given to each a body, as it pleased him, weak or strong, healthy or sickly. This implies, 10. That he gives them various degrees of understanding, and of knowledge, diversified by numberless circumstances. It is hard to say how far this extends; what an amazing difference there is, as to the means of improvement, between one born and brought up in a pious English family, and one born and bred among the Hottentots. Only we are sure the difference cannot be so great, as to necessitate one to be good, or the other to be evil; to force

one into everlasting glory, or the other into everlasting burnings. This cannot be, because it would suppose the character of God as a Creator, to interfere with God as a Governor; wherein he does not, cannot possibly, act according to his own mere sovereign will; but, as he has expressly told us, according to the invariable rules both of justice and mercy.

Whether therefore we can account for it or no, (which indeed we cannot in a thousand cases,) we must absolutely maintain, that God is a rewarder of them that diligently seek him. But he cannot reward the sun for shining, because the sun is not a free agent. Neither could he reward us, for letting our light shine before men, if we acted as necessarily as the sun. All reward, as well as all punishment, pre-supposes free-agency; and whatever creature is incapable of choice, is incapable of either one or the other.

Whenever, therefore, God acts as a Governor, as a rewarder, or punisher, he no longer acts as mere Sovereign, by his own sole will and pleasure; but as an impartial Judge, guided in all things by in-variable justice.

Yet it is true, that, in some cases, mercy rejoices over justice; although severity never does. God may reward more, but he will never punish more, than strict justice requires. It may be allowed that God acts as Sovereign in convincing some souls of sin; arresting them in their mid career, by his resistless power. It seems also, that, at the moment of our conversion, he acts irresistibly. There may likewise be many irresistible touches during the course of our Christian warfare; with regard to which every believer may say,

> "In the time of my distress
> Thou hast my succour been,
> In my utter helplessness
> Restraining me from sin."

But still, as St. Paul might have been either obedient or "disobedient to the heavenly vision," so every individual may, after all that God has done, either improve his grace, or make it of none effect.

Whatever, therefore, it hath pleased God to do, of his sovereign pleasure, as Creator of heaven and earth; and whatever his mercy may do on particular occasions, over and above what justice requires; the general rule stands firm as the pillars of heaven: "The Judge of all the earth will do right. He will judge the world in righteousness," and every man therein, according to the strictest justice. He will punish no man for doing anything which he could not possibly avoid; neither for omitting anything which he could not possibly do. Every punishment supposes the offender might have avoided the offence for which he is punished: Otherwise, to punish him would be palpably unjust, and inconsistent with the character of God our Governor.

Let then these two ideas of God the Creator, the sovereign Creator, and God the Governor, the just Governor, be always kept apart. Let us distinguish them from each other, with the utmost care. So shall we give God the full glory of his sovereign grace, without impeaching his inviolable justice.

Works: "Thoughts Upon God's Sovereignty" (X, 361-63).

4. *God's Activity as Governor or Preserver*

As this all-wise, all-gracious Being created all things, so he sustains all things. He is the Preserver as well as the Creator of everything that exists. "He upholdeth all things by the word of his power"; that is, by his powerful word. Now it must be that he knows everything he has made, and everything he preserves, from moment to moment; otherwise, he could not preserve it, he could not continue to it the being which he has given it. And it is nothing strange that He who is omnipresent, who "filleth heaven and earth," who is in every place, should see what is in every place, where he is intimately present. If the eye of man discerns things at a small distance; the eye of an eagle, what is at a greater; the eye of an angel, what is at a thousand times greater distance; (perhaps taking in the surface of the earth at one view;) how shall not the eye of God see everything, through the whole extent of creation? especially considering, that nothing is distant from Him in whom we all "live, and move, and have our being."

Sermons: "On Divine Providence," 9 (J, VI, 315).

JW

"Without me ye can do nothing!" absolutely, positively nothing! seeing, in Him all things live and move, as well as have their being; seeing, he is not only the true *primum mobile,* containing the whole frame of creation, but likewise the inward, sustaining, acting principle, indeed the only proper agent in the universe; unless so far as he imparts a spark of his active, self-moving nature to created spirits. But more especially "ye can do nothing" right, nothing wise, nothing good, without the direct, immediate agency of the First Cause.

Works: "A Thought on Necessity," V, 1 (X, 476-77).

JW

Are we not better acquainted with his works of providence, than with his works of creation? It is one of the first principles of religion, that his kingdom ruleth over all: So that we may say with confidence, "O Lord our Governor, how excellent is thy name over all the earth!" It is a childish conceit, to suppose chance governs the world, or has any part in the government of it: No, not even in those things that, to a vulgar eye, appear to be perfectly casual. "The lot is cast into the lap; but the disposal thereof is from the Lord." Our blessed Master himself has put this matter beyond all possible doubt: "Not a sparrow," saith he, "falleth to the ground without the will of your Father which is in heaven: Yea," (to express the thing more strongly still,) "even the very hairs of your head are all numbered."

But although we are well apprized of this general truth, that all things are governed by the providence of God; (the very language of the heathen orator, *Deorum moderamine cuncta geri;*) yet how amazingly little do we know of the particulars contained under this general! How little do we understand of his providential dealings, either with regard to nations, or families, or individuals! There are heights and depths in all these which our understanding can in no wise fathom. We can comprehend but a small part of his ways now; the rest we shall know hereafter.

Sermons: "The Imperfection of Human Knowelgde," II, 1-2 (J, VI, 343-44).

JW

Yet there is a difference, . . . in [God's] providential government over the children of men. A pious writer observes, There is a three-fold circle of divine providence. The *outermost circle* includes all the sons of men; Heathens, Mahometans, Jews, and Christians. He causeth his sun to rise upon all. He giveth them rain and fruitful seasons. He pours ten thousand benefits upon them, and fills their hearts with food and gladness. With an *interior circle* he encompasses the whole visible Christian Church, all that name the name of Christ. He has an additional regard to these, and a nearer attention to their welfare. But the *innermost circle* of his providence encloses only the invisible Church of Christ; all real Christians, wherever dispersed in all corners of the earth; all that worship God (whatever denomination they are of) in spirit and in truth. He keeps these as the apple of an eye: he hides them under the shadow of his wings. And it is to these in particular that our Lord says, "Even the hairs of your head are all numbered."

Sermons: "Spiritual Worship," I, 9 (J, VI, 428-29).

JW

It is true, the doctrine of a particular providence (and any but a particular providence is no providence at all) is absolutely out of fashion in England; and a prudent author might write this to gain the favour of his gentle readers. Yet I will not say this is real prudence, because he may lose hereby more than he gains; as the majority, even of Britons, to this day retain some sort of respect for the Bible.

Journal: "Fri. 6 July 1781" (VI, 326).

Equally conspicuous is the wisdom of God in the government of nations, of states and kingdoms; yea, rather, more conspicuous; if infinite can be allowed to admit of any degrees. For the whole inanimate creation, being totally passive and inert, can make no opposition to his will. Therefore, in the natural world all things roll on in an even, uninterrupted course. But it is far otherwise in the moral world. Here evil men and evil spirits continually oppose the divine will, and create numberless irregularities. Here, therefore, is full scope for the exercise of all the riches both of the wisdom and knowledge of God, in counteracting all the wickedness and folly of men, and all the subtlety of Satan, to carry on his own glorious design,—the salvation of lost mankind. Indeed, were he to do this by an absolute decree, and by his own irresistible power, it would imply no wisdom at all. But his wisdom is shown by saving man in such a manner as not to destroy his nature, not to take away the liberty which he has given him.

Sermons: "The Wisdom of God's Counsels," 4 (J, VI, 326).

JW

"All these things are purely natural and accidental; the result of natural causes." But there are two objections to this answer: First, it is untrue: Secondly, it is uncomfortable.

First. If by affirming, "All this is purely natural," you mean, it is not providential, or that God has nothing to do with it, this is not true, that is, supposing the Bible to be true. For supposing this, you may descant ever so long on the natural causes of murrain, winds, thunder, lightning, and yet you are altogether wide of the mark, you prove nothing at all, unless you can prove that God never works in or by natural causes. But this you cannot prove. . . .

A Second objection to your answer is, It is extremely uncomfortable. For if things really be as you affirm; if all these afflictive incidents entirely depend on the fortuitous concourse and agency of blind, material causes; what hope, what help, what resource is left for the poor sufferers by them? . . . Shall they intreat the famine or the pestilence to show mercy? Alas! they are as senseless as you suppose God to be.

However, you who are men of fortune can shift tolerably well, in spite of these difficulties. Your money will undoubtedly procure you food as long as there is any in the kingdom. And if your Physicians cannot secure you from the epidemic disease, your coaches can carry you from the place of infection. Be it so: But you are not out of all danger yet, unless you can drive faster than the wind. Are you sure of this? And are your horses literally swifter than the lightning? Can they leave the panting storm behind? If not, what will you do when it overtakes you? Try your eloquence on the whirlwind. Will it hear your voice? Will it regard either your money, or prayers, or tears? Call upon the lightning. Cry aloud; see whether your voice will "divide the flames of fire." O no! it hath no ears to hear! It devoureth and showeth no pity!

Works: "Serious Thoughts Occasioned by the Late Earthquake at Lisbon" (XI, 6-7).

5. God's Activity as Judge

You subjoin: "The doctrine of Atonement made by Christ is the strongest demonstration that the wrath to be atoned cannot be in God" (page 85). Who talks of "wrath to be atoned"? "The wrath to be atoned" is neither sense nor English, though it is a solecism you perpetually run into (I hope not on purpose to puzzle the cause): that the sin to be atoned cannot be in God we all allow: but it does not affect the question.

Once more, to silence all contradiction at once, to stop the mouths of all gainsayers, you say: "This (that there is no anger, no vindictive justice in God, no punishment at all inflicted by Him) is openly asserted, constantly affirmed and repeated, in the plainest letter of Scripture." Whether this or the very reverse is true will appear from a few out of numberless texts, which I shall barely set down without any comment and leave to your cool consideration.

You say: (1) There is no vindictive, avenging, or punitive justice in God. (2) There is no wrath or anger in God. (3) God inflicts no

punishment on any creature, neither in this world nor that to come.
God says,—

(1) "The just Lord is in the midst of you" (Zeph. iii. 5). "Justice and judgement are the habitation of Thy throne" (Ps. lxxxix. 14). . . . .

(2) "The Lord heard their words, and was wroth" (Deut. i. 34). "The Lord was wroth with me for your sakes" (iii. 26). . . . .

(3) "I will punish the world for their evil, and the wicked for their iniquity" (Isa. xiii. 11). "Behold, the Lord cometh to punish the inhabitants of the earth for their iniquity" (xxvi. 21). . . . .

Now, which am I to believe? God or man?

Letters: "To William Law" (III, 350-51).

JW

Returning from Bedford, I tried another way to reach them. I preached on "Where their worm dieth not, and the fire is not quenched"; and set before them the terrors of the Lord, in the strongest manner I was able. It seemed to be the very thing they wanted. They not only listened with the deepest attention, but appeared to be more affected than I had ever seen them by any discourse whatever.

Journal: "Thur. 26 Feb. 1764" (V, 45).

JW

The Scripture describes God as the Judge of the earth. But how shall God in justice judge the world? (O consider this, as in the presence of God, with reverence and godly fear!) How shall God in justice judge the world, if there be any decree of reprobation?

Works: "Predestination Calmly Considered," 31 (X, 221).

JW

Do you not take the name of God in vain? Do you remember the Sabbath-day, to keep it holy? Do you not speak evil of the ruler of your people? Are you not a drunkard, or a glutton, faring as sumptuously as you can every day; making a god of your belly? Do you not avenge yourself? Are you not a whoremonger or adulterer? Answer plainly to your own heart, before God the Judge of all.

Why then do you say you believe the Scripture? If the Scripture is true, you are lost. You are in the broad way that leadeth to destruction. Your damnation slumbereth not. You are heaping up to yourself wrath against the day of wrath, and revelation of the righteous judgment of God. Doubtless, if the Scripture is true, and you remain thus, it had been good for you if you had never been born.

Works: "An Earnest Appeal to Men of Reason and Religion," 39 (VIII, 15).

JW

In making this supposition, of what God might have justly done [to the elect and the damned alike], you suppose his justice might have been separate from his other attributes, from his mercy in particular. But this never was, nor ever will be; nor indeed is it possible it should. All his attributes are inseparately joined: They cannot be divided, no, not for a moment.

Works: "Predestination Calmly Considered," 23 (X, 217).

6. God's Activity as Redeemer

It was of mere grace, of free love, of undeserved mercy, that God hath vouchsafed to sinful man any way of reconciliation with Himself; that we were not cut away from His hand, and utterly blotted out of His rememberance. Therefore, whatever method He is pleased to appoint, of His tender mercy, of His unmerited goodness, whereby His enemies, who have so deeply revolted from Him, so long and obstinately rebelled against Him, may still find favour in His sight, it is doubtless our wisdom to accept it with all thankfulness.

Sermons: "The Righteousness of Faith," II, 8 (S, I, 143).

Behold then both the justice and mercy of God!—his *justice* in punishing sin, the sin of him in whose loins we were then all contained, on Adam and his whole posterity;—and his *mercy,* in providing an universal remedy for an universal evil; in appointing the Second Adam to die for all who had died in the first; that, "as in Adam all died, so in Christ all" might "be made alive"; that, "as by one man's offence, judgment came up all men to condemnation, so by the righteousness of one, the free gift might "come upon all unto justification of life,"—"justification of *life,*" as being connected with the new birth, the beginning of spiritual life, which leads us, through the life of holiness, to life eternal, to glory.

And it should be particularly observed, that "where sin abounded, grace does much more abound." For not as the condemnation, so is the free gift; but we may gain infinitely more than we have lost. We may now attain both higher degrees of holiness, and higher degrees of glory, than it would have been possible for us to attain. If Adam had not sinned, the Son of God had not died: Consequently that amazing instance of the love of God to man had never existed, which has, in all ages, excited the highest joy, and love, and gratitude from his children. We might have loved God the Creator, God the Preserver, God the Governor; but there would have been no place for love to God the Redeemer. This could have had no being. The highest glory and joy of saints on earth, and saints in heaven, Christ crucified, had been wanting. We could not then have praised him that, thinking it no robbery to be equal with God, yet emptied himself, took upon him the form of a servant, and was obedient to death, even the death of the cross!

Sermons: "On the Fall of Man," II, 9-10 (J, VI, 224).

JW

"God, who is rich in mercy, even when we were dead in sins, hath quickened us together with Christ (by grace ye are saved), that He might show the exceeding riches of His grace in His kindness toward us through Christ Jesus. For by grace are ye saved through faith; and that not of yourselves." Of yourselves cometh neither your faith nor your salvation: "it is the gift of God"; the free, undeserved gift; the faith through which ye are saved, as well as the salvation which He of His own good pleasure, His mere favour, annexes thereto. That ye believe, is one instance of His grace; that believing ye are saved, another. "Not of works, lest any man should boast." For all our works, all our righteousness, which were before our believing, merited nothing of God but condemnation; so far were they from deserving faith, which therefore, whenever given, is not of works. Neither is salvation of the works we do when we believe; for it is then God that worketh in us: and, therefore, that He giveth us a reward for what He Himself worketh, only commendeth the riches of His mercy, but leaveth us nothing whereof to glory.

Sermons: "Salvation by Faith," III, 3 (S, I, 47-48).

JW

[God] "rejoiceth in the prosperity of His servants: He delighteth not to afflict or grieve the children of men." His invariable will is our sanctification, attended with "peace and joy in the Holy Ghost." These are His own free gifts; and we are assured "the gifts of God are," on His part, "without repentance." He never repenteth of what He hath given, or desires to withdraw them from us. Therefore He never *deserts* us, as some speak: it is we only that *desert* Him.

Sermons: "The Wilderness State," II, 1 (S, II, 249).

JW

"This is the victory which overcometh the world, even our faith"; that faith, which is not only an unshaken assent to all that God hath revealed in Scripture—and in particular to those important truths, "Jesus Christ came into the world to save sinners," "He bare our sins in His own body on the tree," "He is the propitiation for our sins, and not for ours only, but also for the sins of the whole world,"—but likewise the revelation of Christ in our hearts; a divine evidence or conviction of His love, His free, unmerited love to me a sinner; a sure confidence in His pardoning mercy, wrought in us by the Holy Ghost; a confidence, whereby every true believer is enabled to bear witness, "I know that my Redeemer liveth," that I have an "Advocate with the Father," and that "Jesus Christ the righteous" is my Lord, and "the propitiation for my sins"—I know He hath "loved me, and given Himself for me"—He hath reconciled me, even me, to God; and I "have redemption through His blood, even the forgiveness of sins."

Sermons: "The Circumcision of the Heart," I, 7 (S, I, 270-71).

Hail! Father, Son, and Holy Ghost,
   One God, in Persons Three!
Of Thee we make our early boast,
   Our songs we make of Thee.

Thou neither canst be felt, or seen;
   Thou art a Spirit pure,
Who from eternity hast been,
   And always shalt endure.

Present alike in every place
   Thy Godhead we adore,
Beyond the bounds of time and space
   Thou dwell'st for evermore.

In wisdom infinite Thou art,
   Thine eye doth all things see;
And every thought of every heart
   Is fully known to Thee.

Whate'er Thou wilt, in earth below
   Thou dost, in heaven above:
But chiefly we rejoice to know
   The' almighty God is Love.

Thou lov'st whate'er Thy hands have made;
Thy goodness we rehearse,
In shining characters display'd
Throughout our universe.

Mercy, and love, and endless grace
O'er all Thy works doth reign;
But mostly Thou delight'st to bless
Thy favourite creature, man.

Wherefore, let every creature give
To Thee the praise design'd:
But chiefly, Lord, the thanks receive,
The hearts of all mankind.

Poetics: "Of God," Hymn I (VI, 371-72).

Supplementary References

GOD'S ATTRIBUTES—*Sermons:* "On Eternity" (J, VI, 189 ff); "The Imperfection of Human Knowledge," I, 1-3 (J, VI, 338-39); "On the Omnipresence of God" (J, VII, 238 ff.); "The Unity of the Divine Being" (J, VII, 264 ff.). *Letters:* "To Mary Bishop" (V, 162); (VI, 213-14). *Notes:* "Luke 4:18."

GOD'S CHARACTER AND PREDESTINATION—*Sermons:* "On the Trinity" (J, VI, 199 ff.); "On Predestination" (J, VI, 225 ff.); "On Divine Providence" (J, VI, 313 ff.). *Works:* "Predestination Calmly Considered" (X, 204 ff.); "A Dialogue between a Predestinarian and His Friend" (X, 259 ff.). *Letters:* "To a Roman Catholic" (III, 8); "To Miss March" (V, 270-71); "To Mrs. Bennis" (V, 284); "To Walter Churchey" (VI, 60). *Journal:* "Wed. 24 Aug. 1743" (III, 84-86). *Notes:* "John 4:24;" "Romans 1:17."

GOD'S ACTIVITY AS CREATOR—*Sermons:* "Upon Our Lord's Sermon on the Mount: VI," III, 4-5 (S, I, 432-34); "God's Approbation of His Works" (J, VI, 206 ff.). *Letters:* "To William Law" (III, 332 ff.). *Journal:* "Wed. 17 Jan. 1770" (V, 351-52); "Thur. 3 Jan. 1771" (V. 399). *Notes:* "Acts 17:24."

GOD'S ACTIVITY AS GOVERNOR OR PRESERVER—*Sermons:* "On Divine Providence," 16-18 (J, VI, 318-20); "The Cause and Cure of Earthquakes" (J, VII, 386 ff.); "Some Account of the Late Work of God in North-America" (J, VII, 409 ff.); "Preached on Occasion of the Death of the Rev. Mr. John Fletcher" (J, VII, 431 ff.). *Works:* "Serious Thoughts Occasioned by the Late Earthquake at Lisbon" (XI, 1 ff.). *Letters:* "To Thomas Church" (II, 256 ff.); "To Samuel Furly" (IV, 7-8); "To Hester Ann Roe" (VI, 339). *Journal:* "Thur. 4 June 1772" (V, 470-72).

GOD'S ACTIVITY AS JUDGE—*Sermons:* "A Caution Against Bigotry," II *passim* (S, II, 112 ff.); "National Sins and Miseries" (J, VII, 400 ff.). *Letters:* "To William Law" (III, 345 ff.). *Notes:* "Romans 5:1; 9:21."

GOD'S ACTIVITY AS REDEEMER—*Sermons:* "God's Love to Fallen Man" (J, VI, 231 ff.); "The General Spread of the Gospel" (J, VI, 277 ff.): *Works:* "The Character of a Methodist" 6-8 (VIII, 342-43); "Predestination Calmly Considered" 29-44 (X, 220-29). *Journal:* "Tues. 3 July 1750" (III, 483); "Mon. 16 June 1755" (IV, 122); "Wed. 19 Sept. 1764" (V, 97). *Notes:* "Luke 15:7."

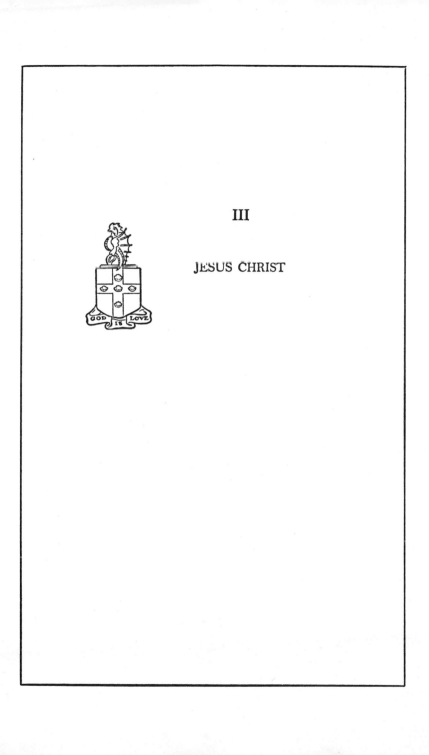

III

JESUS CHRIST

III. JESUS CHRIST

WESLEY'S SPECIFICALLY Christological writings are scattered and fragmentary, yet Christ is central in his theology and essential to every other doctrine. He declares that turning from the atonement is equivalent to embracing deism or paganism; he regards either defection as disastrous to the life of faith. He confesses that the work of Christ is beyond rational comprehension, but testifies that the Scriptures and experience make its reality indisputable. A letter to William Law on this subject shows Wesley to have been accusing, even bitter, because he failed to find in Law's writings the gospel pronouncement of Christ's atoning work for man. Faith in this atoning work is for Wesley the sole way to salvation. As a result of this emphasis on the work of Christ the person of Christ does not receive extensive consideration. Rather Wesley dwells on what God through Christ has done for man, and on what he can do in man, in the life of holiness.

1. Person of Christ

It was in the fulness of time (in just the middle age of the world, as a great man largely proves) that God "brought his first-begotten into the world, made of a woman," by the power of the Highest overshadowing her. He was afterwards manifested to the shepherds; to devout Simeon; to Anna, the Prophetess; and to "all that waited for redemption in Jerusalem."

When he was of due age for executing his priestly office, he was manifested to Israel; preaching the gospel of the kingdom of God in every town and in every city. And for a time he was glorified by all, who acknowledged that he "spake as never man spake"; that "he spake as one having authority," with all the wisdom of God and the power of God. He was manifested by numberless "signs, and wonders, and mighty works which he did," as well as by his whole life; being the only one born of a woman "who knew no sin," who, from his birth to his death, did "all things well"; doing continually "not his own will, but the will of Him that sent him."

Sermons: "The End of Christ's Coming," II, 4-5 (J, VI, 273-74).

In the beginning—(Referring to Gen. i. 1. and Prov. viii, 23.) When all things began to be made by the word: In the beginning of heaven and earth, and this whole frame of created beings, the Word existed, without any beginning. He was when all things began to be, whatsoever had a beginning. *The Word*—So termed Psal. xxxiii. 6, and frequently by the seventy, and in the Chaldee paraphrase. So that St. John did not borrow this expression from Philo, or any heathen writer. He was not yet named Jesus, or Christ. He is *the Word* whom the Father begat or *spoke* from eternity; by whom the Father *speaking* maketh all things; who speaketh the Father to us. We have, in the 18th verse, both a real description of the Word, and the reason why he is so called. *He is the only begotten Son of the Father, who is in the bosom of the Father, and hath declared him. And the word was with God*—Therefore distinct from God the Father. The word rendered *with,* denotes a perpetual tendency as it were of the Son to the Father, in unity of essence. He was *with* God alone; because nothing beside God had then any being. *And the Word was God*—Supreme, eternal, independent. There was no creature, in respect of which he could be styled God in a relative sense. Therefore he is styled so in the absolute sense. The Godhead of the Messiah being clearly revealed in the Old Testament, (Jer. xxiii. 6. Hos. i, 7. Psal. xxiii, 1.) the other evangelists aim at this, to prove that Jesus, a true man, was the Messiah. But when at length, some from hence began to doubt of his Godhead, then St. John expressly asserted it, and wrote in this book, as it were a supplement to the Gospels, as in the Revelation to the prophets.

Notes: "John 1:1."

I believe that Jesus of Nazareth was the Saviour of the world, the Messiah so long foretold; that, being annointed with the Holy Ghost, He was a Prophet, revealing to us the whole will of God; that He was a Priest, who gave Himself a sacrifice for sin, and still makes intercession for transgressors; that He is a King, who has all power in heaven and in earth, and will reign till He has subdued all things to Himself.

I believe He is the proper, natural Son of God, God of God, very God of very God; and that He is the Lord of all, having absolute, supreme, universal dominion over all things; but more peculiarly our Lord, who believe in Him, both by conquest, purchase, and voluntary obligation.

I believe that He was made man, joining the human nature with the divine in one person; being conceived by the singular operation of the Holy Ghost, and born of the blessed Virgin Mary, who, as well after as before she brought Him forth, continued a pure and unspotted virgin.

I believe He suffered inexpressible pains both of body and soul, and at last death, even the death of the cross, at the time that Pontius Pilate governed Judaea under the Roman Emperor; that His body was then laid in the grave, and His soul went to the place of separate spirits; that the third day He rose again from the dead; that He ascended into heaven; where He remains in the midst of the throne of God, in the highest power and glory, as Mediator till the end of the world, as God to all eternity; that in the end He will come down from heaven to judge every man according to his works, both those who shall be then alive and all who have died before that day.

Letters: "To a Roman Catholic," 7 (III, 8-9).

JW

This [verse] *demonstrates* the EQUALITY of the Son with the Father. If our Lord were God only by office or investiture, and not in the unity of the divine essence, and in all respects equal in Godhead with the Father, he could not be honoured *even as,* that is, with the *same* honour that they honoured the Father. *He that honoureth not the Son*

—With the *same* equal honour, greatly dishonoureth *the Father that sent him.*

Notes: "John 5:23."

JW

About noon I preached at Warrington; I am afraid, not to the taste of some of my hearers, as my subject led me to speak strongly and explicitly on the Godhead of Christ. But that I cannot help, for on this I *must* insist as the foundation of all our hope.

Journal: "Tues. 5 April 1768" (V, 253-54).

JW

[Christ's] divine righteousness belongs to His divine nature, as He is 'O ὤν. He that existeth "over all, God blessed for ever"; the Supreme; the Eternal; "equal with the Father as touching His Godhead, though inferior to the Father as touching His manhood." Now this is His eternal, essential immutable holiness; His infinite justice, mercy, and truth; in all which, He and the Father are one.

But I do not apprehend that the divine righteousness of Christ is immediately concerned in the present question. I believe few, if any, do now contend for the imputation of this righteousness to us. Whoever believes the doctrine of imputation, understands it chiefly, if not solely of His human righteousness.

The human righteousness of Christ belongs to Him in His human nature; as He is the "Mediator between God and man, the Man Christ Jesus." This is either internal or external. His internal righteousness is the image of God, stamped on every power and faculty of His soul. It is a copy of His divine righteousness, so far as it can be imparted to a human spirit. It is a transcript of the divine purity, the divine justice, mercy, and truth. It includes love, reverence, resignation to His Father; humility, meekness, gentleness; love to lost mankind, and every other holy and heavenly temper; and all these in the highest degree, without any defect, or mixture of unholiness.

It was the least part of His external righteousness, that He did nothing amiss; that He knew no outward sin of any kind, neither was "guile found in His mouth"; that He never spoke one improper word, nor did one improper action. Thus far it is only a negative righteousness, though such a one as never did, nor ever can, belong to any one that is born of a woman, save Himself alone. But even His outward righteousness was positive too: He did all things well; in every word of His tongue, in every work of His hands, He did precisely the "will of Him that sent Him." In the whole course of His life, He did the will of God on earth, as the angels do it in heaven. All He acted and spoke was exactly right in every circumstance. The whole and every part of His obedience was complete. "He fulfilled all righteousness."

But His obedience implied more than all this: it implied not only doing, but suffering; suffering the whole will of God, from the time He came into the world, till "He bore our sins in His own body upon the tree"; yea, till having made a full atonement for them, "He bowed His head, and gave up the ghost." This is usually termed the *passive* righteousness of Christ; the former, His *active* righteousness. But as the active and passive righteousness of Christ were never, in fact, separated from each other, so we never need separate them at all, either in speaking or even in thinking. And it is with regard to both these conjointly, that Jesus is called "the Lord our Righteousness."

Sermons: "The Lord Our Righteousness," I, 1-4 (S, II, 426-28).

2. *Work of Christ as a Sacrifice for Sin*

The word Christ in Greek, and Messiah in Hebrew, signify anointed, and imply the prophetic, priestly, and royal characters, which were to meet in the Messiah. Among the Jews, anointing was the ceremony whereby prophets, priests, and kings were initiated into those offices. And if we look into ourselves, we shall find a want of Christ in all these respects. We are by nature at a distance from God, alienated from him, and incapable of a free access to him. Hence we want a mediator, an intercessor, in a word, a Christ, in his priestly office. This regards our state with respect to God. And with respect to ourselves, we find a total darkness, blindness, ignorance of God, and the things of God. Now here we want Christ in his prophetic office, to enlighten our minds, and teach us the whole will of God. We find also within us a strange misrule of appetites and passions. For these we want Christ in his royal character, to reign in our hearts, and subdue all things to himself.

Notes: "Matthew 1:16."

JW

We could not rejoice that there is a God, were there not a Mediator also; one who stands between God and men, to reconcile man to God, and to transact the whole affair of our salvation. This excludes all other mediators, as saints and angels, whom the Papists set up, and idolatrously worship as such; just as the Heathens of old set up many mediators, to pacify their superior gods.

Notes: "I Timothy 2:5."

JW

"By one man sin entered into the world, and death by sin. And so death passed upon all men," as being contained in him who was the common father and representative of us all. Thus, "through the offence of one," all are dead, dead to God, dead in sin, dwelling in a corruptible, mortal body, shortly to be dissolved, and under the sentence of death eternal. For as "by one man's disobedience" all "were made sinners"; so, by that offence of one "judgement came upon all men to condemnation" (Rom. v. 12, &c.).

In this state we were, even all mankind, when "God so loved the world, that He gave His only begotten Son, to the end we might not perish, but have everlasting life." In the fullness of time He was made man, another common Head of mankind, a second general Parent and Representative of the whole human race. And as such it was that

"He bore our griefs," "the Lord laying upon Him the iniquities of us all." Then was He "wounded for our transgressions, and bruised for our iniquities." "He made His soul an offering for sin": He poured out His blood for the transgressors; He "bare our sins in His own body on the tree," that by His stripes we might be healed: and by that one oblation of Himself, once offered, He hath redeemed me and all mankind; having thereby "made a full, perfect, and sufficient sacrifice and satisfaction for the sins of the whole world."

In consideration of this, that the Son of God hath "tasted death for every man," God hath now "reconciled the world to Himself, not imputing to them their" former "trespasses." And thus, "as by the offence of one judgement came upon all men to condemnation; even so by the righteousness of one the free gift came upon all men unto justification." So that, for the sake of His well-beloved Son, of what He hath done and suffered for us, God now vouchsafes, on one only condition (which Himself also enables us to perform), both to remit the punishment due to our sins, to reinstate us in His favour, and to restore our dead souls to spiritual life, as the earnest of life eternal.

This, therefore, is the general ground of the whole doctrine of justification. By the sin of the first Adam, who was not only the father, but likewise the representative, of us all, we all fall short of the favour of God; we all became children of wrath; or, as the Apostle expresses it, "judgement came upon all men to condemnation." Even so, by the sacrifice for sin made by the second Adam, as the representative of us all, God is so far reconciled to all the world, that He hath given them a new covenant; the plain condition whereof being once fulfilled, "there is no more condemnation" for us, but "we are justified freely by His grace, through the redemption that is in Jesus Christ."

Sermons: "Justification by Faith," I, 6-9 (S, I, 117-19).

JW

Nothing in the Christian system is of greater consequence than the doctrine of Atonement. It is properly the distinguishing point between Deism and Christianity. "The scriptural scheme of morality," said Lord

Huntingdon, "is what every one must admire; but the doctrine of Atonement I cannot comprehend." Here, then, we divide. Give up the Atonement and the Deists are agreed with us.

This point, therefore, deserves to be more largely considered than my time will permit. But it is the less needful now because I have done it already in my letter to Mr. Law; to which I beg you will give a serious reading, whether you have read it before or no. It is in the nineteenth volume of the *Works*. But it is true I can no more *comprehend* it than his lordship; perhaps I might say than the angels of God, than the highest *created* understanding. Our *reason* is here quickly bewildered. If we attempt to expatiate in this *field*, we "find no end, in wandering mazes lost." But the question is (the only question with me; I regard nothing else), What saith the Scripture? It says, "God was in Christ, reconciling the world unto Himself"; that "He made Him, who knew no sin, to be a sin-offering for us." It says, "He was wounded for our transgressions and bruised for our iniquities." It says, "We have an Advocate with the Father, Jesus Christ the righteous; and He is the atonement for our sins."

But it is certain, had God never been angry, He could never have been reconciled. So that, in affirming this, Mr. Law strikes at the very root of the Atonement, and finds a very short method of converting Deists. Although, therefore, I do not term God, as Mr. Law supposes, "a wrathful Being," which conveys a wrong idea; yet I firmly believe He was angry with all mankind, and that He was reconciled to them by the death of His Son. And I know He was angry with me till I believed in the Son of His love; and yet this is no impeachment to His mercy, that He is just as well as merciful.

But undoubtedly, as long as the world stands, there will be a thousand objections to this scriptural doctrine. For still the preaching of *Christ crucified* will be foolishness to the wise men of the world. However let *us* hold the precious truth fast in our heart as well as in our understanding; and we shall find by happy experience that this is to us the wisdom of God and the power of God.

Letters: "To Mary Bishop" (VI, 297-99).

Is not man here [Law's *Spirit of Love*] represented as having contracted a debt with God which he cannot pay? and God as having, nevertheless, a right to insist upon the payment of it? and a right, if he hath not to pay, of delivering him to the tormentor? And is it not expressly asserted that God will in some cases claim this right, and use it to the uttermost? Upon whom then, lights this imputation of "folly" and of "what is still worse"? "Lord, lay not this sin to their charge! Forgive them; for they know not what they do."

But if the Son of God did not die to atone for our sins, what did He die for?

You answer: "He died,—

"(1) To extinguish our own hell within us" (*Spirit of Prayer,* Part II, p. 159).

Nay, the Scripture represents this not as the first but the second end of His death.

"(2) To show that He was above the world, death, hell, and Satan" (pages 130-1).

Where is it written that He died for this end? Could He not have done this without dying at all?

"(3) His death was the only possible way of overcoming all the evil that was in fallen man" (page 129).

This is true, supposing He atoned for our sins. But if this supposition be not made, His death was not the only possible way whereby the Almighty could have overcome all things.

"(4) Through this He got power to give the same victory to all His brethren of the human race" (page 132).

Had He not this power before? Otherwise, how was He Ὁ Ὤν, "He that is," "God over all, blessed for ever"?

If Christ died for no other ends than these, what need was there of His being more than a creature?

Letters: "To William Law" (III, 352-53).

JW

[Hence I cannot look on Dr. Taylor's treatise] as any other than old Deism in a new dress; seeing it saps the very foundation of all revealed religion, whether Jewish or Christian. "Indeed, my L—," said an eminent man to a person of quality, "I cannot see that we have much need of Jesus Christ." And who might not say, upon this supposition, "I cannot see that we have much need of Christianity?" Nay, not any at all; for "they that are whole have no need of a Physician"; and the Christian Revelation speaks of nothing else but the great "Physician" of our souls; nor can Christian philosophy, whatever be thought of the Pagan, be more properly defined than in Plato's word: It is . . . "the only true method of healing a distempered soul." But what need of this, if we are in perfect health? If we are not diseased, we do not want a cure. If we are not sick, why should we seek for a medicine to heal our sickness? What room is there to talk of our being renewed in "knowledge" or "holiness, after the image wherein we were created," if we never have lost that image? if we are as knowing and holy now, nay, far more so, than Adam was immediately after his creation? If, therefore, we take away this foundation, that man is by nature foolish and sinful, "fallen short of the glorious image of God," the Christian system falls at once; nor will it deserve so honourable an appellation, as that of a "cunningly devised fable."

Works: Preface to "The Doctrine of Original Sin" (IX, 193-94).

JW

The sinner being first convinced of his sin and danger by the Spirit of God, stands trembling before the awful tribunal of divine justice; and has nothing to plead but his own guilt and the merits of a Mediator. Christ here interposes. Justice is satisfied: the sin is remitted, and pardon is applied to the soul, by a divine faith wrought by the Holy Ghost, who then begins the great work of inward sanctification. Thus God justifies the ungodly; and yet remains just and true to all its attributes! But let none hence presume to continue in sin. For to the impenitent God is a consuming fire.

Notes: "Romans 4:5."

3. Other Consequences of Christ's Work

The Son of God strikes at the root of that grand work of the devil,—pride; causing the sinner to humble himself before the Lord, to abhor himself, as it were, in dust and ashes. He strikes at the root of self-will; enabling the humbled sinner to say in all things, "Not as I will, but as thou wilt." He destroys the love of the world; delivering them that believe in him from "every foolish and hurtful desire"; from the "desire of the flesh, the desire of the eyes, and the pride of life." He saves them from seeking, or expecting to find, happiness in any creature. As Satan turned the heart of man from the Creator to the creature; so the Son of God turns his heart back again from the creature to the Creator. Thus it is, by manifesting himself, he destroys the works of the devil; restoring the guilty outcast from God, to his favour, to pardon and peace; the sinner in whom dwelleth no good thing, to love and holiness; the burdened, miserable sinner, to joy unspeakable, to real, substantial happiness.

But it may be observed, that the Son of God does not destroy the whole work of the devil in man, as long as he remains in this life. He does not yet destroy bodily weakness, sickness, pain, and a thousand infirmities incident to flesh and blood. He does not destroy all that weakness of understanding, which is the natural consequence of the soul's dwelling in a corruptible body. . . . . It is to remove from us all temptation to pride, and all thought of independency, (which is the very thing that men in general so earnestly covet under the name of *liberty,*) that he leaves us encompassed with all these infirmities, particularly weakness of understanding; till the sentence takes place, "Dust thou art, and unto dust thou shalt return!"

Then error, pain and all bodily infirmities cease: All these are destroyed by death. And death itself, "the last enemy" of man, shall be destroyed at the resurrection. The moment that we hear the voice of the archangel and the trump of God, "then shall be fulfilled the saying that is written, Death is swallowed up in victory." "This corruptible" body "shall put on incorruption; this mortal" body "shall put on immortality"; and the Son of God, manifested in the clouds of heaven, shall destroy this last work of the devil!

Here then we see in the clearest, strongest light, what is real religion: A restoration of man by Him that bruises the serpent's head, to all that the old serpent deprived him of; a restoration, not only to the favour but likewise to the image of God, implying not barely deliverance from sin, but the being filled with the fulness of God. It is plain, if we attend to the preceding considerations, that nothing short of this is Christian religion. Every thing else, whether negative or external, is utterly wide of the mark.

Sermons: "The End of Christ's Coming," III, 2-5 (J, VI, 275-76).

JW

I went on to Leeds, and, after preaching, met the select society, consisting of about sixty members, most of whom can testify that "the blood of Jesus Christ cleanseth from all sin."

Journal: "Sat. 29 June 1782" (VI, 359).

JW

In every state we need Christ in the following respects, (1) Whatever grace we receive, it is a free gift from him. (2) We receive it as his purchase, merely in consideration of the price he paid. (3) We have this grace, not only from Christ, but in him. For our perfection is not like that of a tree, which flourishes by the sap derived from its own root, but, as was said before, like that of a branch which, united to the vine, bears fruit; but, severed from it, is dried up and withered. (4) All our blessings, temporal, spiritual, and eternal, depend on his intercession for us, which is one branch of his priestly office, whereof therefore we have always equal need. (5) The best of men still need Christ in his priestly office, to atone for their omissions, their shortcomings, (as some not improperly speak,) their mistakes in judgment and practice, and their defects of various kinds. For these are all deviations from the perfect law, and consequently need an atonement. Yet that they are not properly sins, we apprehend may appear from the words of St. Paul, "He that loveth, hath fulfilled the law; for love is the fulfilling of the law." (Romans xiii. 10.) Now, mistakes, and whatever infirmities necessarily flow from the corruptible state of the body, are noway contrary to love; nor therefore, in the Scripture sense, sin.

Works: "Plain Account of Christian Perfection," 19 (XI, 395-96).

For he that is dead—With Christ, *is freed from* the guilt of past, and from the power of present *sin,* as dead men from the commands of their former masters.

Notes: "Romans 6:7."

Through the obedience and death of Christ, (1) The bodies of all men become immortal after the resurrection (2) Their souls receive a capacity of spiritual life. And, (3) An actual spark or seed thereof. (4) All believers become children of grace, reconciled to God; and, (5) Made partakers of the divine nature.

Works: "Minutes of Some Late Conversations," Mon. June 25, 1744 (VIII, 277-78).

In what sense is this righteousness imputed to believers? In this: all believers are forgiven and accepted, not for the sake of anything in them, or of anything that ever was, that is, or ever can be done by them, but wholly and solely for the sake of what Christ hath done and suffered for them. I say again, not for the sake of anything in them, or done by them, of their own righteousness or works: "Not for works of righteousness which we have done, but of His own mercy

He saved us." "By grace ye are saved through faith; . . . not of works, lest any man should boast"; but wholly and solely for the sake of what Christ hath done and suffered for us. We are "justified freely by His grace, through the redemption that is in Jesus Christ." And this is not only the means of our obtaining the favour of God, but of our continuing therein. It is thus we come to God at first; it is by the same we come unto Him ever after. We walk in one and the same new and living way, till our spirit returns to God.

Sermons: "The Lord Our Righteousness," II, 5 (S, II, 430).

JW

To preach Christ, as a workman that needeth not to be ashamed, is to preach Him, not only as our great High-Priest, "taken from among men, and ordained for men, in things pertaining to God"—as such "reconciling us to God by His blood," and "ever living to make intercession for us";—but likewise as the Prophet of the Lord, "who of God is made unto us wisdom"; who, by His Word and His Spirit, is with us always, "guiding us into all truth";—yea, and as remaining a King for ever; as giving laws to all whom He has bought with His blood; as restoring those to the image of God, whom He had first reinstated in His favour; as reigning in all believing hearts until He has "subdued all things to Himself,"—until He hath utterly cast out all sin, and brought in everlasting righteousness.

Sermons: "The Law Established Through Faith: II," I, 6 (S, II, 76-77).

JW

Jesus, my Lord, attend
Thy fallen creature's cry,
And show Thyself the sinner's Friend,
And set me up on high:
From hell's oppressive power,
From earth and sin release,
And to Thy Father's grace restore,
And to Thy perfect peace.

For this, alas! I mourn
In helpless unbelief,
But Thou my wretched heart canst turn,
And heal my sin and grief;
Salvation in Thy name
To dying souls is given,
And all may, through Thy merit, claim
A right to life and heaven.

Thy blood and righteousness
I make my only plea,
My present and eternal peace
Are both derived from Thee:
Rivers of life Divine
From Thee their Fountain flow,
And all who know that love of Thine
The joy of angels know.

O then impute, impart
To me Thy righteousness,
And let me taste how good Thou art,
How full of truth and grace:
That Thou canst here forgive
I long to testify,
And justified by faith to live,
And in that faith to die.

Poetics: Hymn I (IV, 207-8).

SUPPLEMENTARY REFERENCES

PERSON OF CHRIST—*Sermons:* "Upon Our Lord's Sermon on the Mount: I," Introduction (S, I, 315-21); "The Signs of the Times," I (J, VI, 305-ff.); "Spiritual Worship," I, 2-10 (J, VI, 426-29); "On Knowing Christ after the Flesh," (J, VII, 291 ff.). *Journal:* "Wed. 14 Jan. 1756 (IV, 145 ff.). *Notes:* "John 3:13; 8:16."

WORK OF CHRIST AS A SACRIFICE FOR SIN—*Sermons:* "Justification by Faith," I, 7-9 (S, I, 118-19); "The Law Established Through Faith: II," I, 6 (S, II, 76); "The End of Christ's Coming" (J, VI, 267 ff.). *Letters:* "To Lady Maxwell" (IV, 301); "To Ann Bolton" (V, 86). *Journal:* "Thur. 29 July 1780" (VI, 288); "Thur. 29 March 1787" (VII, 254-55). *Notes:* "John 10:18;" "Romans 3:23-26; 8:3;" "II Corinthians 5: 19-21."

OTHER CONSEQUENCES OF CHRIST'S WORK—*Sermons:* "The Lord Our Righteousness" (S, II, 423 ff.). *Works:* "A Dialogue Between an Antinomian and His Friend" (X, 266 ff.); "Thoughts on the Imputed Righteousness of Christ," 1-15 (X, 312-15); "Preface to a Treatise on Justification" (X, 332). *Letters:* "To James Hutton" (I, 253); "To James Hervey" (III, 371 ff.); "To Peggy Dale" (IV, 319). *Journal:* "Tues. 1 Dec. 1767" (V, 243-44); "Thur. 9 Oct. 1777" (VI, 173). *Notes:* "II Corinthians 3:18"; "Ephesians 1:21-22."

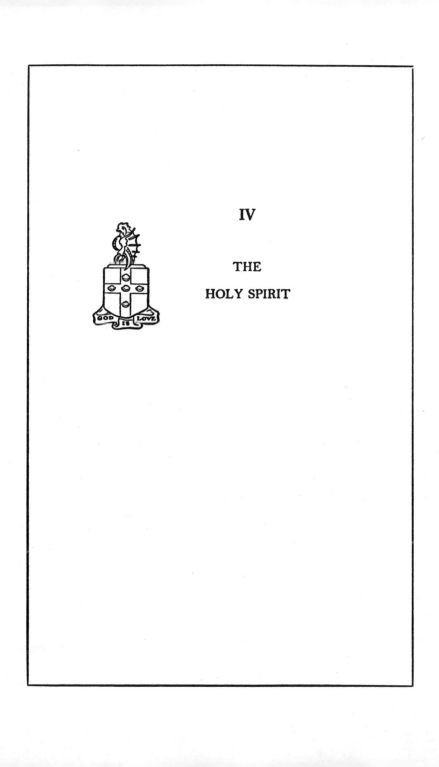

IV

THE

HOLY SPIRIT

IV. THE HOLY SPIRIT

THE HOLY SPIRIT as the instrument of God's love plays a very important role in Wesley's theology. The experiential basis of Wesley's thought perceives God's Spirit entering into human life and bearing witness to its presence. Thus the Holy Spirit is central in the description of the meeting of God and man. The doctrine of assurance, one theological formulation of the Spirit's work, was repeatedly labeled "enthusiasm." Wesley therefore takes great pains to guard it against perversion. He considers the doctrine of assurance too important to relinquish simply because it is subject to distortion. He guards it by insisting that those who claim the assurance of the Spirit's working must also show the fruits of the Spirit in their lives. The conclusive certainty of God's grace is to be attended by effects in the lives of believers which are discernible by others of the religious community.

1. Redemptive Work of the Holy Spirit

I believe the infinite and eternal Spirit of God, equal with the Father and the Son, to be not only perfectly holy in Himself, but the immediate cause of all holiness in us; enlightening our understandings, rectifying our wills and affections, renewing our natures, uniting our persons to Christ, assuring us of the adoption of sons, leading us in our actions, purifying and sanctifying our souls and bodies, to a full and eternal enjoyment of God.

Letters: "To a Roman Catholic" 8 (III, 9).

JW

There can be no point of greater importance to him who knows that it is the Holy Spirit which leads us into all truth and into all holiness, than to consider with what temper of soul we are to entertain his divine presence; so as not either to drive him from us, or to disappoint him of the gracious ends for which his abode with us is designed; which is not the amusement of our understanding, but the conversion and entire sanctification of our hearts and lives.

These words of the Apostle contain a most serious and affectionate exhortation to this purpose. "Grieve not the Holy Spirit of God, whereby ye are sealed unto the day of redemption."

The title "holy," applied to the Spirit of God, does not only denote that he is holy in his own nature, but that he makes us so; that he is the great fountain of holiness to his Church; the Spirit from whence flows all the grace and virtue, by which the stains of guilt are cleansed, and we are renewed in all holy dispositions, and again bear the image of our Creator. Great reason, therefore, there was for the Apostle to give this solemn charge concerning it, and the highest obligation lies upon us all to consider it with the deepest attention.

Sermons: "On Grieving the Holy Spirit," Introduction (J, VII, 485-86).

JW

The author of faith and salvation is God alone. It is he that works in us both to will and to do. He is the sole Giver of every good gift, and the sole Author of every good work. There is no more of power than of merit in man; but as all merit is in the Son of God, in what he has done and suffered for us, so all power is in the Spirit of God. And therefore every man, in order to believe unto salvation, must receive the Holy Ghost. This is essentially necessary to every Christian, not in order to his working miracles, but in order to faith, peace, joy, and love—the ordinary fruits of the Spirit.

Although no man on earth can explain the particular manner wherein the Spirit of God works on the soul, yet whosoever has these fruits, cannot but know and *feel* that God has wrought them in his heart.

Sometimes He acts more particularly on the understanding, opening or enlightening it, (as the Scripture speaks,) and revealing, unveiling, discovering to us "the deep things of God."

Sometimes He acts on the wills and affections of men; withdrawing them from evil, inclining them to good, inspiring (breathing, as it were) good thoughts into them: So it has frequently been expressed by an easy natural metaphor, strictly analogous to רוח, πνεῦμα, *spiritus,* and the words used in most modern tongues also, to denote the third person in the everblessed Trinity. But however it be expressed, it is certain all true faith, and the whole work of salvation, every good thought, word, and work, is altogether by the operation of the Spirit of God.

Works: "A Farther Appeal to Men of Reason and Religion," I, 6 (VIII, 49).

JW

The Holy Spirit prepares us for his inward kingdom, by removing the veil from our heart, and enabling us to know ourselves as we are known of him; by "convincing us of sin," of our evil nature, our evil tempers, and our evil words and actions; all of which cannot but partake of the corruption of the heart from which they spring. He then convinces us of the desert of our sins; so that our mouth is stopped, and we are constrained to plead guilty before God. At the same time, we "receive the spirit of bondage unto fear"; fear of the wrath of God, fear of the punishment which we have deserved; and, above all, fear of death, lest it should consign us over to eternal death. Souls that are thus convinced feel they are so fast in prison, that they cannot get forth. They feel themselves at once altogether sinful, altogether guilty, and altogether helpless. But all this conviction implies a species of faith; being "an evidence of things not seen"; nor indeed possible to be seen or known, till God reveals them unto us.

Sermons: "On the Discoveries of Faith," 12 (J, VII, 235).

JW

I believe firmly, and that in the most literal sense, that "without God we can do nothing"; that we cannot think, or speak, or move an hand or an eye without the concurrence of the divine energy; and that all our natural faculties are God's gift, nor can the meanest be exerted without the assistance of His Spirit. What, then, do I mean by saying that faith, hope, and love are not the effect of any or all our natural faculties? I mean this: that, supposing a man to be now void of faith and hope and love, he cannot effect any degree of them in himself by any possible exertion of his understanding and of any or all his other natural faculties, though he should enjoy them in the utmost perfection. A distinct power from God, not implied in any of these, is indispensably necessary before it is possible he should arrive at the very lowest degree of Christian faith or hope or love. In order to his having any of these (which, on this very consideration, I suppose St. Paul terms the "fruits of the Spirit") he must be created anew, thoroughly and inwardly changed by the operation of the Spirit of God; by a power equivalent to that which raises the dead and which calls the things which are not as though they were.

Letters: "To 'John Smith,'" 7 (II, 71).

JW

There is an irreconcilable variability in the operations of the Holy Spirit on the souls of men, more especially as to the manner of justification. Many find Him rushing upon them like a torrent, while they experience

The o'erwhelming power of saving grace.

This has been the experience of many; perhaps of more in this late visitation than in any other age since the times of the Apostles. But in others He works in a very different way:

He designs His influence to infuse,

Sweet, refreshing, as the silent dews.

It has pleased Him to work the latter way in you from the beginning; and it is not improbable He will continue (as He has begun) to work in a gentle and almost insensible manner. Let Him take His own way:

He is wiser than you; He will do all things well. Do not reason against Him; but let the prayer of your heart be,

Mould as Thou wilt Thy passive clay!

Letters: "To Mary Cooke" (VII, 298).

But we—Not only the apostles, but all true believers, *have this treasure*—Of divine light, love, glory, *in earthern vessels*—In frail, feeble, perishing bodies. He proceeds to show, that afflictions, yea, death itself, are so far from hindering the ministration of the Spirit, that they even further it, sharpen the ministers, and increase the fruit; that the excellency of the power which works these in us, may undeniably appear to be of God.

Notes: "II Corinthians 4:7."

2. *Witness of the Spirit (Assurance)*

I observed many years ago, "It is hard to find words in the language of men, to explain the deep things of God. Indeed, there are none that will adequately express what the Spirit of God works in His children. But perhaps one might say (desiring any who are taught of God, to correct, soften, or strengthen the expression), by the testimony of the Spirit, I mean, an inward impression on the soul, whereby the Spirit of God immediately and directly witnesses to my spirit, that I am a child of God; that Jesus Christ hath loved me, and given Himself for me; that all my sins are blotted out, and I, even I, am reconciled to God."

After twenty years' further consideration, I see no cause to retract any part of this. Neither do I conceive how any of these expressions may be altered, so as to make them more intelligible. I can only add, that if any of the children of God will point out any other expressions which are more clear, or more agreeable to the Word of God, I will readily lay these aside.

Meantime let it be observed, I do not mean hereby, that the Spirit of God testifies this by any outward voice; no, nor always by an inward voice, although He may do this sometimes. Neither do I suppose, that He always applies to the heart (though He often may) one or more texts of Scripture. But He so works upon the soul by His immediate influence, and by a strong, though inexplicable operation, that the stormy wind and troubled waves subside, and there is a sweet calm; the heart resting as in the arms of Jesus, and the sinner being clearly satisfied that God is reconciled, that all his "iniquities are forgiven, and his sins covered."

Sermons: "The Witness of the Spirit: II," II, 2-4 (S, II, 344-45).

JW

"But how may one who has the real witness in himself distinguish it from presumption?" How, I pray, do you distinguish day from night? How do you distinguish light from darkness; or the light of a star, or a glimmering taper, from the light of the noonday sun? Is there not an inherent, obvious, essential difference between the one and the other? And do you not immediately and directly perceive that difference, provided your senses are rightly disposed? In like manner, there is an inherent, essential difference between spiritual light and spiritual darkness; and between the light wherewith the Sun of Righteousness shines upon our heart, and that glimmering light which arises only from "sparks of our own kindling": and this difference also is immediately and directly perceived, if our spiritual senses are rightly disposed.

To require a more minute and philosophical account of the manner whereby we distinguish these, and of the *criteria,* or intrinsic marks, whereby we know the voice of God, is to make a demand which can never be answered; no, not by one who has the deepest knowledge of God. . . .

Suppose God were now to speak to any soul, "Thy sins are forgiven thee," He must be willing that soul should know His voice; otherwise He would speak in vain. And He is able to effect this; for, whenever He wills, to do is present with Him. And He does effect it: that soul is absolutely assured, "This voice is the voice of God." But yet he who hath that witness in himself cannot explain it to one who hath it not; nor indeed is it to be expected that he should. Were there any natural medium to prove, or natural method to explain, the things of God to unexperienced men, then the natural man might discern and know the things of the Spirit of God. But this is utterly contrary to the assertion of the Apostle, that "he cannot know them, because they are spiritually discerned"; even by spiritual senses, which the natural man hath not.

"But how shall I know that my spiritual senses are rightly disposed?" This also is a question of vast importance; for if a man mistake in this, he may run on in endless error and delusion. "And how am I assured that this is not my case; and that I do not mistake the voice of the Spirit?" Even by the testimony of your own spirit: by "the answer of a good conscience toward God." By the fruits which He hath wrought in your spirit, you shall know the testimony of the Spirit of God. Hereby you shall know that you are in no delusion, that you have not deceived your own soul. The immediate fruits of the Spirit, ruling in the heart, are "love, joy, peace, bowels of mercies, humbleness of mind, meekness, gentleness, long-suffering." And the outward fruits are, the doing good to all men; the doing no evil to any; and the walking in the light—a zealous, uniform obedience to all the commandments of God.

By the same fruits shall you distinguish this voice of God from any delusion of the devil. That proud spirit cannot humble thee before God. He neither can nor would soften thy heart, and melt it first into earnest mourning after God, and then into filial love. It is not the adversary of God and man that enables thee to love thy neighbour; or to put on meekness, gentleness, patience, temperance, and the whole armour of God. He is not divided against himself, or a destroyer of sin, his own work. No; it is none but the Son of God who cometh "to destroy the works of the devil." As surely therefore as holiness is of God, and as sin is the work of the devil, so surely the witness thou hast in thyself is not of Satan, but of God.

Well then mayest thou say, "Thanks be unto God for His unspeakable gift!" Thanks be unto God, who giveth me to "know in whom I have believed"; who hath "sent forth the Spirit of His Son into my heart, crying, Abba, Father," and even now, "bearing witness with my spirit that I am a child of God"! And see, that not only thy lips, but thy life show forth His praise. He hath sealed thee for His own; glorify Him then in thy body and thy spirit, which are His. Beloved, if thou hast this hope in thyself, purify thyself, as He is pure. While thou beholdest what manner of love the Father hath given thee, that thou shouldest be called a child of God, cleanse thyself "from all filthiness of flesh and spirit, perfecting holiness in the fear of God"; and let all thy thoughts, words, and works be a spiritual sacrifice, holy, acceptable to God through Christ Jesus!

Sermons: "The Witness of the Spirit: I," II, 9-14 (S, I, 216-18).

JW

I mean an assurance that I am now in a state of salvation; you [mean] an assurance that I shall persevere therein. The very definition of the term cuts off your second and third observation. As to the first, I would take notice: (1) No kind of assurance (that I know), or of faith, or repentance, is essential to their salvation who die infants. (2) I believe God is ready to give all true penitents who fly to His free grace in Christ a fuller sense of pardon than they had before they fell. I know this to be true of several; whether these are exempt cases, I know not. (3) Persons that were of a melancholy and gloomy constitution, even to some degree of madness, I have known in a moment (let it be called a miracle, I quarrel not) brought into a state of firm, lasting peace and joy.

Letters: "To his Brother Samuel" (I, 290).

JW

Q. 10. But does not matter of fact prove, that justifying faith does not necessarily imply assurance? For can you believe that such a person as J.A., or E.V., who have so much integrity, zeal, and fear of God, and walk so unblamably in all things, is void of justifying faith? Can you suppose such as these to be under the wrath and under the curse of God; especially if you add to this, that they are continually longing, striving, praying for the assurance which they have not?

A. This contains the very strength of the cause; and inclines us to think that some of these may be exempt cases. But, however that be, we answer.

(1) It is dangerous to ground a general doctrine on a few particular experiments.

(2) Men may have many good tempers, and a blameless life, (speaking in a loose sense,) by nature and habit, with preventing grace; and yet not have faith and the love of God.

(3) It is scarce possible for us to know all the circumstances relating to such persons, so as to judge certainly concerning them.

(4) But this we know, if Christ is not revealed in them, they are not yet Christian believers.

Works: "Minutes of Some Late Conversations," Tues. June 16, 1747 (VIII, 293).

J.W.

Q. 16. But how do you know, that you are sanctified, saved from your inbred corruption?

A. I can know it no otherwise than I know that I am justified. "Hereby know we that we are of God," in either sense, "by the Spirit that he hath given us."

We know it by the witness and by the fruit of the Spirit. And, First, by the witness. As, when we were justified, the Spirit bore witness with our spirit, that our sins were forgiven; so, when we were sanctified he bore witness, that they were taken away. Indeed, the witness of sanctification is not always clear at first; (as neither is that of justification;) neither is it afterward always the same, but, like that of justification, sometimes stronger and sometimes fainter. Yea, and sometimes it is withdrawn. Yet, in general, the latter testimony of the Spirit is both as clear and as steady as the former.

Work: "A Plain Account of Christian Perfection" 25 (XI, 420).

JW

One of our preachers that was (I mean Hampson) has lately made a discovery that there is no such thing in any believer as a *direct, immediate* testimony of the Spirit that he is a child of God, that the Spirit testifies this *only* by the fruits, and consequently that the witness and the fruits are *all one.* Let me have your deliberate thoughts on this head. It seems to me to be a point of no small importance. I am afraid lest we should get back again unawares into justification by works.

Letters: "To Samuel Furly" (V, 8).

JW

A divine conviction of my being reconciled to God is, I think, directly implied, not in a divine evidence or conviction of something else, but in a divine conviction that Christ loved me and gave Himself for me, and still more clearly in the Spirit's bearing witness with my spirit that I am a child of God.

I see no reason either to retract or soften the expression "God's mercy in some cases obliges Him to act thus and thus." Certainly, as His own nature obliges Him (in a very clear and sound sense) to act according to truth and justice in all things; so in some sense His love obliged Him to give His only Son, that whosoever believeth in Him might not perish. So much for the phrase. My meaning is, The same compassion which moves God to pardon a mourning, broken-hearted sinner moves Him to comfort that mourner by witnessing to his spirit that his sins are pardoned.

You think "full assurance excludes all doubt." I think so too. But there may be faith without full assurance. And these lower degrees of faith do not exclude doubts, which frequently mingle therewith, more or less. But this you cannot allow. You say it cannot be shaken without being overthrown; and trust I shall be "convinced upon reflection that the distinction between 'shaken' and 'destroyed' is absolutely without a difference." Hark! The wind rises: the house *shakes,* but it is not *overthrown;* it *totters,* but it is not *destroyed.*

You add: "Assurance is quite a distinct thing from faith. Neither does it depend upon the same agent. Faith is an act of my mind; assurance an act of the Holy Ghost." I answer: (1) The assurance in question is no other than the full assurance of faith; therefore it cannot be a distinct thing from faith, but only so high a degree of faith as excludes all doubt and fear. (2) This *plerophory,* or full assurance, is doubtless wrought in us by the Holy Ghost. But so is every degree of true faith; yet the mind of man is the subject of both. I believe feebly; I believe without all doubt.

Your next remark is: "The Spirit's witnessing that we are accepted cannot be the faith whereby we are accepted." I allow it. A conviction that we are justified cannot be implied in justifying faith.

You subjoin: "A sure trust that God hath accepted me is not the same thing with knowing that God has accepted me." I think it is the same thing with some degree of that knowledge. But it matters not whether it be so or no. I will not contend for a term. I contend only for this,—that every true Christian believer has "a sure trust and confidence in God that through the merits of Christ he is reconciled to God"; and that in consequence of this he is able to say, "The life which I now live, I live by faith in the Son of God, who loved me, and gave Himself for me."

Letters: "To Richard Tompson" (III, 161-62).

JW

In the evening I went very unwillingly to a society in Aldersgate Street, where one was reading Luther's preface to the *Epistle to the Romans.* About a quarter before nine, while he was describing the change which God works in the heart through faith in Christ, I felt my heart strangely warmed. I felt I did trust in Christ, Christ alone for salvation; and an assurance was given me that He had taken away *my* sins, even *mine,* and saved *me* from the law of sin and death.

Journal: "May 24, 1738" (I, 475-76).

3. Fruits of the Spirit

Let none ever presume to rest in any supposed testimony of the Spirit, which is separate from the fruit of it. If the Spirit of God does really testify that we are the children of God, the immediate consequences will be the fruit of the Spirit, even "love, joy, peace, long-suffering, gentleness, goodness, fidelity, meekness, temperance." And however this fruit may be clouded for a while, during the time of strong temptation, so that it does not appear to the tempted person, while Satan is sifting him as wheat; yet the substantial part of it remains, even under the thickest cloud. It is true, joy in the Holy Ghost may be withdrawn, during the hour of trial; yea, the soul may be "exceeding sorrowful," while "the hour and power of darkness" continue; but even this is generally restored with increase, till we rejoice "with joy unspeakable and full of glory."

The second inference is, Let none rest in any supposed fruit of the Spirit without the witness. There may be foretastes of joy, of peace, of love, and those not delusive, but really from God, long before we have the witness in ourselves; before the Spirit of God witnesses with our spirits that we have "redemption in the blood of Jesus, even the forgiveness of sins." Yea, there may be a [degree] of long-suffering, of gentleness, of fidelity, meekness, temperance (not a shadow thereof, but a real degree, by the preventing grace of God), before we "are accepted in the Beloved," and, consequently, before we have a testimony of our acceptance: but it is by no means advisable to rest here; it is at the peril of our souls if we do. If we are wise, we shall be continually crying to God, until His Spirit cry in our heart, "Abba, Father!" This is the privilege of all the children of God, and without this we can never be assured that we are His children. Without this we cannot retain a steady peace, nor avoid perplexing doubts and fears. But when we have once received this Spirit of adoption, this "peace, which passeth all understanding," and which expels all painful doubt and fear, will "keep our hearts and minds in Christ Jesus." And when this has brought forth its genuine fruit, all inward and outward holiness, it is undoubtedly the will of Him that calleth us, to give us always what He has once given: so that there is no need that we should ever more be deprived of either the testimony of God's Spirit or the testimony of our own, the consciousness of our walking in all righteousness and true holiness.

Sermons: "The Witness of the Spirit: II," V, 3-4 (S, II, 358-59).

JW

In [Acts IV] we read, that when the Apostles and brethren had been praying, and praising God, "the place was shaken where they were assembled together, and they were all filled with the Holy Ghost." Not that we find any visible appearance here, such as had been in the former instance: nor are we informed that the *extraordinary gifts* of the Holy Ghost were then given to all or any of them; such as the gifts of "healing, of working" other "miracles, of prophecy, of discerning spirits, the speaking with divers kinds of tongues, and the interpretation of tongues" (I Cor. xii. 9, 10).

Whether these gifts of the Holy Ghost were designed to remain in the Church throughout all ages, and whether or no they will be restored at the nearer approach of the "restitution of all things," are questions which it is not needful to decide. But it is needful to observe this, that, even in the infancy of the Church, God divided them with a sparing hand. Were all even then prophets? Were all workers of miracles? Had all the gifts of healing? Did all speak with tongues? No, in no wise. Perhaps not one in a thousand. Probably none but the teachers in the Church, and only some of them (I Cor. xii. 28-30). It was, therefore, for a more excellent purpose than this, that "they were all filled with the Holy Ghost."

It was, to give them (what none can deny to be essential to all
Christians in all ages) the mind which was in Christ, those holy fruits
of the Spirit, which whosoever hath not, is none of His; to fill them
with "love, joy, peace, long-suffering, gentleness, goodness" (Gal. v.
22-24); to endue them with faith (perhaps it might be rendered
fidelity), with meekness and temperance; to enable them to crucify
the flesh, with its affections and lusts, its passions and desires; and in
consequence of that inward change, to fulfil all outward righteousness;
to "walk as Christ also walked," in "the work of faith, in the patience
of hope, the labour of love" (I Thess. i. 3).

Sermons: "Scriptural Christianity," Introduction, 2-4 (S, I, 92-94).

JW

Spirit of Faith, come down,
Reveal the things of God,
And make to us the Godhead known,
And witness with the blood:
'Tis Thine the blood to' apply,
And give us eyes to see
Who did for every sinner die
Hath surely died for *me*.

No man can truly say
That Jesus is the Lord,
Unless Thou take the veil away,
And breathe the living word:
Then, only then we feel
Our interest in His blood,
And cry with joy unspeakable
Thou art my Lord, my God!

. . . .

Inspire the living faith,
(Which whosoe'er receives
The witness in himself he hath,

FRUITS OF THE SPIRIT

And consciously believes;)
The faith that conquers all,
And doth the mountain move,
And saves whoe'er on Jesus call,
And perfects them in love.

Poetics: Hymn XXVII (IV, 196-97).

SUPPLEMENTARY REFERENCES

REDEMPTIVE WORK OF THE HOLY SPIRIT—*Sermons:* "The Lord Our Righteousness," II, 12 (S, II, 433-34). *Works:* "A Farther Appeal to Men of Reason and Religion: I," III (VIII, 58 ff.); I, v (VIII, 76 ff.). *Letters:* "To Dr. Lavington, Bishop of Exeter" (III, 295 ff.); "To Dr. Warburton, Bishop of Gloucester" (IV, 371 ff.); "To Philothea Briggs" (V, 241).

WITNESS OF THE SPIRIT (ASSURANCE)—*Sermons:* "The Witness of the Spirit: I" (S, I, 202 ff.); "The Nature of Enthusiasm" (S, II, 86 ff.); "The Witness of the Spirit: II" (S, II, 343 ff.); "On Grieving the Holy Spirit" (J, VII, 485 ff.). *Letters:* "To 'John Smith'" (II, 42 ff; 57 ff; 68 ff; 87 ff; 97 ff; 133 ff.); "To Thomas Church" (II, 204 ff.); "To Dr. Rutherforth" (V, 358-59). *Journal:* "Sat. 22 April 1738" (I, 454-55); "Wed. 17 Jan. 1739" (II, 130). *Notes:* "Hebrews 6:11;" "I Timothy 6:11."

FRUITS OF THE SPIRIT—*Sermons:* "Scriptural Christianity" (S, I, 92 ff.); "The First-Fruits of the Spirit" (S, I, 162-77); "The Witness of the Spirit: I, II, 12-14 (S, I, 217-8); "The Witness of Our Own Spirit" (S, I, 221 ff.); "The Witness of the Spirit: II," III (S, II, 346-52). *Letters:* "To Benjamin Ingham" (II, 80 ff.). *Journal:* "Fri. 22 June 1739" (II, 226); "Tues. 31 July 1739" (II, 249 ff.); "Sat. 1 Aug. 1741" (II, 483-84). *Notes:* "Matthew 7:15-16."

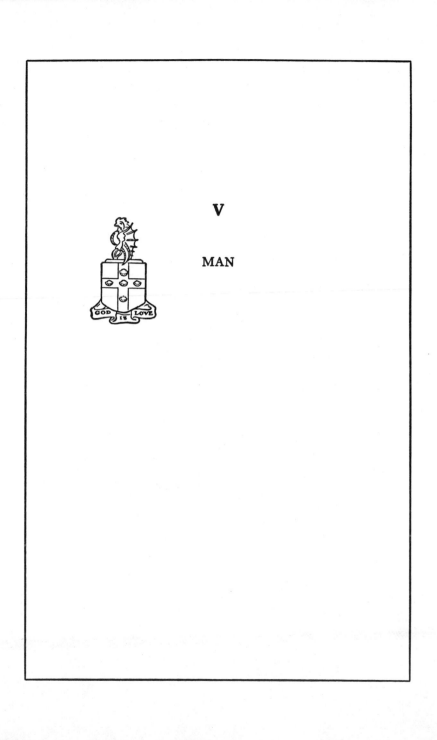

V

MAN

V. MAN

WESLEY'S DOCTRINE of man receives full meaning when seen in its relation to salvation. The image of God in man which is defaced by sin is restored by the redemptive process. Wesley distinguishes between the guilt of sin, which is forgiven in justification, and the depravity or power of sin, which is removed in sanctification. The distinction is only briefly outlined, however, and never developed in detail. Wesley indicates that purely "natural man" does not exist. This theological abstraction is valuable, for each man, of himself, exhibits the universality and depth of sin and has no claim to goodness. However, the truth is that by virtue of the atonement God bestows preventing grace on all men who thus stand as debtors to his grace. Because of the conjunction of the ideas of natural man and prevenient grace many of Wesley's sermons follow a common pattern, affirming first man's incapacity and then his capacity for salvation. Wesley can say without theological contradiction, "You can do nothing to save yourself," and "You must work out your own salvation." The former assertion is emphasized in this chapter, the latter in the next chapter. Wesley's conception of grace is basic to his idea of free will; liberty, in matters of other than an indifferent nature, is entirely dependent on God's grace.

1. Image of God

In the image of God was man made; holy as He that created him is holy; merciful as the Author of all is merciful; perfect as his Father in heaven is perfect. As God is love, so man, dwelling in love, dwelt in God, and God in him. God made him to be an "image of His own eternity," an incorruptible picture of the God of glory. He was accordingly pure, as God is pure, from every spot of sin. He knew not evil in any kind or degree, but was inwardly and outwardly sinless and undefiled. He "loved the Lord his God with all his heart, and with all his mind, and soul, and strength."

To man, thus upright and perfect, God gave a perfect law, to which He required full and perfect obedience. He required full obedience in every point, and this to be performed without any intermission, from the moment man became a living soul, till the time of his trial should be ended. No allowance was made for any falling short. As, indeed, there was no need of any; man being altogether equal to the task assigned, and thoroughly furnished for every good word and work.

Sermons: "Justification by Faith," I, 1-2 (S, I, 116).

JW

"Man was made in the image of God." But "God is a Spirit:" so therefore was man: (Only that spirit, being designed to dwell on earth, was lodged in an earthly tabernacle.) As such, he had an innate principle of self-motion. And so, it seems, has every spirit in the universe; this being the proper distinguishing difference between spirit and matter, which is totally, essentially passive and inactive, as appears from a thousand experiments. He was, after the likeness of his Creator, endued with understanding; a capacity of apprehending whatever objects were brought before it, and of judging concerning them. He was endued with a will, exerting itself in various affections and passions: And, lastly, with liberty, or freedom of choice; without which all the rest would have been in vain, and he would have been no more capable of serving his Creator than a piece of earth or marble; he would have been as incapable of vice or virtue, as any part of the inanimate creation. In these, in the power of self-motion, understanding, will and liberty, the natural image of God consisted. . . .

What then is the barrier between men and brutes? the line which they cannot pass? It was not reason. Set aside that ambiguous term: Exchange it for the plain word, understanding: And who can deny that brutes have this? We may as well deny that they have sight or hearing. But it is this: Man is capable of God; the inferior creatures are not. We have no ground to believe that they are, in any degree, capable of knowing, loving, or obeying God. This is the specific difference between man and brute; the great gulf which they cannot pass over.

Sermons: "The General Deliverance," I, 1, 5 (J, VI, 242-44).

JW

Why must we be born again? What is the foundation of this doctrine? The foundation of it lies near as deep as the creation of the world; in the scriptural account whereof we read, "And God," the three-one God, "said, Let us make man in our image, after our likeness. So God created man in His own image, in the image of God created He him" (Gen. i. 26, 27):—not barely in his *natural image,* a picture of His own immortality; a spiritual being, endued with understanding, freedom of will, and various affections; nor merely in his *political image,* the governor of this lower world, having "dominion over the fishes of the sea, and over all the earth": but chiefly in his *moral image;* which, according to the Apostle, is "righteousness and true holiness" (Eph. iv. 24). In this image of God was man made. "God is love"; accordingly, man at his creation was full of love; which was the sole principle of all his tempers, thoughts, words, and actions. God is full of justice, mercy, and truth; so was man as he came from the hands of his Creator. God is spotless purity; and so man was in the beginning pure from every sinful blot; otherwise God could not have pronounced him, as well as all the other work of His hands, "very good" (Gen. i. 31). This he could not have been, had he not been pure from sin, and filled with righteousness and true holiness. For there is no medium: if we suppose an intelligent creature not to love God, not to be righteous and holy, we necessarily suppose him not to be good at all; much less to be "very good."

Sermons: "The New Birth," I, 1 (S, II, 227-28).

111

"God created man in his own image; in the image of God created he him!" Mark the emphatical repetition. God did not make him mere matter, a piece of senseless, unintelligent clay; but a spirit, like himself, although clothed with a material vehicle. As such he was endued with understanding; with a will including various affections; and with liberty, a power of using them in a right or wrong manner, of choosing good or evil. Otherwise neither his understanding nor his will would have been to any purpose; for he must have been as incapable of virtue or holiness as the stock of a tree. Adam, in whom all mankind were then contained, freely preferred evil to good. He chose to do his own will, rather than the will of his Creator. He "was not deceived," but knowingly and deliberately rebelled against his Father and his King. In that moment he lost the moral image of God, and, in part, the natural: He commenced unholy, foolish, and unhappy.

Sermons: "On the Fall of Man," II, 6 (J, VI, 222-23).

2. Fall and Its Results

[Man's] liberty . . . necessarily included a power of choosing or refusing either good or evil. Indeed it has been doubted whether man could then choose evil, knowing it to be such. But it cannot be doubted, he might mistake evil for good. He was not infallible; therefore, not impeccable. And this unravels the whole difficulty of the grand question, *Unde malum?* "How came evil into the world?" It came from "Lucifer, son of the morning." It was the work of the devil. "For the devil," saith the Apostle, "sinneth from the beginning"; that is, was the first sinner in the universe, the author of sin, the first being who, by the abuse of his liberty, introduced evil into the creation. He,

—Of the first,
If not the first archangel,

was self-tempted to think too highly of himself. He freely yielded to the temptation; and gave way, first to pride, then to self-will. He said, "I will sit upon the sides of the north: I will be like the Most High." He did not fall alone, but soon drew after him a third part of the stars of heaven; in consequence of which they lost their glory and happiness, and were driven from their former habitation.

"Having great wrath," and perhaps envy, at the happiness of the creatures whom God had newly created, it is not strange that he should desire and endeavour to deprive them of it. In order to this, he concealed himself in the serpent, who was the most subtile, or intelligent, of all the brute creatures; and, on that account, the least liable to raise suspicion. Indeed, some have (not improbably) supposed that the serpent was then endued with reason and speech. Had not Eve known he was so, would she have admitted any parley with him? Would she not have been frightened rather than deceived? as the Apostle observes she was. To deceive her, Satan mingled truth with falsehood: —"Hath God said, Ye may not eat of every tree of the garden?"—and soon after persuaded her to disbelieve God, to suppose his threatening should not be fulfilled. She then lay open to the whole temptation:—To "the desire of the flesh"; for the tree was "good for food": To "the desire of the eyes"; for it was "pleasant to the eyes": And to "the pride of life"; for it was "to be desired to make one wise," and consequently honoured. So unbelief begot pride. She thought herself wiser than God; capable of finding a better way to happiness than God had taught her. It begot self-will: She was determined to do her own will, not the will of Him that made her. It begot foolish desires; and completed all by outward sin: "She took of the fruit, and did eat."

Sermons: "The End of Christ's Coming," I, 8-9 (J, VI, 271-72).

JW

As by one man—Adam; who is mentioned, and not Eve, as being the representative of mankind. *Sin entered into the world*—Actual sin, and its consequences, a sinful nature. *And death*—With all its attendants. *It entered into the world,* when it entered into being; or till then it did not exist, *by sin*—Therefore it could not enter before sin. *Even so death passed upon all men*—Namely, by one man, *in that*—So

113

the word is used also: 2 Cor. v. 4. *All sinned*—In Adam. These words assign the reason why death came upon *all men:* infants themselves not excepted, *in that all sinned....*

Death reigned—And how vast is his kingdom! Scarce can we find any king, who has as many subjects, as are the kings whom he hath conquered! *Even over them that had not sinned after the likeness of Adam's transgression*—Even over infants who had never sinned, as Adam did, in their own persons: and over others, who had not, like him, sinned against an express law. *Who is the figure of him that was to come*—Each of them being a public person, and a federal head of mankind. The one, the fountain of sin and death to mankind by his offence; the other, of righteousness and life by his free gift.

Thus far the apostle shows the agreement between the first and second Adam: afterward he shows the difference between them. The agreement may be summed up thus: As by one man sin entered into the world, and death by sin; so by one man righteousness entered into the world, and life by righteousness. As death passed upon all men, in that all had sinned; so life passed upon all men, (who are in the second Adam by faith) in that all are justified. And as death through the sin of the first Adam, reigned *even over them who had not sinned after the likeness of Adam's transgression: so* through the righteousness of Christ, even those who have not obeyed, after the likeness of his obedience, shall reign in life. We may add, As the sin of Adam, without the sins which we afterward committed, brought us death; so the righteousness of Christ, without the good works which we afterward performed, brings us life; although still every good, as well as evil work, will receive its due reward.

Notes: "Romans 5:12, 14."

JW

"But if parents were wise and virtuous themselves, and then endeavoured to bring up their children virtuously, there would be less wickedness in the world." There would: But this does not reach the point; nor, that "undisciplined children contract bad habits." I have known wise and virtuous parents who did earnestly labour to bring up their children virtuously; and disciplined them with all possible care, from the very first dawn of reason; yet these very children showed bad tempers before it was possible they should "contract bad habits." They daily evidenced the wrong state of all their faculties, both of their understanding, will, and affections; just contrary both to the examples and instructions of all that were round about them. Here, then, these wrong tempers were not owing to "the fault of careless or ungodly parents"; nor could be rationally accounted for, but by supposing those children to have a natural propensity to evil.

Works: "The Doctrine of Original Sin," II (IX, 295).

JW

[Natural] circumstances are considered by some as the source of the general calamities that befall mankind; that, in consequence of these great changes, the years of his life are reduced to a smaller number, and he, and all living creatures with him, rendered the remediless victims of affliction and sorrow. Whatever degree of plausibility may be considered as attached to this doctrine, one thing is most certain, and that is, that man, by his own folly and imprudence, is his own greatest punisher; and if the world itself were better, it would make no great difference to him, unless he himself were better also.

A Compendium of Natural Philosophy (I, 480).

JW

What benefit accrues to the brute creation from the sufferings wherein their whole race is involved through the sin of the first man? The fact cannot be denied; daily experience attests what we read in the oracles of God, that "the whole creation groaneth together, and travaileth in pain to this day"; a considerable part of it groans to God, under the wantonness or cruelty of man. . . . When man, the lord of the visible creation, rebelled against God, every part of the creation began to suffer on account of his sin. And to suffering on account of sin, I can give no properer name than that of punishment.

Work: "The Doctrine of Original Sin," III, 2 (IX, 318-19).

JW

My reason for believing [that Adam is a federal head or representative of mankind] is this: Christ was the representative of mankind, when God "laid on him the iniquities of us all, and he was wounded for our transgressions." But Adam was a type or figure of Christ; therefore, he was also, in some sense, our representative; in consequence of which, "all died" in him as "in Christ all shall be made alive."

But as neither representative, nor federal head, are scripture words, it is not worth while to contend for them. The thing I mean is this: The state of all mankind did so far depend on Adam, that, by his fall, they all fell into sorrow, and pain, and death, spiritual and temporal. And all this is noways inconsistent with either the justice or goodness of God, provided all may recover through the Second Adam, whatever they lost through the first; nay, and recover it with unspeakable gain; since every additional temptation they feel, by that corruption of their nature which is antecedent to their choice, will, if conquered by grace, be a means of adding to that "exceeding and eternal weight of glory."...

And if you ask me, how, in what determinate manner, sin is propagated; how it is transmitted from father to son: I answer plainly, I cannot tell; no more than I can tell how man is propagated, how a body is transmitted from father to son. I know both the one and the other fact; but I can account for neither.

Thus much, however, is plain: That "God is the maker of every man who comes into the world." For it is God alone who gives man power to propagate his species. Or rather, it is God himself who does the work by man as an instrument; man (as you observed before) having no other part in producing man, than the oak has in producing an acorn. God is really the producer of every man, every animal, every vegetable in the world; as he is the true *primum mobile,* the spring of all motion throughout the universe. So far we agree. But when you subsume, "If it is the power of God whereby a sinful species is propagated, whereby a sinful father begets a sinful son, then God is the author of sin; that sinfulness is chargeable upon him." Here we divide; I cannot allow the consequences, because the same argument would make God chargeable with all the sinful actions of men. For it is the power of God whereby the murderer lifts up his arm, whereby the adulterer perpetrates his wickedness; full as much as it is his power whereby an acorn produces an oak, or a father a son. But does it follow, that God is chargeable with the sin? You know it does not follow. The power of God, vulgarly termed *nature,* acts from age to age, under its fixed rules. Yet he who this moment supplies the power by which a sinful action is committed is not chargeable with the sinfulness of that action. In like manner, it is the power of God which, from age to age, continues the human species; yet He who this moment supplies the power whereby a sinful nature is propagated (according to the fixed rules established in the lower world) is not chargeable with the sinfulness of that nature. This distinction you must allow, as was observed before, or charge God with all the sin committed under heaven. And this general answer may suffice any sincere and modest inquirer, without entangling himself in those minute particulars which are beyond the reach of human understanding.

Works: "The Doctrine of Original Sin," III, 6, 7 (IX, 332, 335).

JW

Q. 15. In what sense is Adam's sin imputed to all mankind?

A. In Adam all die; that is, (1) Our bodies then became mortal. (2) Our souls died; that is, were disunited from God. And hence, (3) We are all born with a sinful, devilish nature. By reason whereof, (4) We are children of wrath, liable to death eternal. (Rom. v. 18; Ephes. ii. 3.)

Works: "Minutes of Some Late Conversations," Monday, June 25, 1744 (VIII, 277).

How exactly does matter of fact, do all things round us, even the face of the whole world, agree with this account [*i.e.* the fall of Adam]! Open your eyes! Look around you! See darkness that may be felt; see ignorance and error; see vice in ten thousand forms; see consciousness of guilt, fear, sorrow, shame, remorse, covering the face of the earth! See misery, the daughter of sin. See, on every side, sickness and pain, inhabitants of every nation under heaven; driving on the poor, helpless sons of men, in every age, to the gates of death! So they have done well nigh from the beginning of the world. So they will do, till the consummation of all things.

Sermons: "On the Fall of Man," II, 7 (J, VI, 223).

I spent two or three hours in the House of Lords. I had frequently heard that this was the most venerable assembly in England. But how was I disappointed! What is a lord but a sinner, born to die!

Journal: "Tues. 25 Jan. 1785" (VII, 46).

3. Guilt and Depravity of Original Sin

"Unto the woman he said, I will greatly multiply thy sorrow and," or in, "thy conception: In sorrow" or pain "thou shalt bring forth children";—yea, above any other creature under heaven; which original curse we see is entailed on her latest posterity. "And thy desire shall be to thy husband, and he shall rule over thee." It seems, the latter part of this sentence is explanatory of the former. Was there, till now, any other inferiority of the woman to the man than that which we may conceive in one angel to another? "And unto Adam he said, Because thou hast hearkened unto the voice of thy wife, and hast eaten of the tree of which I commanded thee, saying, Thou shalt not eat of it; cursed is the ground for thy sake.—Thorns and thistles shall it bring forth unto thee":—Useless, yea, and hurtful productions; whereas nothing calculated to hurt or give pain had at first any place in the creation. "And thou shalt eat the herb of the field":—Coarse and vile, compared to the delicious fruits of paradise! "In the sweat of thy face shalt thou eat bread, till thou return unto the ground: For out of it wast thou taken: For dust thou art, and unto dust shalt thou return."

Sermons: "On the Fall of Man," I, 4 (J, VI, 218-19).

JW

What, then, can we answer when He shall say, "Pay me that thou owest"? We are utterly insolvent; we have nothing to pay; we have wasted all our substance. Therefore, if He deal with us according to the rigour of His law, if He exact what He justly may, He must command us to be "bound hand and foot, and delivered over to the tormentors."

Indeed we are already bound hand and foot by the chains of our own sins. These, considered with regard to ourselves, are chains of iron and fetters of brass. They are wounds wherewith the world, the flesh, and the devil have gashed and mangled us all over. They are diseases that drink up our blood and spirits, that bring us down to the chambers of the grave. But, considered as they are here, with regard to God, they are debts immense and numberless. Well, therefore, seeing we have nothing to pay, may we cry unto Him, that He would frankly forgive us all!

Sermons: "Upon Our Lord's Sermon on the Mount: VI," III, 13 (S, I, 441-42).

JW

Man did disobey God. He "ate of the tree, of which God commanded him, saying, Thou shalt not eat of it." And in that day he was condemned by the righteous judgement of God. Then also the sentence, whereof he was warned before, began to take place upon him. For the moment he tasted that fruit, he died. His soul died, was separated from God; separate from whom the soul has no more life than the body has when separate from the soul. His body, likewise, became corruptible and mortal; so that death then took hold on this also. And being already dead in spirit, dead to God, dead in sin, he hastened on to death everlasting; to the destruction both of body and soul, in the fire never to be quenched.

Sermons: "Justification by Faith," I, 5 (S, I, 117).

Our old man—Coeval with our being, and as old as the fall, our evil nature; a strong and beautiful expression for that entire depravity and corruption, which by nature spreads itself over the whole man, leaving no part uninfected.

Notes: "Romans 6:6."

[Christians] suppose Adam to have been created holy and wise, like his Creator; and yet capable of falling from it. They suppose farther, that through temptations, of which we cannot possibly judge, he did fall from that state; and that hereby he brought pain, labour, and sorrow on himself and all his posterity; together with death, not only temporal, but spiritual, and (without the grace of God) eternal. And it must be confessed, that not only a few Divines, but the whole body of Christians in all ages, did suppose this, till after seventeen hundred years a sweet-tongued orator arose, not only more enlightened than silly Adam, but than any of his wise posterity, and declared that the whole supposition was folly, nonsense, inconsistency, and blasphemy!

Works: "The Doctrine of Original Sin," II (IX, 291).

Know thyself to be a sinner, and what manner of sinner thou art. Know that corruption of thy inmost nature, whereby thou art very far gone from original righteousness, whereby "the flesh lusteth" always "contrary to the Spirit," through that "carnal mind" which "is enmity against God," which "is not subject to the law of God, neither indeed can be." Know that thou art corrupted in every power, in every faculty of thy soul; that thou art totally corrupted in every one of these, all the foundations being out of course. The eyes of thine understanding are darkened, so that they cannot discern God, or the things of God. The clouds of ignorance and error rest upon thee, and cover thee with the shadow of death. Thou knowest nothing yet as thou oughtest to know, neither God, nor the world, nor thyself. Thy will is no longer the will of God, but is utterly perverse and distorted, averse from all good, from all which God loves, and prone to all evil, to every abomination which God hateth. Thy affections are alienated from God, and scattered abroad over all the earth. All thy passions, both thy desires and aversions, thy joys and sorrows, thy hopes and fears, are out of frame, are either undue in their degree, or placed on undue objects. So that there is no soundness in thy soul; but "from the crown of the head, to the sole of the foot" (to use the strong expression of the prophet), there are only "wounds, and bruises, and putrefying sores."

Sermons: "The Way to the Kingdom," II, 1 (S, I, 155-56).

JW

By the grace of God, know thyself. Know and feel that thou wast shapen in wickedness, and in sin did thy mother conceive thee; and that thou thyself hast been heaping sin upon sin, ever since thou couldest discern good from evil. Own thyself guilty of eternal death; and renounce all hope of ever being able to save thyself. Be it all thy hope, to be washed in His blood, and purified by His Spirit, "who Himself bore" all "thy sins in His own body upon the tree." And if thou knowest He hath taken away thy sins, so much the more abase thyself before Him, in a continual sense of thy total dependence on Him for every good thought, and word, and work, and of thy utter inability to all good unless He "water thee every moment."

Sermons: "Upon Our Lord's Sermon on the Mount: XIII," III, 6 (S, II, 34).

[Man's] guilt is now also before his face: he knows the punishment he has deserved, were it only on account of his carnal mind, the entire, universal corruption of his nature: how much more, on account of all his evil desires and thoughts, of all his sinful words and actions! He cannot doubt for a moment, but the least of these deserves the damnation of hell—"the worm that dieth not, and the fire that never shall be quenched." Above all, the guilt of "not believing on the name of the only-begotten Son of God" lies heavy upon him. How, saith he, shall I escape, who "neglect so great a salvation"! "He that believeth not is condemned already," and "the wrath of God abideth on him."

Sermons: "Upon Our Lord's Sermon on the Mount: I," I, 5 (S, I, 324).

JW

Come to me . . . I alone (for none else can) *will* freely *give you* (what ye cannot purchase) *rest* from the guilt of sin by justification, and from the power of sin by sanctification.

Notes: "Matthew 11:28."

4. Original Sin and Actual Sins

From this infection of our nature (call it original sin, or what you please) spring many, if not all, actual sins. And this St. James (i. 14) plainly intimates. . . . And irregular desire is (not so much a fruit as a) part of original sin. For to say, "Eve had irregular desires before she sinned," (p. 127) is a contradiction; since all irregular desire is sin.

Another proof that actual sins spring from original, is, "Out of the heart proceed evil thoughts, murders, adulteries, fornications, thefts, false witness, blasphemies" (Matt. xv. 19.)

"But what has this text to do with Adam's sin?" It has much to do with the point it is brought to prove; namely, that actual sin proceeds from original; evil works, from an evil heart. Do not, therefore, triumph over these venerable men, (as you have done again and again,) because a text cited in proof of one clause of a proposition does not prove the whole.

But "neither of those texts proves that all our wickedness proceeds from our being corrupted by Adam's sin." (page 128) But they both prove what they were brought to prove,—that all outward wickedness proceeds from inward wickedness. Those pious men, therefore, did not mix "the forgery of their own imagination with the truth of God."

Works: "The Doctrine of Original Sin," II (IX, 274-75).

JW

How wide do those parent sins extend, from which all the rest derive their being; that carnal mind which is enmity against God, pride of heart, self-will, and love of the world! Can we fix any bounds to them? Do they not diffuse themselves through all our thoughts, and mingle with all our tempers? Are they not the leaven which leavens, more or less, the whole mass of our affections? May we not, on a close and faithful examination of ourselves, perceive these roots of bitterness continually springing up, infecting all our words, and tainting all our actions? And how innumerable an offspring do they bring forth, in every age and nation! Even enough to cover the whole earth with darkness and cruel habitations.

Sermons: "Upon Our Lord's Sermon on the Mount: XI," I, 3 (S, I, 534).

JW

What manner of branches canst thou expect to grow from such an evil root? Hence springs unbelief; ever departing from the living God; saying, "Who is the Lord, that I should serve Him? Tush! Thou God carest not for it." Hence independence; affecting to be like the Most High. Hence pride, in all its forms; teaching thee to say, "I am rich, and increased in goods, and have need of nothing." From this evil fountain flow forth the bitter streams of vanity, thirst of praise, ambition, covetousness, the lust of the flesh, the lust of the eye, and the pride of life. From this arise anger, hatred, malice, revenge, envy, jealousy, evil surmisings: from this, all the foolish and hurtful lusts that now "pierce thee through with many sorrows," and, if not timely prevented, will at length drown thy soul in everlasting perdition.

And what fruits can grow on such branches as these? Only such as are bitter and evil continually. Of pride cometh contention, vain boasting, seeking and receiving praise of men, and so robbing God of that glory which He cannot give unto another. Of the lust of the flesh, come gluttony or drunkenness, luxury or sensuality, fornication, uncleanness; variously defiling that body which was designed for a temple of the Holy Ghost: of unbelief, every evil word and work. But the time would fail, shouldest thou reckon up all; all the idle words thou hast spoken, provoking the Most High, grieving the Holy One of Israel; all the evil works thou hast done, either wholly evil in themselves, or, at least, not done to the glory of God. For thy actual sins are more than thou art able to express, more than the hairs of thy head. Who can number the sands of the sea, or the drops of rain, or thy iniquities?

Sermons: "The Way of the Kingdom," II, 2-3 (S, I, 156-57).

JW

Is it sin which occasions darkness? What sin? Is it outward sin of any kind? Does your conscience accuse you of committing any sin, whereby you grieve the Holy Spirit of God? Is it on this account that He is departed from you, and that joy and peace are departed with Him? And how can you expect they should return, till you put away the accursed thing? "Let the wicked forsake his way"; "cleanse your hands, ye sinner"; "put away the evil of your doings"; so shall your "light break out of obscurity"; the Lord will return and "abundantly pardon."

If, upon the closest search, you can find no sin of commission which causes the cloud upon your soul, inquire next, if there be not some sin of omission which separates between God and you. Do you "not suffer sin upon your brother"? Do you reprove them that sin in your sight? Do you walk in all the ordinances of God? in public, family, private prayer? If not, if you habitually neglect any one of these known duties, how can you expect that the light of His countenance should continue to shine upon you? Make haste to "strengthen the things that remain"; then your soul shall live. "To-day, if ye will hear His voice," by His grace supply what is lacking. When you hear a voice behind you saying, "This is the way, walk thou in it," harden not your heart; be no more "disobedient to the heavenly calling." Till the sin, whether of omission or commission, be removed, all comfort is false and deceitful. It is only skinning the wound over, which still festers and rankles beneath. Look for no peace within, till you are at peace with God; which cannot be without "fruits meet for repentance."

But perhaps you are not conscious of even any sin of omission which impairs your peace and joy in the Holy Ghost. Is there not, then, some inward sin, which, as a root of bitterness, springs up in your heart to trouble you? Is not your dryness, and barrenness of soul occasioned by your heart's "departing from the living God"? Has not "the foot of pride come against" you? . . . Have you not been offended at any of your brethren, looking at their (real or imagined) sin, so as to sin yourself against the great law of love, by estranging your heart from them? . . . Have not you given way to any foolish desire? to any kind or degree of inordinate affection? How then can the love of God have place in your heart, till you put away your idols? . . . It is vain to hope for a recovery of His light, till you pluck out the right eye, and cast it from you. O let there be no longer delay!

Sermons: "The Wilderness State," III, 2-4 (S, II, 256-58).

5. Natural Man

The Scripture represents [the state of *natural man*] as a state of sleep: the voice of God to him is, "Awake, thou that sleepest." For his soul is in a deep sleep: his spiritual senses are not awake: they discern neither spiritual good nor evil. The eyes of his understanding are closed; they are sealed together, and see not. Clouds and darkness continually rest upon them; for he lies in the valley of the shadow of death. Hence, having no inlets for the knowledge of spiritual things, all the avenues of his soul being shut up, he is in gross, stupid ignorance of whatever he is most concerned to know. He is utterly ignorant of God, knowing nothing concerning Him as he ought to know. He is totally a stranger to the law of God, as to its true, inward, spiritual meaning. He has no conception of that evangelical holiness, without which no man shall see the Lord; nor of the happiness which they only find whose "life is hid with Christ in God."

And, for this very reason, because he is fast asleep, he is, in some sense, at rest. Because he is blind, he is also secure: he saith, "Tush, there shall no harm happen unto me." The darkness which covers him on every side, keeps him in a kind of peace; so far as peace can consist with the works of the devil, and with an earthly, devilish mind. He *sees* not that he stands on the edge of the pit; therefore he *fears* it not. He cannot *tremble* at the danger he does not *know*. He has not understanding enough to fear. Why is it that he is in no dread of God? Because he is totally ignorant of Him: if not saying in his heart, "There is no God"; or, that "He sitteth on the circle of the heavens, and humbleth" not "Himself to behold the things which are done on earth"; yet satisfying himself as well, to all Epicurean intents and purposes, by saying, "God is merciful"; confounding and swallowing up all at once in that unwieldy idea of mercy all His holiness and essential hatred of sin; all His justice, wisdom, and truth. He is in no dread of the vengeance denounced against those who obey not the blessed law of God, because he understands it not. He imagines the main point is, to *do thus,* to be *outwardly* blameless; and sees not that it extends to every temper, desire, thought, motion of the heart. Or he fancies that the obligation hereto is ceased; that Christ came to "destroy the Law and the Prophets"; to save His people *in,* not *from,* their sins; to bring them to heaven without holiness—notwithstanding His own words, "Not one jot or tittle of the law shall pass away, till all things are fulfilled"; and, "Not every one that saith unto Me, Lord, Lord!

shall enter into the kingdom of heaven; but he that doeth the will of My Father which is in heaven."

He is secure, because he is utterly ignorant of himself. Hence he talks of "repenting by-and-by"; he does not indeed exactly know when, but some time or other before he dies; taking it for granted, that this is quite in his own power. For what should hinder his doing it, if he will? If he does but once set a resolution, no fear but he will make it good!

But this ignorance never so strongly glares, as in those who are termed *men of learning*. If a natural man be one of these, he can talk at large of his rational faculties, of the freedom of his will, and the absolute necessity of such freedom, in order to constitute man a moral agent. He reads, and argues, and proves to a demonstration, that every man may do as he will; may dispose his own heart to evil or good, as it seems best in his own eyes. Thus the god of this world spreads a double veil of blindness over his heart, lest, by any means, "the light of the glorious gospel of Christ should shine" upon it.

From the same ignorance of himself and God, there may sometimes arise, in the natural man, a kind of *joy,* in congratulating himself upon his own wisdom and goodness; and what the world calls joy he may often possess. He may have pleasure in various kinds; either in gratifying the desires of the flesh, or the desire of the eye, or the pride of life; particularly if he has large possessions; if he enjoy an affluent fortune; then he may "clothe" himself "in purple and fine linen, and fare sumptuously every day." And so long as he thus doeth well unto himself, men will doubtless speak good of him. They will say, "He is a happy man." For, indeed, this is the sum of worldly happiness; to dress, and visit, and talk, and eat, and drink, and rise up to play.

It is not surprising, if one in such circumstances as these, dosed with the opiates of flattery and sin, should imagine, among his other waking dreams, that he walks in great *liberty.* How easily may he persuade himself, that he is at liberty from all *vulgar errors,* and from the *prejudice* of education; judging exactly right, and keeping clear of all extremes. "I am free," may he say, "from all the *enthusiasm* of weak and narrow souls; from *superstition,* the disease of fools and cowards, always righteous over much; and from *bigotry,* continually incident

to those who have not a free and generous way of thinking." And too
sure it is, that he is altogether free from the "wisdom which cometh
from above," from holiness, from the religion of the heart, from the
whole mind which was in Christ.

For all this time he is the servant of sin. He commits sin, more or
less, day by day. Yet he is not troubled: he "is in no bondage," as
some speak; he feels no condemnation. He contents himself (even
though he should profess to believe that the Christian Revelation is
of God) with, "Man is frail. We are all weak. Every man has his
infirmity." Perhaps he quotes Scripture: "Why, does not Solomon say,
The righteous man falls into sin seven times a day? And, doubtless,
they are all hypocrites or enthusiasts who pretend to be better than
their neighbors." If, at any time, a serious thought fix upon him, he
stifles it as soon as possible, with, "Why should I fear, since God is
merciful, and Christ died for sinners?" Thus, he remains a willing
servant of sin, content with the bondage of corruption; inwardly and
outwardly unholy, and satisfied therewith; not only not conquering
sin, but not striving to conquer, particularly that sin which doth so
easily beset him.

Such is the state of every *natural man;* whether he be a gross,
scandalous transgressor, or a more reputable and decent sinner, having
the form, though not the power, of godliness.

Sermons: "The Spirit of Bondage and of Adoption," I, 1-8 (S, I, 181-85).

JW

All men [are] "Atheists in the world." But Atheism itself does
not screen us from idolatry. In his natural state, every man born into
the world is a rank idolater. Perhaps, indeed, we may not be such
in a vulgar sense of the word. We do not, like the idolatrous Heathens,
worship molten or graven images. We do not bow down to the stock
of a tree, to the work of our own hands. We do not pray to the angels
or saints in heaven, any more than to the saints that are upon the
earth. But what then? We have set up our idols in our hearts; and to
these we bow down, and worship them: we worship ourselves, when

we pay that honour to ourselves which is due to God only. Therefore all pride is idolatry; it is ascribing to ourselves what is due to God alone. And although pride was not made for man, yet where is the man that is born without it? But hereby we rob God of His unalienable right, and idolatrously usurp His glory.

But pride is not the only sort of idolatry which we are all by nature guilty of. Satan has stamped his own image on our heart in self-will also. "I will," said he, before he was cast out of heaven, "I will sit upon the sides of the north": I will do my own will and pleasure, independently on that of my Creator. The same does every man born into the world say, and that in a thousand instances; nay, and avow it too, without ever blushing upon the account, without either fear or shame. . . .

So far we bear the image of the devil, and tread in his steps. But at the next step we leave Satan behind; we run into an idolatry whereof he is not guilty: I mean, love of the world; which is now as natural to every man, as to love his own will. What is more natural to us than to seek happiness in the creature, instead of the Creator—to seek that satisfaction in the works of His hands, which can be found in God only? What more natural than "the desire of the flesh"? that is, of the pleasure of sense in every kind? . .

And so is "the desire of the eye": The desire of the pleasures of the imagination. These arise either from great, or beautiful, or uncommon objects—if the two former do not coincide with the latter; for perhaps it would appear, upon a diligent inquiry, that neither grand nor beautiful objects please any longer than they are new; that when the novelty of them is over, the greatest part, at least, of the pleasure they give is over; and in the same proportion as they become familiar, they become flat and insipid. . . .

A third symptom of this fatal disease—the love of the world, which is so deeply rooted in our nature—is "the pride of life"; the desire of praise, of the honour that cometh of men. This the greatest admirers of human nature allow to be strictly natural; as natural as the sight, or hearing, or any other of the external senses. And are they ashamed of it, even men of letters, men of refined and improved understanding? So far from it, that they glory therein! . . . But would one imagine that these men had ever heard of Jesus Christ or His Apostles; or that they knew who it was that said, "How can ye believe who receive honour one of another, and seek not the honour which cometh of God only?" But if this be really so, if it be impossible to believe, and consequently to please God, so long as we receive or seek honour one of another, and seek not the honour which cometh of God only; then in what a condition are all mankind! the Christians as well as Heathens! . . .

And, first, from hence we may learn one grand fundamental difference between Christianity, considered as a system of doctrines, and the most refined Heathenism. Many of the ancient Heathens have largely described the vices of particular men. They have spoken much against their covetousness, or cruelty; their luxury, or prodigality. Some have dared to say, that "no man is born without vices of one kind or another." But still, as none of them were apprised of the fall of man, so none of them knew of his total corruption. They knew not that all men were empty of all good, and filled with all manner of evil. They were wholly ignorant of the entire depravation of the whole human nature, of every man born into the world, in every faculty of his soul, not so much by those particular vices which reign in particular persons, as by the general flood of Atheism and idolatry, of pride, self-will, and love of the world. This, therefore, is the first grand distinguishing point between Heathenism and Christianity. The one acknowledges that many men are infected with many vices, and even born with a proneness to them; but supposes withal, that in some the natural good much over-balances the evil: the other declares that all men are "conceived in sin," and "shapen in wickedness"—that hence there is in every man a "carnal mind, which is enmity against God. . . ."

Hence we may, secondly, learn, that all who deny this, call it "original sin," or by any other title, are but heathens still, in the fundamental point which differences Heathenism from Christianity. They may, indeed, allow, that men have many vices; that some are born with us; and that consequently, we are not born altogether so wise or so virtuous as we should be; there being few that will roundly affirm, "We are born with as much propensity to good as to evil, and that every man is, by nature, as virtuous and wise as Adam was at his creation." But here is the *shibboleth:* Is man by nature filled with all manner of evil? Is he void of all good? Is he wholly fallen? Is his soul totally corrupted? Or to come back to the text, is "every imagination of the thoughts of his heart only evil continually"? Allow this, and you are so far a Christian. Deny it, and you are but an Heathen still.

Sermons: "Original Sin," II, 7-III, 2 (S, II, 218-23).

I preached at Bath. Some of the rich and great were present, to whom, as to the rest, I declared with all plainness of speech: (1) that, by nature, they were all children of wrath; (2) that all their natural tempers were corrupt and abominable; and, (3) all their words and works, which could never be any better but by faith; and that (4) a natural man has no more faith than a devil, if so much. One of them, my Lord——, stayed very patiently till I came to the middle of the fourth head. Then, starting up, he said, " 'Tis hot! 'tis very hot," and got downstairs as fast as he could.

Journal: "Mon. 24 Jan. 1743" (III, 65).

6. *Free Will*

In the evening I preached at Dundee, and on *Tuesday* the 24th went on to Arbroath. In the way I read Lord K[ames]'s plausible *Essays on the Principles of Morality and Natural Religion.* Did ever man take so much pains to so little purpose as he does in his essay on "Liberty and Necessity"? *Cui bono?* What good would it do to mankind if he could convince them that they are a mere piece of clockwork; that they have no more share in directing their own actions than in directing the sea or north wind? He owns that "if men saw themselves in this light all sense of moral obligation, of right and wrong, of good or ill desert, would immediately cease." Well, my lord sees himself in this light; consequently, if his own doctrine is true, he has no "sense of moral obligation, of right or wrong, of good or ill desert." Is he not, then, excellently well qualified for a judge? Will he condemn a man for not "holding the wind in his fist"?

Journal: "Mon. 23, May 1774" (VI, 21).

JW

Q. 23. Wherein may we come to the very edge of Calvinism?
A. In ascribing all good to the free grace of God. (2) In denying all natural free-will, and all power antecedent to grace. And (3) In excluding all merit from man; even for what he has or does by the grace of God.

Works: "Minutes of Some Late Conversations," Aug. 1, 1745 (VIII, 285).

JW

Why Dr. E. should quarrel with me concerning natural free-will, I cannot conceive, unless for quarrelling's sake. For it is certain, on this head, if no other, we are precisely of one mind. I believe that Adam, before his fall, had such freedom of will, that he might choose either good or evil; but that, since the fall, no child of man has a natural power to choose anything that is truly good. Yet I know (and who does not?) that man has still freedom of will in things of an indifferent nature. Does not Dr. E. agree with me in this? O why should we seek occasion of contention!

Works: "Some Remarks on 'A Defence of the Preface to the Edinburgh Edition of Aspasio Vindicated,'" 5 (X, 350).

JW

Both Mr. F. [letcher] and Mr. W. [esley] absolutely deny natural free-will. We both steadily assert that the will of man is by nature free only to evil. Yet we both believe that every man has a measure of free-will restored to him by grace.

Works: "Some Remarks on Mr. Hill's 'Review of all the Doctrines Taught by Mr. John Wesley,'" 64 (X, 392).

JW

I am conscious to myself of one more property, commonly called liberty. This is very frequently confounded with the will; but is of a very different nature. Neither is it a property of the will, but a distinct property of the soul capable of being exerted with regard to all the faculties of the soul, as well as all the motions of the body. It is a power of self-determination; which, although it does not extend to all our thoughts and imaginations, yet extends to our words and actions in general, and not with many exceptions. I am full as certain of this, that I am free, with respect to these, to speak or not to speak, to act or not to act, to do this or the contrary, as I am of my own existence. I have not only what is termed, a "liberty of contradiction,"—a power to do or not to do; but what is termed, a "liberty of contrariety,"—a power to act one way, or the contrary. To deny this would be to deny the constant experience of all human kind. Every one feels that he has an inherent power to move this or that part of his body, to move it or not, and to move this way or the contrary, just as he pleases. I can, as I choose, (and so can every one that is born of a woman,) open or shut my eyes; speak, or be silent; rise, or sit down; stretch out my hand, or draw it in; and use any of my limbs according to my pleasure, as well as my whole body. And although I have not an absolute power over my own mind, because of the corruption of my own nature; yet, through the grace of God assisting me, I have a power to choose and do good, as well as evil. I am free to choose whom I will serve; and if I choose the better part, to continue therein even unto death.

Sermons: "What is Man?" 11 (J, VII, 228-29).

JW

MAN

O my false, deceitful heart,
Desperately false thou art,
Foul as hell, when fair in show;
Who can all the mazes know?
He the stars may reckon o'er,
Tell the sands that bound the shore,
Count the drops that make the sea,
Comprehend eternity.

Foolish heart, unjust and vain!
Pride was never made for man;
Glory dost thou still pursue;
Glory all to God is due.
What hast thou whereof to boast?
God alone is good and just;
Only His be all the praise;
What we are, we are by grace.

Wretched heart, with woes opprest!
Ever roving after rest:
Wilt thou still pretend to own
Bliss is found in God alone?
While thy foolish wishes go
After empty joys below,
False imaginary ease,
Dreams of creature happiness.

. . . .

O my Lord, what must I do?
Only Thou the way canst show,
Thou canst save me in this hour,
I have neither will nor power:
God if over all Thou art,
Greater than the sinful heart,

FREE WILL

Let it now on me be shown,
Take away the heart of stone.

Poetics: "Jeremiah XVII. 9" (II, 86-89).

SUPPLEMENTARY REFERENCES

IMAGE OF GOD—*Sermons:* "The General Deliverance," I, 1-2 (J, VI, 242-43); "What is Man?" (J, VII, 167 ff.); "The Heavenly Treasure in Earthen Vessels," Introduction. 2 (J, VII, 344-45). *Works:* "The Doctrine of Original Sin," Preface (IX, 192 ff.; 293 ff.). *Notes:* "I Corinthians 11:7;" "II Corinthians 1:22;" "Hebrews 2:6."

FALL AND ITS RESULTS—*Sermons:* "Original Sin" (S, II, 210 ff.); "On the Fall of Man" (J, VI, 215 ff.); "The General Deliverance" (J, VI, 241 ff.). *Works:* "A Farther Appeal to Men of Reason and Religion," III (VIII, 201 ff.); "The Doctrine of Original Sin," I (IX, 196 ff.). *Letters:* "To Dr. Taylor" (IV, 67-68); "To Samuel Sparrow" (V, 327 ff.).

GUILT AND DEPRAVITY OF ORIGINAL SIN—*Sermons:* "The Way to the Kingdom," II, 4 (S, I, 157); "Upon Our Lord's Sermon on the Mount: XI," I, 1-6 (S, I, 533-36); "Spiritual Idolatry" (J, VI, 435 ff.); "On Friendship with the World" (J, VI, 452 ff.); "On the Deceitfulness of the Human Heart," Introduction. (J, VII, 335 ff.). *Works:* "The Doctrine of Original Sin," II, III (IX, 238 ff.). *Letters:* "To Howell Harris" (II, 8-9); "To Mrs. Savage" (V, 330); "To Samuel Furly" (VIII, 271-72). *Journal:* "Jan. 1738" (I, 423-24). *Notes:* "Romans 6:6."

ORIGINAL SIN AND ACTUAL SINS—*Sermons:* "The Great Privilege of Those that are Born of God," II, 7 (S, I, 307). *Works:* "The Doctrine of Original Sin" (IX, 273-74; 312). *Notes:* "Colossians 2:11, 13;" "James 1:14, 15."

NATURAL MAN—*Sermons:* "The Righteousness of Faith," II, 5-6 (S, I, 141-42); "The Spirit of Bondage and of Adoption," I (S, I, 179 ff.); "Self-Denial," I, 3 (S, II, 286); "What is Man?" (J, VII, 167 ff.). "On Living Without God," 7-8 (J, VII, 351). *Letters:* "To John Valton" (IV, 229-30). *Journal:* "May 1738" (I, 470). *Notes:* "I Corinthians 2:14-16;" "Ephesians 2:12."

FREE WILL—*Sermons:* "Free Grace," 29 (J, VII, 385). *Works:* "Predestination Calmly Considered," 45-50 (X, 229-32.). *Letters:* "To Elizabeth Ritchie" (VI, 89).

135

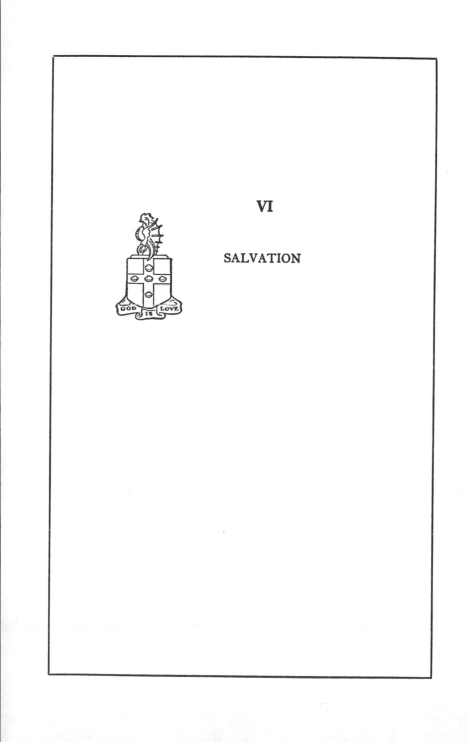

VI

SALVATION

GOD IS LOVE

VI. SALVATION

IN HIS conception of salvation Wesley combines a sense of complete dependence on God with a sense of man's complete responsibility and, thereby, makes intelligible the universality of God's redemptive plan over against the apparently limited number of the redeemed. Basic to the relation of dependence and responsibility is prevenient grace, enabling man to reject or to be taken over by God's grace. Man is never wholly devoid of grace; the grace he possesses makes action imperative. Wesley also joins emphases on the impossibility of righteousness as a condition of justification and the necessity of perfection for final salvation. The guilt of sin, occasioned in all men by Adam's fall, is taken away in justification; the depravity of sin is overcome by a gradual growth in holiness until entire sanctification removes its lingering power.

Wesley weds justification and sanctification, makes faith the condition of both, and sets eternity as the goal toward which both move. In his terminology the distinction between entire sanctification and the consequent life (Christian perfection) is never clear. The former is considered here as the second work of salvation through faith; the latter as an ideal of the ethical life. Wesley's view of sanctification requires a redefinition of sin in terms of conscious violation of the law of love. This is radically different from that alienation of sin, prior to justification, which brings men to despair. The distinction appears explicity in later years in two sermons, "Sin in Believers" and "Repentance of Believers."

1. General Nature of Salvation

Salvation begins with what is usually termed (and very properly) *preventing grace;* including the first wish to please God, the first dawn of light concerning his will, and the first slight transient conviction of having sinned against him. All these imply some tendency toward life; some degree of salvation; the beginning of a deliverance from a blind, unfeeling heart, quite insensible of God and the things of God. Salvation is carried on by *convincing grace,* usually in Scripture termed *repentance;* which brings a larger measure of self-knowledge, and a farther deliverance from the heart of stone. Afterwards we experience the proper Christian salvation; whereby, "through grace," we "are saved by faith"; consisting of those two grand branches, justification and sanctification. By justification we are saved from the guilt of sin, and restored to the favour of God; by sanctification we are saved from the power and root of sin, and restored to the image of God. All experience, as well as Scripture, show this salvation to be both instantaneous and gradual. It begins the moment we are justified, in the holy, humble, gentle, patient love of God and man. It gradually increases from that moment, as "a grain of mustard-seed, which, at first, is the least of all seeds," but afterwards puts forth large branches, and becomes a great tree; till, in another instant, the heart is cleansed from all sin, and filled with pure love to God and man. But even that love increases more and more, till we "grow up in all things into Him that is our Head"; till we attain "the measure of the stature of the fulness of Christ."

Sermons: "On Working Out Our Own Salvation," II, 1 (J, VI, 509).

JW

[The clergy who dissent from the Church of England] speak of justification, either as the same thing with sanctification, or as something consequent upon it. I believe justification to be wholly distinct from sanctification, and necessarily antecedent to it.

They speak of our own holiness, or good works, as the cause of our justification; or that for the sake of which, on account of which, we are justified before God. I believe neither our own holiness nor good works are any part of the cause of our justification; but that the death and righteousness of Christ are the whole and sole cause of it; or that for the sake of which, on account of which, we are justified before God.

They speak of good works as a condition of justification, necessarily previous to it. I believe no good work can be previous to justification, nor, consequently, a condition of it; but that we are justified (being till that hour ungodly, and, therefore, incapable of doing any good work) by faith alone, faith without works, faith (though producing all, yet) including no good work.

They speak of sanctification (or holiness) as if it were an outward thing—as if it consisted chiefly, if not wholly, in those two points: (1) the doing no harm; (2) the doing good (as it is called); that is, the using the means of grace, and helping our neighbour. I believe it to be an inward thing, namely, the life of God in the soul of man; a participation of the divine nature; the mind that was in Christ; or, the renewal of our heart after the image of Him that created us.

They speak of the new birth as an outward thing—as if it were no more than baptism; or, at most, a change from outward wickedness to outward goodness, from vicious to (what is called) a virtuous life. I believe it to be an inward thing; a change from inward wickedness to inward goodness; an entire change of our inmost nature from the image of the devil (wherein we are born) to the image of God; a change from the love of the creature to the love of the Creator; from earthly and sensual to heavenly and holy affections—in a word, a change from the tempers of the spirits of darkness to those of the angels of God in heaven.

There is therefore a wide, essential, fundamental, irreconcilable difference between us; so that if they speak the truth as it is in Jesus, I am found a false witness before God. But if I teach the way of God in truth, they are blind leaders of the blind.

Journal: "Thur. 13 Sept. 1739" (II, 275-76).

JW

Whatsoever else [salvation by faith] imply, it is a present salvation. It is something attainable, yea, actually attained, on earth, by those who are partakers of this faith. For thus saith the Apostle to the believers at Ephesus, and in them to the believers of all ages, not, *Ye shall be* (though that also is true), but, *"Ye are saved* through faith."

Ye are saved (to comprise all in one word) from sin. This is the salvation which is through faith. This is that great salvation foretold by the angel, before God brought His First-begotten into the world: "Thou shalt call His name Jesus; for He shall save His people from their sins." And neither here, nor in other parts of holy writ, is there any limitation or restriction. All His people, or, as it is elsewhere expressed, "all that believe in Him," He will save from all their sins; from original and actual, past and present sin, "of the flesh and of the spirit." Through faith that is in Him, they are saved both from the guilt and from the power of it.

First, from the guilt of all past sin: for, whereas all the world is guilty before God, insomuch that should He "be extreme to mark what is done amiss, there is none that could abide it": and whereas, "by the law is" only "the knowledge of sin," but no deliverance from it, so that, "by" fulfilling "the deeds of the law, no flesh can be justified in His sight": now, "the righteousness of God, which is by faith of Jesus Christ, is manifested unto all that believe." Now, "they are justified freely by His grace, through the redemption that is in Jesus Christ." "Him God hath set forth to be a propitiation through faith in His blood, to declare His righteousness for (or by) the remission of the sins that are past." Now hath Christ taken away "the curse of the law, being made a curse for us." He hath "blotted out the handwriting that was against us, taking it out of the way, nailing it to His cross." "There is therefore no condemnation now to them which" believe "in Christ Jesus."

And being saved from guilt, they are saved from fear. Not indeed from a filial fear of offending; but from all servile fear; from that fear which hath torment; from fear of punishment; from fear of the wrath of God, whom they now no longer regard as a severe Master, but as an indulgent Father. "They have not received again the spirit of bondage, but the Spirit of adoption, whereby they cry, Abba, Father: the Spirit itself also bearing witness with their spirits, that they are the children of God." They are also saved from the fear, though not from the possibility, of falling away from the grace of God, and coming short of the great and precious promises. [They are sealed with the Holy Spirit of Promise, which is the earnest of their inheritance (Eph. i. 13).] Thus have they "peace with God through our Lord Jesus Christ. They rejoice in hope of the glory of God. And the love of God is shed abroad in their hearts, through the Holy Ghost, which is given unto them." And hereby they are persuaded (though perhaps not at all times, nor with the same fullness of persuasion), that "neither death, nor life, nor things present, nor things to come, nor height, nor depth, nor any other creature, shall be able to separate them from the love of God, which is in Christ Jesus our Lord."

Again: through this faith they are saved from the power of sin, as well as from the guilt of it. So the Apostle declares, "Ye know that He was manifested to take away our sins; and in Him is no sin. Whosoever abideth in Him sinneth not" (1 John iii. 5, &c.). Again: "little children, let no man deceive you. He that committeth sin is of the devil. Whosoever believeth is born of God. And whosoever is born of God doth not commit sin; for His seed remaineth in him: and he cannot sin, because he is born of God." Once more: "We know that whosoever is born of God sinneth not; but he that is begotten of God keepeth himself, and that wicked one toucheth him not" (1 John v. 18).

He that is, by faith, born of God sinneth not (1) by any habitual sin; for all habitual sin is sin reigning: but sin cannot reign in any that believeth. Nor (2) by an wilful sin; for his will, while he abideth in the faith, is utterly set against all sin, and abhorreth it as deadly poison. Nor (3) by any sinful desire; for he continually desireth the holy and perfect will of God; and any tendency to an unholy desire, he by the grace of God, stifleth in the birth. Nor (4) doth he sin by infirmities, whether in act, word, or thought; for his infirmities have no concurrence of his will; and without this they are not properly sins. Thus, "he that is born of God doth not commit sin": and though he cannot say he hath not sinned, yet now "he sinneth not."

This then is the salvation which is through faith, even in the present world: a salvation from sin, and the consequences of sin, both often expressed in the word *justification;* which, taken in the largest sense, implies a deliverance from guilt and punishment, by the atonement of

Christ actually applied to the soul of the sinner now believing on Him, and a deliverance from the [whole body] of sin, through Christ *formed in his heart*. So that he who is thus justified, or saved by faith, is indeed *born again*. He is *born again of the Spirit* unto new life, which "is hid with Christ in God." [He is a new creature: old things are passed away: all things in him are become new.] And as a new-born babe he gladly receives the ἄδολον, *"sincere* milk of the word, and grows thereby"; going on in the might of the Lord his God, from faith to faith, from grace to grace, until at length, he comes unto "a perfect man, unto the measure of the stature of the fullness of Christ."

Sermons: "Salvation by Faith," II, 1-7 (S, I, 41-45).

2. Salvation Through Grace

All the blessings which God hath bestowed upon man are of His mere grace, bounty, or favour; His free, undeserved favour; favour altogether undeserved; man having no claim to the least of His mercies. It was free grace that "formed man of the dust of the ground, and breathed into him a living soul," and stamped on that soul the image of God, and "put all things under his feet." The same free grace continues to us, at this day, life, and breath, and all things. For there is nothing we are, or have, or do, which can deserve the least thing at God's hands. "All our works, Thou, O God, hast wrought in us." These, therefore, are so many more instances of free mercy: and whatever righteousness may be found in man, this is also the gift of God.

Wherewithal then shall a sinful man atone for any the least of his sins? With his own works? No. Were they ever so many or holy, they are not his own, but God's. But indeed they are all unholy and sinful themselves, so that every one of them needs a fresh atonement. Only corrupt fruit grows on a corrupt tree. And his heart is altogether corrupt and abominable; being "come short of the glory of God," the glorious righteousness at first impressed on his soul, after the image of his great Creator. Therefore, having nothing, neither righteousness nor works, to plead, his mouth is utterly stopped before God.

If then sinful men find favour with God, it is "grace upon grace!" If God vouchsafe still to pour fresh blessings upon us, yea, the greatest of all blessings, salvation; what can we say to these things, but, "Thanks be unto God for His unspeakable gift!" And thus it is. Herein "God commendeth His love toward us, in that, while we were yet sinners, Christ died" to save us. "By grace" then "are ye saved through faith." Grace is the source, faith the condition, of salvation.

Sermons: "Salvation by Faith," Introduction, 1-3 (S, I, 37-38).

JW

If you ask, "Why, how are men capable of performing duty?" I answer, By grace; though not by nature. And a measure of this is given to all men.

Works: "The Doctrine of Original Sin" (IX, 273).

JW

You know how God wrought in *your own* soul, when he first enabled you to say, "The life I now live, I live by faith in the Son of God, who loved me, and gave himself for me." He did not take away your understanding; but enlightened and strengthened it. He did not destroy any of your affections; rather they were more vigorous than before. Least of all did he take away your liberty; your power of choosing good or evil: He did not *force* you; but, being *assisted* by his grace, you, like Mary, *chose* the better part. Just so has he *assisted* five in one house to make that happy *choice;* fifty or five hundred in one city; and many thousands in a nation;—without depriving any of them of that liberty which is essential to a moral agent.

Not that I deny, that there are exempt cases, wherein

The' o'erwhelming power of saving grace

does, for a time, work as irresistibly as lightning falling from heaven.

145

But I speak of God's general manner of working, of which I have known innumerable instances; perhaps more within fifty years last past, than any one in England or in Europe. And with regard even to these exempt cases; although God does work irresistibly *for the time,* yet I do not believe there is any human soul in which God works irresistibly *at all times.* Nay, I am fully persuaded there is not. I am persuaded, there are no men living that have not many times "resisted the Holy Ghost," and made void "the counsel of God against themselves." Yea, I am persuaded, every child of God has had, at some time, "life and death set before him," eternal life and eternal death; and has in himself the casting voice. So true is that well-known saying of St. Austin, (One of the noblest he ever uttered,) *Qui fecit nos sine nobis, non salvabit nos sine nobis:* "He that made us without ourselves, will not save us without ourselves." Now in the same manner as God *has* converted so many to himself without destroying their liberty, he *can* undoubtedly convert whole nations, or the whole world; and it is as easy to him to convert a world, as one individual soul.

Sermons: "The General Spread of the Gospel," 11-12 (J, VI, 280-81).

JW

There are no works of supererogation; we can never do more than our duty; seeing all we have is not our own, but God's; all we can do is due to Him. We have not received this or that, or many things only, but everything from Him: therefore, everything is His due. He that gives us all, must needs have a right to all: so that if we pay Him anything less than all, we cannot be faithful stewards.

Sermons: "The Good Steward," IV, 3 (S, II, 479).

JW

The grace or love of God, whence cometh our salvation, is FREE IN ALL, and FREE FOR ALL.

It is free IN ALL to whom it is given. It does not depend on any power or merit in man; no, not in any degree, neither in whole, nor in part. It does not in anywise depend either on the good works or righteousness of the receiver; not on anything he has done, or anything he is. It does not depend on his endeavours. It does not depend on his good tempers, or good desires, or good purposes and intentions; for all these flow from the free grace of God; they are the streams only, not the fountain. They are the fruits of free grace, and not the root. They are not the cause, but the effects of it. Whatsoever good is in man, or is done by man, God is the author and doer of it. Thus is his grace free in all; that is, no way depending on any power or merit in man, but on God alone, who freely gave us his own Son, and "with him freely giveth us all things."

Sermons: "Free Grace," 2-3 (J, VII, 373-74).

3. Prevenient Grace

We are to observe that great and important truth which ought never to be out of our remembrance: "It is God that worketh in us both to will and to do of his good pleasure." The meaning of these words may be made more plain by a small transposition of them: "It is God that of his good pleasure worketh in you both to will and to do." This position of the words, connecting the phrase, *of his good pleasure,* with the word *worketh,* removes all imagination of merit from man, and gives God the whole glory of his work. Otherwise, we might have had some room for boasting, as if it were our own desert, some goodness in us, or some good thing done by us, which first moved God to work. But this expression cuts off all such vain conceits, and clearly shows his motive to work lay wholly in himself, in his own mere grace, in his unmerited mercy.

It is by this alone he is impelled to work in man both to will and to do. The expression is capable of two interpretations; both of which are unquestionably true. First, *to will,* may include the whole of inward; *to do,* the whole of outward religion. And if it be thus understood, it implies, that it is God that worketh both inward and outward holiness. Secondly, *to will,* may imply every good desire; *to do,* whatever results therefrom. And then the sentence means, God breathes into us every good desire, and brings every good desire to good effect. . . .

Nothing can so directly tend to hide pride from man as a deep, lasting conviction of this. For if we are thoroughly sensible that we have nothing which we have not received, how can we glory as if we had not received it? If we know and feel that the very first motion of good is from above, as well as the power which conducts it to the end; if it is God that not only infuses every good desire, but that accompanies and follows it, else it vanishes away; then it evidently follows, that "he who glorieth" must "glory in the Lord.". . .

First. God worketh in you; therefore, you *can* work: Otherwise it would be impossible. If he did not work, it would be impossible for you to work out your own salvation. "With man this is impossible," saith our Lord, "for a rich man to enter into the kingdom of heaven." Yea, it is impossible for any man, for any that is born of a woman, unless God work in him. Seeing all men are, by nature, not only sick, but "dead in trespasses and in sins," it is not possible for them to do anything well till God raises them from the dead. It was impossible for Lazarus to come forth, till the Lord had given him life. And it is equally impossible for us to *come* out of our sins, yea, or to make the least motion toward it, till He who hath all power in heaven and earth calls our dead souls into life.

Yet this is no excuse for those who continue in sin, and lay the blame upon their Maker, by saying, "It is God only that must quicken us; for we cannot quicken our own souls." For allowing that all the souls of men are dead in sin by *nature,* this excuses none, seeing there is no man that is in a state of mere nature; there is no man, unless he has quenched the Spirit, that is wholly void of the grace of God. No man living is entirely destitute of what is vulgarly called *natural conscience.* But this is not natural: It is more properly termed, *preventing grace.* Every man has a greater or less measure of this, which waiteth not for the call of man. Every one has, sooner or later, good desires; although the generality of men stifle them before they can strike deep root, or produce any considerable fruit. Every one has some measure of that light, some faint glimmering ray, which, sooner or later, more or less, enlightens every man that cometh into the world. And every one, unless he be one of the small number whose conscience is seared as with a hot iron, feels more or less uneasy when he acts contrary to the light of his own conscience. So that no man sins because he has not grace, but because he does not use the grace which he hath.

Therefore, in as much as God works in you, you are now able to work out your own salvation. Since he worketh in you of his own good pleasure, without any merit of yours, both to will and to do, it is possible for you to fulfil all righteousness. It is possible for you to "love God, because he hath first loved us"; and to "walk in love," after the pattern of our great Master. We know, indeed, that word of his to be absolutely true: "Without me ye can do nothing." But, on the other hand, we know, every believer can say, "I can do all things through Christ that strengtheneth me.". . .

Secondly. God worketh in you; therefore, you *must* work: You must be "workers together with him," (they are the very words of the Apostle,) otherwise he will cease working. The general rule on which his gracious dispensations invariably proceed is this: "Unto him that hath shall be given: But from him that hath not,"—that does not improve the grace already given,—"shall be taken away what he assuredly hath." (So the words ought to be rendered.) Even St. Augustine, who is generally supposed to favour the contrary doctrine, makes that just remark, *Qui fecit nos sine nobis, non salvabit nos sine nobis:* "He that made us without ourselves, will not save us without ourselves." He will not save us unless we "save ourselves from this untoward generation"; unless we ourselves "fight the good fight of faith, and lay hold on eternal life"; unless we "agonize to enter in at the strait gate," "deny ourselves, and take up our cross daily," and labour by every possible means to "make our own calling and election sure."

Sermons: "On Working Out Our Own Salvation," I, 1 *passim* (J, VI, 508-09, 511-13).

JW

[Have not Christians,] in common with other men, . . . an immaterial principle, a spiritual nature, endued with understanding, and

149

affections, and a degree of liberty; of a self-moving, yea, and self-governing power? (Otherwise we were mere machines; stocks, and stones:) And, . . . all that is vulgarly called natural conscience; implying some discernment of the difference between moral good and evil, with an approbation of the one, and disapprobation of the other, by an inward monitor, excusing or accusing? Certainly, whether this is natural or superadded by the grace of God, it is found, at least in some small degree, in every child of man. Something of this is found in every human heart, passing sentence concerning good and evil, not only in all Christians, but in all Mahometans, all Pagans, yea, the vilest of savages.

Sermons: "The Heavenly Treasure in Earthen Vessels," I, 1 (J, VII, 345).

JW

Conscience, . . . is that faculty whereby we are at once conscious of our own thoughts, words, and actions; and of their merit or demerit, of their being good or bad; and, consequently, deserving either praise or censure. And some pleasure generally attends the former sentence; some uneasiness the latter: But this varies exceedingly, according to education and a thousand other circumstances.

Can it be denied that something of this is found in every man born into the world? And does it not appear as soon as the understanding opens, as soon as reason begins to dawn? Does not every one then begin to know that there is a difference between good and evil; how imperfect soever the various circumstances of this sense of good and evil may be? Does not every man, for instance, know, unless blinded by the prejudices of education, . . . that it is good to honour his parents? Do not all men, however uneducated or barbarous, allow, it is right to do to others as we would have them do to us? And are not all who know this condemned in their own mind when they do anything contrary thereto? as, on the other hand, when they act suitable thereto, they have the approbation of their own conscience?

This faculty seems to be what is usually meant by those who speak of natural conscience; an expression frequently found in some of our best authors, but yet not strictly just. For though in one sense it may be termed natural, because it is found in all men; yet, properly speaking, it is not natural, but a supernatural gift of God, above all his natural endowments. No; it is not nature, but the Son of God, that is "the true light, which enlighteneth every man that cometh into the world." So that we may say to every human creature, "He," not nature, "hath showed thee, O man, what is good." And it is his Spirit who giveth thee an inward check, who causeth thee to feel uneasy, when thou walkest in any instance contrary to the light which he hath given thee.

Sermons: "On Conscience," I, 3-5 (J, VII, 187-88).

4. Repentance

A stupid, senseless wretch is going on in his own way, not having God in all his thoughts, when God comes upon him unawares, perhaps by an awakening sermon or conversation, perhaps by some awful providence, or, it may be, by an immediate stroke of His convincing Spirit, without any outward means at all. Having now a desire to flee from the wrath to come, he purposely goes to *hear* how it may be done. If he finds a preacher who speaks to the heart, he is amazed and begins searching the Scriptures, whether these things are so. The more he *hears* and *reads,* the more convinced he is; and the more he meditates thereon day and night. Perhaps he finds some other book which explains and enforces what he has heard and read in Scripture. And by all these means, the arrows of conviction sink deeper into his soul. He begins also to *talk* of the things of God, which are ever uppermost in his thoughts; yea, and to talk with God; to *pray* to Him; although, through fear and shame, he scarce knows what to say. But whether he can speak or no, he cannot but pray, were it only in "groans which cannot be uttered." Yet, being in doubt, whether "the high and lofty One that inhabiteth eternity" will regard such a sinner as him, he wants to pray with those who know God, with the faithful, in the

great congregation. But here he observes others go up to the table of
the Lord. He considers, "Christ has said, 'Do this!' How is it that I do
not? I am too great a sinner. I am not fit. I am not worthy." After
struggling with these scruples awhile, he breaks through. And thus
he continues in God's way, in hearing, reading, meditating, praying,
and partaking of the Lord's supper, till God, in the manner that
pleases Him, speaks to his heart, "Thy faith hath saved thee. Go in
peace."

Sermons: "The Means of Grace," V, 1 (S, I, 257-58).

JW

Repentance is of two sorts; that which is termed legal, and that
which is styled evangelical repentance. The former (which is the
same that is spoken of here), is a thorough conviction of sin. The
latter is a change of heart (and consequently of life) from all sin to
all holiness.

Notes: "Matthew 3:8."

JW

[Natural man] not only sees, but feels in himself, by an emotion of
soul which he cannot describe, that for the sins of his heart, were his
life without blame (which yet it is not, and cannot be; seeing "an
evil tree cannot bring forth good fruit"), he deserves to be cast into
the fire that never shall be quenched. He feels that "the wages," the just
reward, "of sin," of his sin above all, "is death"; even the second death,
the death which dieth not, the destruction of body and soul in hell.

Here ends his pleasing dream, his delusive rest, his false peace, his
vain security. His joy now vanishes as a cloud; pleasures, once loved,
delight no more. They pall upon the taste: he loathes the nauseous
sweet; he is weary to bear them. The shadows of happiness flee away,
and sink into oblivion: so that he is stripped of all, and wanders to
and fro, seeking rest, but finding none.

The fumes of those opiates being now dispelled, he feels the anguish of a wounded spirit. He finds that sin let loose upon the soul (whether it be pride, anger, or evil desire, whether self-will, malice, envy, revenge, or any other) is perfect misery: he feels sorrow of heart for the blessings he has lost, and the curse which is come upon him; remorse for having thus destroyed himself, and despised his own mercies; fear, from a lively sense of the wrath of God, and of the consequences of His wrath, of the punishment which He has justly deserved, and which he sees hanging over his head; fear of death, as being to him the gate of hell, the entrance of death eternal; fear of the devil, the executioner of the wrath and righteous vengeance of God; fear of men, who, if they were able to kill his body, would thereby plunge both body and soul into hell,—fear, sometimes arising to such a height, that the poor, sinful, guilty soul is terrified with everything, with nothing, with shades, with a leaf shaken of the wind. Yea, sometimes it may even border upon distraction, making a man "drunken though not with wine," suspending the exercise of the memory, of the understanding, of all the natural faculties. Sometimes it may approach to the very brink of despair; so that he who trembles at the name of death, may yet be ready to plunge into it every moment, to "choose strangling rather than life." Well may such a man roar, like him of old, for the very disquietness of his heart. Well may he cry out, "The spirit of a man may sustain his infirmities; but a wounded spirit who can bear?"

Now he truly desires to break loose from sin, and begins to struggle with it. But though he strive with all his might, he cannot conquer: sin is mightier than he. He would fain escape; but he is so fast in prison, that he cannot get forth. He resolves against sin, but yet sins on: He sees the snare, and abhors and runs into it. So much does his boasted reason avail—only to enhance his guilt, and increase his misery! Such is the freedom of his will; free only to evil; free to "drink in iniquity like water"; to wander farther and farther from the living God, and do more "despite to the Spirit of grace."

The more he strives, wishes, labours to be free, the more does he feel his chains, the grievous chains of sin, wherewith Satan binds and "leads him captive at his will"; his servant he is, though he repine ever so much; though he rebel, he cannot prevail. He is still in bondage and fear, by reason of sin: generally, of some outward sin, to which he is peculiarly disposed, either by nature, custom, or outward circumstances; but always, of some inward sin, some evil temper or unholy affection. And the more he frets against it the more it prevails; he may bite, but cannot break his chain. Thus he toils without end, repenting and sinning, and repenting and sinning again, till at length the poor, sinful, helpless wretch is even at his wit's end, and can barely groan, "O wretched man that I am! who shall deliver me from the body of this death?"

Sermons: "The Spirit of Bondage and of Adoption," II, 4-8 (S, I, 187-89).

JW

It is the ordinary method of the Spirit of God to convict sinners by the law. It is this which, being set home on the conscience, generally breaketh the rocks in pieces. It is more especially this part of the word of God which is ζῶν καὶ ἐνεργής,—*quick and powerful,* full of life and energy, "and sharper than any two-edged sword." This, in the hand of God and of those whom He hath sent, pierces through all the folds of a deceitful heart, and "divides asunder even the soul and the spirit"; yea, as it were, the very "joints and marrow." By this is the sinner discovered to himself. All his fig-leaves are torn away, and he sees that he is "wretched, and poor, and miserable, and blind, and naked." The law flashes conviction on every side. He feels himself a mere sinner. He has nothing to pay. His "mouth is stopped," and he stands "guilty before God."

Sermons: "The Original, Nature, Property, and Use of the Law," IV, 1 (S, II, 52).

JW

In the afternoon I heard a sermon wherein it was asserted that our repentance was not sincere, but feigned and hypocritical, (1) if we relapsed into sin soon after repenting; especially if (2) we did not avoid all the occasions of sin; or if (3) we relapsed frequently; and most of all if (4) our hearts were hardened thereby. Oh what a hypocrite was I (if this be so) for near twice ten years! But I know it is not so. I know every one under the law is even as I was. Every one, when he begins to see his fallen state, and to feel the wrath of God abiding on him, relapses into the sin that most easily besets him, soon after repenting of it. Sometimes he avoids, and at many other times cannot persuade himself to avoid, the occasions of it. Hence his relapses are frequent, and of consequence his heart is hardened more and more. And yet all this time he is sincerely striving against sin. He can say unfeignedly, without hypocrisy, "The thing which I do, I approve not; the evil which I would not, that I do." "To will is" even then "present with" him; "but how to perform that which is good" he "finds not." Nor can he, with all his sincerity, avoid any one of these four marks of hypocrisy till, "being justified by faith," he hath, "peace with God, through Jesus Christ our Lord."

Journal: "Fri. 31 Aug. 1739" (II, 266).

JW

I preached again at Plaistow on "Blessed are those that mourn." It pleased God to give us in that hour two living instances of that piercing sense both of the guilt and power of sin, that dread of the wrath of God, and that full conviction of man's inability either to remove the power, or atone for the guilt, of sin (called by the world, despair); in which properly consist that poverty of spirit, and mourning, which are the gate of Christian blessedness.

Journal: "Mon. 17 Sept. 1739" (II, 278 79).

JW

We must repent, before we can believe the gospel. We must be cut off from dependence upon ourselves, before we can truly depend upon Christ. We must cast away all confidence in our own righteousness, or we cannot have a true confidence in His. Till we are delivered from trusting in anything that we do, we cannot thoroughly trust in what He has done and suffered. First, we receive the sentence of death in ourselves: then, we trust in Him that lived and died for us.

Sermons: "The Lord Our Righteousness," II, 11 (S, II, 433).

JW

God does undoubtedly command us both to repent, and to bring forth fruits meet for repentance; which if we willingly neglect, we cannot reasonably expect to be justified at all: therefore both repentance, and fruits meet for repentance, are, in some sense, necessary to justification. But they are not necessary in the *same sense* with faith, nor in the *same degree*. Not in the *same degree;* for those fruits are necessary *conditionally;* if there be time and opportunity for them. Otherwise a man may be justified without them, as was the *thief* upon the cross (if we may call him so; for a late writer has discovered that he was no thief, but a very honest and respectable person!); but he cannot be justified without faith; this is impossible. Likewise, let a man have ever so much repentance, or ever so many of the fruits meet for repentance, yet all this does not at all avail; he is not justified till he believes. But the moment he believes, with or without those fruits, yea, with more or less repentance, he is justified.—Not in the *same sense;* for repentance and its fruits are only *remotely* necessary; necessary in order to faith; whereas faith is *immediately* and *directly* necessary to justification. It remains, that faith is the only condition which is *immediately* and *proximately* necessary to justification.

Sermons: "The Scripture Way of Salvation," III, 2 (S, II 451-52).

5. Faith

Faith, in general, is defined by the Apostle, πραγμάτων ἔλεγχος οὐ βλεπομένων—*an evidence,* a divine *evidence and conviction* (the word means both) *of things not seen;* not visible, not perceivable either by sight, or by any other of the external senses. It implies both a super-natural *evidence* of God, and of the things of God; a kind of spiritual *light* exhibited to the soul, and a supernatural *sight* or perception there-of. Accordingly, the Scripture speaks of God's giving sometimes light, sometimes a power of discerning it. So St. Paul: "God, who com-manded light to shine out of darkness, hath shined in our hearts, to give us the light of the knowledge of the glory of God in the face of Jesus Christ." And elsewhere the same Apostle speaks of "the eyes of" our "understanding being opened." By this two-fold operation of the Holy Spirit, having the eyes of our soul both *opened* and *enlightened,* we see the things which the natural "eye hath not seen, neither the ear heard." We have a prospect of the invisible things of God; we see the *spiritual world,* which is all round about us, and yet no more dis-cerned by our natural faculties than if it had no being. And we see the *eternal world;* piercing through the veil which hangs between time and eternity. Clouds and darkness then rest upon it no more, but we already see the glory which shall be revealed.

Taking the word in a more particular sense, faith is a divine *evidence* and *conviction* not only that "God was in Christ, reconciling the world unto Himself," but also that Christ loved *me,* and gave Himself for *me.* It is by this faith (whether we term it the *essence,* or rather a *property* thereof) that we *receive Christ;* that we receive Him in all His offices, as our Prophet, Priest, and King. It is by this that He is "made of God unto us wisdom, and righteousness, and sanctification, and redemption."

"But is this the *faith of assurance,* or *faith of adherence?*" The Scripture mentions no such distinction. The Apostle says, "There is one faith, and one hope of our calling"; one Christian, saving faith; "as there is one Lord," in whom we believe, and "one God and Father of us all." And it is certain, this faith necessarily implies an *assurance* (which is here only another word for *evidence,* it being hard to tell the difference between them) that Christ loved me, and gave Himself for me. For "he that believeth" with the true living faith "hath the witness in himself": "the Spirit witnesseth with his spirit that he is a child of God." "Because he is a son, God hath sent forth the Spirit of His Son into his heart, crying, Abba, Father"; giving him an assurance that he is so, and a childlike confidence in Him. But let it be observed, that, in the very nature of the thing, the assurance goes before the confidence. For a man cannot have a childlike confidence in God till he knows he is a child of God. Therefore, confidence, trust, reliance, adherence, or whatever else it be called, is not the first, as some have supposed, but the second, branch or act of faith.

It is by this faith we are saved, justified, and sanctified; taking that word in its highest sense.

Sermons: "The Scripture Way of Salvation," II, 1-4 (S, II, 448-51).

JW

By affirming that this faith is the term or *condition of justification,* I mean, first, that there is no justification without it. "He that believeth not is condemned already"; and so long as he believeth not, that condemnation cannot be removed, but "the wrath of God abideth on him." As "there is no other name given under heaven" than that of Jesus of Nazareth, no other merit whereby a condemned sinner can ever be saved from the guilt of sin, so there is no other way of obtaining a share in His merit, than *by faith in His name.* So that as long as we are without this faith, we are "strangers to the covenant of promise," we are "aliens from the commonwealth of Israel, and without God in the world." Whatsoever virtues (so called) a man may have—I speak of those unto whom the gospel is preached for "what have I to do to judge them that are without?"—whatsoever good works (so accounted) he may do, it profiteth not; he is still a *child of wrath,* still under the curse, till he believes in Jesus.

Faith, therefore, is the *necessary* condition of justification; yea, and the *only necessary* condition thereof. This is the second point carefully to be observed; that, the very moment God giveth faith (for *it is the gift of God*) to the "ungodly" that "worketh not," that "faith is counted to him for righteousness." He hath no righteousness at all, antecedent to this; not so much as negative righteousness, or innocence. But "faith is imputed to him for righteousness" the very moment that he believeth. Not that God (as was observed before) thinketh him to be what he is not. But as "He made Christ to be sin for us," that is, treated Him as a sinner, punishing Him for our sins, so He counteth us righteous, from the time we believe in Him: that is, He doth not punish us for our sins; yea, treats us as though we were guiltless and righteous.

Surely the difficulty of assenting to this proposition, that "faith is the *only condition* of justification," must arise from not understanding it. We mean thereby thus much, that it is the only thing without which no one is justified; the only thing that is immediately, indispensably, absolutely requisite in order to pardon. As on the one hand, though a man should have everything else without faith, yet he cannot be justified; so, on the other, though he be supposed to want everything else, yet if he hath faith, he cannot but be justified. For suppose a sinner of any kind or degree, in a full sense of his total ungodliness, of his utter inability to think, speak, or do good, and his absolute meetness for hell-fire; suppose, I say, this sinner, helpless and hopeless, casts himself wholly on the mercy of God in Christ (which indeed he cannot do but by the grace of God), who can doubt but he is forgiven in that moment? Who will affirm that any more is *indispensably required,* before that sinner can be justified?

Now, if there ever was one such instance from the beginning of the world (and have there not been, and are there not, ten thousand times ten thousand?), it plainly follows, that faith is, in the above sense, the sole condition of justification.

Sermons: "Justification by Faith," IV, 4-6 (S, I, 126-27).

JW

"But what is that faith whereby we are sanctified,—saved from sin, and perfected in love?" It is a divine evidence and conviction, first, that God hath promised it in the holy Scriptures. . . .

It is a divine evidence and conviction, secondly, that what God hath promised He is able to perform. . . .

It is, thirdly, a divine evidence and conviction that He is able and willing to do it now. And why not? Is not a moment to Him the same as a thousand years? He cannot want more time to accomplish whatever is His will. And He cannot want or stay for any more *worthiness* or *fitness* in the persons He is pleased to honour. . . .

To this confidence, that God is both able and willing to sanctify us now, there needs to be added one thing more,—a divine evidence and conviction that He doeth it. . . .

If you seek it by faith, you may expect it *as you are;* and if as you are, then expect it *now.* It is of importance to observe, that there is an inseparable connexion between these three points,—expect it *by faith;* expect it *as you are;* and expect it *now.* To deny one of them, is to deny them all; to allow one, is to allow them all.

Sermons: "The Scripture Way of Salvation," III, 14-18 (S, II, 457-60).

JW

[Faith] is not a bare assent to this proposition, "Jesus is the Christ"; nor indeed to all the propositions contained in our creed, or in the Old and New Testament. It is not merely an assent to any or all these credible things, as credible. To say this, were to say (which who could hear?) that the devils were born of God; for they have this faith. They, trembling, believe, both that Jesus is the Christ, and that all Scripture, having been given by inspiration of God, is true as God is true. It is not only an assent to divine truth, upon the testimony of God, or upon the evidence of miracles; for *they* also heard the words of His mouth, and knew Him to be a faithful and true witness. They could not but receive the testimony He gave, both of Himself, and of the Father which sent Him. They saw likewise the mighty works which He did, and thence believed that He "came forth from God." Yet, notwithstanding this faith, they are still "reserved in chains of darkness and unto the judgement of the great day."

For all this is no more than a dead faith. The true, living, Christian faith, which whosoever hath is born of God, is not only assent, an act of the understanding; but a disposition, which God hath wrought in his heart; "a sure trust and confidence in God, that, through the merits of Christ, his sins are forgiven, and he reconciled to the favour of God." This implies, that a man first renounce himself; that, in order to be "found in Christ," to be accepted through Him, he totally rejects all "confidence in the flesh"; that, "having nothing to pay," having no trust in his own works or righteousness of any kind, he comes to God as a lost, miserable, self-destroyed, self-condemned, undone, helpless sinner; as one whose mouth is utterly stopped, and who is altogether "guilty before God." Such a sense of sin (commonly called "despair" by those who speak evil of the things they know not), together with a full conviction, such as no words can express, that of Christ only cometh our salvation, and an earnest desire of that salvation, must precede a living faith, a trust in Him, who "for us paid our ransom by His death, and [for us] fulfilled the law in His life." This faith then, whereby we are born of God, is "not only a belief of all the articles of our faith, but also a true confidence of the mercy of God through our Lord Jesus Christ."

Sermons: "The Marks of the New Birth," I, 2-3 (S, I, 284-85).

To believe in God implies, to trust in Him as our strength, without whom we can do nothing, who every moment endues us with power from on high, without which it is impossible to please Him; as our help, our only help in time of trouble, who compasseth us about with songs of deliverance; as our shield, our defender, and the lifter up of our head above all our enemies that are round about us.

It implies, to trust in God as our happiness; as the centre of spirits; the only rest of our souls; the only good who is adequate to all our capacities, and sufficient to satisfy all the desires He hath given us.

It implies (what is nearly allied to the other), to trust in God as our end; to have an eye to Him in all things; to use all things only as means of enjoying Him: wheresoever we are, or whatsoever we do, to see Him that is invisible, looking on us well pleased, and to refer all things to Him in Christ Jesus.

Sermons: "Upon Our Lord's Sermon on the Mount: IX," 4 (S, I, 498).

Q. 7. What are the immediate fruits of justifying faith?

A. Peace, joy, love, power over all outward sin, and power to keep down inward sin.

Q. 8. Does any one believe, who has not the witness in himself, or any longer than he sees, loves, obeys God?

A. We apprehend not; seeing God being the very essence of faith; love and obedience, the inseparable properties of it.

Q. 9. What sins are consistent with justifying faith?

A. No wilful sin. If a believer wilfully sins, he casts away his faith. Neither is it possible he should have justifying faith again, without previously repenting.

Q. 10. Must every believer come into a state of doubt, or fear, or darkness? Will he do so, unless by ignorance, or unfaithfulness? Does God otherwise withdraw himself?

A. It is certain, a believer need never again come into condemnation. It seems he need not come into a state of doubt, or fear, or darkness; and that (ordinarily at least) he will not, unless by ignorance or unfaithfulness. Yet it is true, that the first joy does seldom last long; that it is commonly followed by doubts and fears; and that God frequently permits great heaviness before any large manifestation of himself.

Q. 11. Are works necessary to the continuance of faith?

A. Without doubt; for a man may forfeit the free gift of God, either by sins of omission or commission.

Q. 12. Can faith be lost but for want of works?

A. It cannot but through disobedience.

Q. 13. How is faith "made perfect by works"?

A. The more we exert our faith, the more it is increased.

Works: "Minutes of Some Late Conversations," Mon., June 25, 1744, (VIII, 276-77).

6. Justification by Faith (Pardon and Acceptance)

It is evident from what has been already observed, that [justification] is not the being made actually just and righteous. This is *sanctification;*

which is, indeed, in some degree, the immediate fruit of justification, but, nevertheless, is a distinct gift of God, and of a totally different nature. The one implies, what God does for us through His Son; the other, what He works in us by His Spirit. So that, although some rare instances may be found, wherein the term *justified* or *justification* is used in so wide a sense as to include *sanctification* also; yet, in general use, they are sufficiently distinguished from each other, both by St. Paul and the other inspired writers.

Neither is that far-fetched conceit, that justification is the clearing us from accusation, particularly that of Satan, easily proveable from any clear text of holy writ. In the whole scriptural account of this matter, as above laid down, neither that accuser nor his accusation appears to be at all taken in. It cannot indeed be denied, that he is the "accuser" of men, emphatically so called. But it does in no wise appear, that the great Apostle hath any reference to this, more or less, in all that he hath written touching justification, either to the Romans or the Galatians.

It is also far easier to take for granted, than to prove from any clear scripture testimony, that justification is the clearing us from the accusation brought against us by the law: at least, if this forced, un-natural way of speaking mean either more or less than this, that whereas we have transgressed the law of God, and thereby deserved the damnation of hell, God does not inflict on those who are justified the punishment which they had deserved.

Least of all does justification imply, that God is deceived in those whom He justifies; that He thinks them to be what, in fact, they are not; that He accounts them to be otherwise than they are. It does by no means imply, that God judges concerning us contrary to the real nature of things; that He esteems us better than we really are, or believes us righteous when we are unrighteous. Surely no. The judge-ment of the all-wise God is always according to truth. Neither can it ever consist with His unerring wisdom, to think that I am innocent, to judge that I am righteous or holy, because another is so. He can no more, in this manner, confound me with Christ, than with David or Abraham. Let any man, to whom God hath given understanding, weigh this without prejudice; and he cannot but perceive, that such a notion of justification is neither reconcileable to reason nor Scripture.

The plain scriptural notion of justification is pardon, the forgiveness of sins. It is that act of God the Father, whereby, for the sake of the propitiation made by the blood of His Son, He "showeth forth His righteousness" (or mercy) "by the remission of the sins that are past." This is the easy, natural account of it given by St. Paul, throughout this whole epistle. So he explains it himself, more particularly in this, and in the following chapter. Thus, in the next verses but one to the text, "Blessed are they," saith he, "whose iniquities are forgiven, and whose sins are covered: blessed is the man to whom the Lord will not impute sin." To him that is justified or forgiven, God "will not impute sin" to his condemnation. He will not condemn him on that account, either in this world or in that which is to come. His sins, all his past sins, in thought, word and deed, are covered, are blotted out, shall not be remembered or mentioned against him, any more than if they had not been. God will not inflict on that sinner what he deserved to suffer, because the Son of His love hath suffered for him. And from the time we are "accepted through the Beloved," "reconciled to God through His blood," He loves, and blesses, and watches over us for good, even as if we had never sinned.

Indeed the Apostle in one place seems to extend the meaning of the word much farther, where he says, "Not the hearers of the law, but the doers of the law, shall be justified." Here he appears to refer our justification to the sentence of the great day. And so our Lord Himself unquestionably doth, when He says, "By thy words thou shalt be justified"; proving thereby that "for every idle word men shall speak, they shall give an account in the day of judgement"; but perhaps we can hardly produce another instance of St. Paul's using the word in that distant sense. In the general tenor of his writings, it is evident he doth not; and least of all in the text before us, which undeniably speaks, not of those who have already "finished their course," but of those who are now just *setting out,* just beginning to "run the race which is set before them."

But this is the third thing which was to be considered, namely, Who are they that are justified? And the Apostle tells us expressly, the ungodly: "He" (that is, God) "justifieth the ungodly"; the ungodly of every kind and degree; and none but the ungodly. As "they that are righteous need no repentance," so they need no forgiveness. It is only sinners that have any occasion for pardon: it is sin alone which admits of being forgiven. Forgiveness, therefore, has an immediate reference to sin, and, in this respect, to nothing else. It is our *unrighteousness* to which the pardoning God is *merciful:* it is our *iniquity* which He "remembereth no more."

This seems not to be at all considered by those who so vehemently contend that a man must be sanctified, that is, holy, before he can be justified; especially by such of them as affirm, that universal holiness or obedience must precede justification. (Unless they mean that justification at the last day, which is wholly out of the present question.) So far from it, that the very supposition is not only flatly impossible (for where there is no love of God, there is no holiness, and there is no love of God but from a sense of His loving us), but also grossly, intrinsically absurd, contradictory to itself. For it is not a saint but a sinner that is forgiven, and under the notion of a sinner. God justifieth not the godly, but the ungodly; not those that are holy already, but the unholy. Upon what condition He doeth this, will be considered quickly: but whatever it is, it cannot be holiness. To assert this, is to say the Lamb of God takes away only those sins which were taken away before.

Sermons: "Justification by Faith," II, 1-III, 2 (S, I, 119-22).

JW

I believe, three things must go together in our justification: Upon God's part, his great mercy and grace; upon Christ's part, the satisfaction of God's justice, by the offering his body, and shedding his blood; and upon our part, true and living faith in the merits of Jesus Christ. So that in our justification there is not only God's mercy and grace, but his justice also. And so the grace of God does not shut out the righteousness of God in our justification; but only shuts out the righteousness of man, that is, the righteousness of our works.

And therefore St. Paul requires nothing on the part of man, but only a true and living faith. Yet this faith does not shut out repentance, hope, and love, which are joined with faith in every man that is justified. But it shuts them out from the office of justifying. So that although they are all present together in him that is justified, yet they justify not all together.

Neither does faith shut out good works, necessarily to be done afterwards. But we may not do them to this intent,—to be justified by doing them. Our justification comes freely, of the mere mercy of God; for whereas all the world was not able to pay any part towards their ransom, it pleased him, without any of our deserving, to prepare for us Christ's body and blood, whereby our ransom might be paid, and his justice satisfied. Christ, therefore, is now the righteousness of all them that truly believe in him.

But let it be observed, the true sense of those words, "We are justified by faith in Christ only," is not, that this our own act, "to believe in Christ," or this our faith which is within us, justifies us; for that were to account ourselves to be justified by some act or virtue that is within us; but that although we have faith, hope, and love within us, and do never so many good works, yet we must renounce the merit of all, of faith, hope, love, and all other virtues and good works, which we either have done, shall do, or can do, as far too weak to deserve our justification; for which, therefore, we must trust only in God's mercy, and the merits of Christ. For it is he alone that taketh away our sins. To him alone are we to go for this; forsaking all our virtues, good words, thoughts, and works, and putting our trust in Christ only.

In strictness, therefore, neither our faith nor our works justify us, that is, deserve the remission of our sins. But God himself justifies us, of his own mercy, through the merits of his Son only. Nevertheless, because by faith we embrace the promise of God's mercy and of the remission of our sins, therefore the Scripture says, that faith does justify, yea, faith without works. And it is all one to say, "Faith without works," and "Faith alone, justifies us." Therefore the ancient Fathers from time to time speak thus: "Faith alone justifies us." And because we receive faith, through the only merits of Christ, and not through the merit and virtue we have, or work we do; therefore in that respect we renounce, as it were, again, faith, works, and all other virtues. For our corruption through original sin is so great, that all our faith, charity, words, and works, cannot merit or deserve any part of our justification for us. And therefore we thus speak, humbling ourselves before God, and giving Christ all the glory of our justification.

Works: "The Principles of a Methodist," 3-7 (VIII, 361-63).

JW

Such has been my judgment for these threescore years, without any material alteration. Only, about fifty years ago I had a clearer view than before of justification by faith; and in this, from that very hour, I never varied, no not a hair's breadth. Nevertheless, an ingenious man has publicly accused me of a thousand variations. I pray God, not to lay this to his charge! I am now on the borders of the grave; but, by the grace of God, I still witness the same confession. Indeed, some have supposed, that when I began to declare, "By grace ye are saved through faith," I retracted what I had before maintained: "Without holiness no man shall see the Lord." But it is an entire mistake: These scriptures well consist with each other; the meaning of the former being plainly this,—By faith we are saved from sin, and made holy. The imagination, that faith *supersedes* holiness, is the marrow of Antinomianism.

Sermons: "On the Wedding Garment," 18 (J, VII, 316-17).

JW

There is something so absolutely inconsistent, between the being justified by grace, and the being justified by works, that if you suppose either, you of necessity exclude the other. For what is given to works is the payment of a debt; whereas grace implies an unmerited favour. So that the same benefit cannot, in the very nature of things, be derived from both.

Notes: "Romans 11:6."

In the afternoon I was informed how many wise and learned men (who cannot in terms deny it, because our Articles and Homilies are not yet repealed) *explain* justification by faith. They say: (1) Justification is twofold: the first in this life, the second at the last day. (2) Both these are by faith alone; that is, by objective faith, or by the merits of Christ, which are the object of our faith. And this, they say, is all that St. Paul and the Church mean by "We are justified by faith only." But they add (3) We are not justified by subjective faith alone, that is, by the faith which is in us. But works also must be added to this faith, as a joint condition both of the first and second justification.

The sense of which hard words is plainly this: God accepts us both here and hereafter only for the sake of what Christ has done and suffered for us. This alone is the *cause* of our justification. But the *condition* thereof is, not *faith alone,* but *faith and works* together.

In flat opposition to this I cannot but maintain (at least, till I have a clearer light): (1) That the justification which is spoken of by St. Paul to the Romans, and in our Articles, is *not twofold.* It is one, and no more. It is the present remission of our sins, or our first acceptance with God. (2) It is true that the merits of Christ are the *sole cause* of this our justification; but it is not true that this is all which St. Paul and our Church mean by our being justified by faith only; neither is it true that either St. Paul or the Church mean, by faith, the merits of Christ. But (3) By our being justified by faith only, both St. Paul and the Church mean that the *condition* of our justification is *faith alone,* and *not good works;* inasmuch as "all works done before justification have in them the nature of sin." Lastly, that faith which is the sole condition of justification is the faith which is in us by the grace of God.

Journal: "Thurs. 13 Dec. 1739" (II, 326).

7. *New Birth (Regeneration)*

Before a child is born into the world he has eyes, but sees not; he has ears, but does not hear. He has a very imperfect use of any other sense. He has no knowledge of any of the things of the world, or any natural understanding. To that manner of existence which he then has, we do not even give the name of life. It is then only when a man is born, that we say he begins to live. For as soon as he is born, he begins to see the light, and the various objects with which he is encompassed. His ears are then opened, and he hears the sounds which successively strike upon them. At the same time, all the other organs of sense begin to be exercised upon their proper objects. He likewise breathes, and lives in a manner wholly different from what he did before. How exactly doth the parallel hold in all these instances! While a man is in a mere natural state, before he is born of God, he has, in a spiritual sense, eyes and sees not; a thick impenetrable veil lies upon them: he has ears, but hears not; he is utterly deaf to what he is most of all concerned to hear. His other spiritual senses are all locked up: he is in the same condition as if he had them not. Hence he has no knowledge of God; no intercourse with Him; he is not at all acquainted with Him. He has no true knowledge of the things of God, either of spiritual or eternal things; therefore, though he is a living man, he is a dead Christian. But as soon as he is born of God, there is a total change in all these particulars. The "eyes of his understanding are opened" (such is the language of the great Apostle); and, He who of old "commanded light to shine out of darkness shining on his heart, he sees the light of the glory of God," His glorious love, "in the face of Jesus Christ." His ears being opened, he is now capable of hearing the inward voice of God, saying, "Be of good cheer; thy sins are forgiven thee"; "Go and sin no more." This is the purport of what God speaks to his heart; although perhaps not in these very words. He is now ready to hear whatsoever "He that teacheth man knowledge" is pleased, from time to time, to reveal to him. He "feels in his heart," to use the language of our Church, "the mighty working of the Spirit of God"; not in a gross, carnal sense, as the men of the world stupidly and wilfully misunderstand the expression; though they have been told again and again, we mean thereby neither more nor less than this: he feels, is inwardly sensible of, the graces which the Spirit of God works in his heart. He feels, he is conscious of, a "peace which passeth all understanding." He many times feels such a joy in God as is "unspeakable, and full of glory." He feels "the love of God shed abroad in his heart by the Holy Ghost which is given unto him"; and all his spiritual senses are then exercised to discern spiritual good and evil. By the use of these, he is daily increasing in the knowledge of God, of Jesus Christ whom He hath sent, and of all the things pertaining to His inward kingdom. And now he may be properly said to live: God having quickened him by His Spirit, he is alive to God through Jesus Christ. He lives a life which the world knoweth not of, a "life which is hid with Christ in God." God is continually breathing, as it were, upon the soul; and his soul is breathing unto God. Grace is descending into his heart; and prayer and praise ascending to heaven: and by this intercourse between God and man, this fellowship with the Father and the Son, as by a kind of spiritual respiration, the life of God in the soul is sustained; and the child of God grows up, till he comes to the "full measure of the stature of Christ."

Sermons: "The New Birth," II, 4 (S, II, 232-34).

JW

"If any man be in Christ, he is a new creature: old things are passed away; behold, all things are become new."

First: His judgements are new: his judgement of *himself,* of *happiness,* of *holiness.*

He judges himself to be altogether fallen short of the glorious image of God; to have no good thing abiding in him, but all that is corrupt and abominable. In a word, to be wholly earthly, sensual, and devilish —a motley mixture of beast and devil.

Thus, by the grace of God in Christ, I judge of myself. Therefore I am, in this respect, a new creature.

Again: his judgement concerning *happiness* is new. He would as soon expect to dig it out of the earth as to find it in riches, honour, pleasure (so called), or indeed in the enjoyment of any creature. He knows there can be no happiness on earth but in the enjoyment of God and in the foretaste of those "rivers of pleasure which flow at His right hand for evermore."

NEW BIRTH (REGENERATION)

Thus, by the grace of God in Christ, I judge of happiness. Therefore I am, in this respect, a new creature.

Yet again: his judgement concerning *holiness* is new. He no longer judges it to be an outward thing—to consist either in doing no harm, in doing good, or in using the ordinances of God. He sees it is the life of God in the soul; the image of God fresh stamped on the heart; an entire renewal of the mind in every temper and thought, after the likeness of Him that created it.

Thus, by the grace of God in Christ, I judge of holiness. Therefore I am, in this respect, a new creature.

Journal: "Sat. 14 Oct 1738" (II, 89-90).

If any doctrines within the whole compass of Christianity may be properly termed "fundamental," they are doubtless these two,—the doctrine of justification, and that of the new birth: the former relating to that great work which God does *for us,* in forgiving our sins; the latter, to the great work which God does *in us,* in renewing our fallen nature. In order of time, neither of these is before the other; in the moment we are justified by the grace of God, through the redemption that is in Jesus, we are also "born of the Spirit"; but in order of *thinking,* as it is termed, justification precedes the new birth. We first conceive His wrath to be turned away, and then His Spirit to work in our hearts.

Sermons: "The New Birth," Introduction, 1 (S, II, 226-27).

The new birth is not the same with sanctification. This is indeed taken for granted by many; particularly by an eminent writer, in his late treatise on the nature and grounds of Christian Regeneration. To waive several other weighty objections which might be made to that tract, this is a palpable one: it all along speaks of regeneration as a progressive work, carried on in the soul by slow degrees, from the time of our first turning to God. This is undeniably true of sanctification; but of regeneration, the new birth, it is not true. This is a part of sanctification, not the whole; it is the gate to it, the entrance into it. When we are born again, then our sanctification, our inward and outward holiness begins; and thenceforward we are gradually to "grow up in Him who is our Head." This expression of the Apostle admirably illustrates the difference between one and the other, and farther points out the exact analogy there is between natural and spiritual things. A child is born of a woman in a moment, or at least in a very short time: afterward he gradually and slowly grows, till he attains to the stature of a man. In like manner, a child is born of God in a short time, if not in a moment. But it is by slow degrees that he afterward grows up to the measure of the full stature of Christ. The same relation, therefore, which there is between our natural birth and our growth, there is also between our new birth and our sanctification.

Sermons: "The New Birth," IV, 3 (S, II, 239-40).

JW

Thus have I plainly laid down those marks of the new birth which I find laid down in Scripture. Thus doth God Himself answer that weighty question, What is it to be born of God? Such, if the appeal be made to the oracles of God, is "every one that is born of the Spirit." This it is, in the judgement of the Spirit of God, to be a son or a child of God: it is, so to *believe* in God, through Christ, as "not to commit sin," and to enjoy at all times, and in all places, that "peace of God which passeth all understanding." It is, so to *hope* in God through the Son of His love, as to have not only the "testimony of a good conscience," but also the Spirit of God "bearing witness with your spirits, that ye are the children of God"; whence cannot but spring the rejoicing [evermore] in Him through whom ye "have received the atonement." It is, so to *love* God, who hath thus loved you, as you never did love any creature: so that ye are constrained to love all men as yourselves; with a love not only ever burning in your hearts, but flaming out in all your actions and conversations, and making your whole life one "labour of love," one continued obedience to those commands, "Be ye merciful, as God is merciful"; "Be ye holy, as I the Lord am holy"; "Be ye perfect, as your Father which is in heaven in perfect."

Sermons: "The Marks of the New Birth," IV, 1 (S, I, 294).

8. Sin in Believers

Is there then sin in him that is in Christ? Does sin *remain* in one that believes in Him? Is there any sin in them that are born of God, or are they wholly delivered from it? Let no one imagine this to be a question of mere curiosity; or that it is of little importance whether it be determined one way or the other. Rather it is a point of the utmost moment to every serious Christian; the resolving of which very nearly concerns both his present and eternal happiness.

And yet I do not know that ever it was controverted in the primitive Church. Indeed there was no room for disputing concerning it, as all Christians were agreed. And so far as I have ever observed, the whole body of ancient Christians, who have left us anything in writing, declare with one voice, that even believers in Christ, till they are "strong in the Lord and in the power of His might," have need to "wrestle with flesh and blood," with an evil nature, as well as "with principalities and powers." . . .

I use indifferently the words, *regenerate, justified,* or *believers;* since, though they have not precisely the same meaning (the first implying an inward, actual change, the second a relative one, and the third the means whereby both the one and the other are wrought), yet they come to one and the same thing; as every one that believes, is both justified and born of God.

By sin, I here understand inward sin; any sinful temper, passion, or affection; such as pride, self-will, love of the world, in any kind or degree; such as lust, anger, peevishness; any disposition contrary to the mind which was in Christ.

The question is not concerning *outward sin;* whether a child of God *commit sin* or no. We all agree and earnestly maintain, "He that committeth sin is of the devil." We agree, "Whosoever is born of God doth not commit sin." Neither do we now inquire whether inward sin will *always* remain in the children of God; whether sin will continue in the soul as long as it continues in the body; nor yet do we inquire whether a justified person may *relapse* either into inward or outward sin; but simply this, Is a justified or regenerate man freed from *all sin* as soon as he is justified? Is there then no sin in his heart?— nor ever after, unless he fall from grace? . . .

There are in every person, even after he is justified, two contrary principles, nature and grace, termed by St. Paul, the *flesh* and the *Spirit.* Hence, although even babes in Christ are *sanctified,* yet it is only in part. In a degree, according to the measure of their faith, they are spiritual; yet in a degree they are carnal. Accordingly, believers are continually exhorted to watch against the flesh, as well as the world and the devil. And to this agrees the constant experience of the children of God. While they feel this witness in themselves, they feel a will not wholly resigned to the will of God. They know they are in Him; and yet find an heart ready to depart from Him, a proneness to evil in many instances, and a backwardness to that which is good. The contrary doctrine is wholly new; never heard of in the Church of Christ, from the time of His coming into the world, till the time of Count Zinzendorf; and it is attended with the most fatal consequences. It cuts off all watching against our evil nature, against the Delilah which we are told is gone, though she is still lying in our bosom. It tears away the shield of weak believers, deprives them of their faith, and so leaves them exposed to all the assaults of the world, the flesh, and the devil.

Let us, therefore, hold fast the sound doctrine "once delivered to the saints," and delivered down by them, with the written word, to all succeeding generations: that, although we are renewed, cleansed, purified, sanctified, the moment we truly believe in Christ, yet we are not then renewed, cleansed, purified altogether; but the flesh, the evil nature, still *remains* (though subdued), and wars against the Spirit. So much the more let us use all diligence in "fighting the good fight of faith." So much the more earnestly let us "watch and pray" against the enemy within. The more carefully let us take to ourselves, and "put on, the whole armour of God"; that, although "we wrestle" both "with flesh and blood, and with principalities, and powers, and wicked spirits in high places," we "may be able to withstand in the evil day, and having done all, to stand."

Sermons: "On Sin in Believers," I, 1-2, II, 1-3, V, 1-2 (S, II, 361, 365, 377-78).

JW

We should likewise be convinced, that as sin remains in our hearts, so it *cleaves* to all our words and actions. Indeed it is to be feared, that many of our words are more than mixed with sin; that they are sinful altogether; for such undoubtedly is all *uncharitable conversation;* all which does not spring from brotherly love; all which does not agree with that golden rule, "What ye would that others should do to you, even so do unto them." . . .

And how much sin, if their conscience is thoroughly awake, may they find cleaving to *their actions* also! Nay, are there not many of these, which, though they are such as the world would not condemn, yet cannot be commended, no, nor excused, if we judge by the Word of God? Are there not many of their actions which, they themselves know, are not to the glory of God? many, wherein they did not even aim at this; which were not undertaken with an eye to God? . . .

Again: how many *sins of omission* are they chargeable with! We know the words of the Apostle: "To him that knoweth to do good, and doeth it not, to him it is sin." But do they not know a thousand instances, wherein they might have done good, to enemies, to strangers, to their brethren, either with regard to their bodies or their souls, and they did it not? . . .

But besides these outward omissions, may they not find in themselves *inward defects* without number? defects of every kind: they have not the love, the fear, the confidence they ought to have, toward God. They have not the love which is due to their neighbour, to every child of man; no, nor even that which is due to their brethren, to every child of God, whether those that are at a distance from them, or those with whom they are immediately connected.

Sermons: "The Repentance of Believers," I, 11, 13-15, (S, II, 385-88).

JW

The conviction we feel of inbred sin is deeper and deeper every day. The more we grow in grace, the more do we see of the desperate wickedness of our heart. The more we advance in the knowledge and love of God, through our Lord Jesus Christ (as great a mystery as this may appear to those who know not the power of God unto salvation), the more do we discern of our alienation from God, of the enmity that is in our carnal mind, and the necessity of our being entirely renewed in righteousness and true holiness.

Sermons: "Upon Our Lord's Sermon on the Mount: I," I, 13 (S, I, 329).

JW

You see the unquestionable progress from grace to sin: thus it goes on, from step to step. (1) The divine seed of loving, conquering faith, remains in him that is born of God. "He keepeth himself," by the grace of God, and "cannot commit sin." (2) A temptation arises; whether from the world, the flesh, or the devil, it matters not. (3) The Spirit of God gives him warning that sin is near, and bids him more abundantly watch unto prayer. (4) He gives way, in some degree, to the temptation, which now begins to grow pleasing to him. (5) The Holy Spirit is grieved; his faith is weakened; and his love of God grows cold. (6) The Spirit reproves him more sharply, and saith, "This is the way; walk thou in it." (7) He turns away from the painful voice of God, and listens to the pleasing voice of the tempter. (8) Evil desire begins and spreads in his soul, till faith and love vanish away: he is then capable of committing outward sin, the power of the Lord being departed from him.

Sermons: "The Great Privilege of Those that are Born of God," II, 9 (S, I, 309).

Nothing is sin, strictly speaking, but a voluntary transgression of a known law of God. Therefore every voluntary breach of the law of love is sin; and nothing else, if we speak properly. To strain the matter farther is only to make way for Calvinism. There may be ten thousand wandering thoughts and forgetful intervals without any breach of love, though not without transgressing the Adamic law. But Calvinists would fain confound these together. Let love fill your heart, and it is enough!

Letters: "To Mrs. Bennis" (V, 322).

JW

In speaking from those words, "In many things we offend all," I observed (1) as long as we live, our soul is connected with the body; (2) as long as it is thus connected it cannot think but by the help of bodily organs; (3) as long as these organs are imperfect we are liable to mistakes, both speculative and practical; (4) yea, and a mistake may occasion my loving a good man less than I ought; which is a defec-. tive, that is, a wrong temper; (5) for all these we need the atoning blood, as indeed for every defect or omission. Therefore (6) all may have need to say daily, "Forgive us our trespasses."

Journal: "Fri. 24 July 1761" (IV, 471).

JW

Whenever our heart is eagerly athirst for all the great and precious promises; when we pant after the fullness of God, as the hart after the water-brook; when our soul breaketh out in fervent desire, "Why are His chariot-wheels so long a-coming?"—[Satan] will not neglect the opportunity of tempting us to murmer against God. He will use all his wisdom, and all his strength, if haply, in an unguarded hour, we may be influenced to repine at our Lord for thus delaying His coming. At least, he will labour to excite some degree of fretfulness or impatience; and, perhaps, of envy at those whom we believe to have already attained the prize of our high calling. He well knows, that, by giving way to any of these tempers, we are pulling down the very thing we would build up. But *thus* following after perfect holiness, we become more unholy than before. Yea, there is great danger that our last state should be worse than the first; like them of whom the Apostle speaks in those dreadful words, "It had been better for them not to have known the way of righteousness, than, after they have known it, to turn from the holy commandment delivered to them."

Sermons: "Satan's Devices," I, 13 (S, II, 199).

9. Repentance of Believers

There is a repentance and a faith, which are, more especially, necessary at the beginning: a repentance, which is a conviction of our utter sinfulness, and guiltiness, and helplessness; and which precedes our receiving that kingdom of God, which, our Lord observes, is "within us"; and a faith, hereby we receive that kingdom, even "righteousness, and peace, and joy in the Holy Ghost."

But, notwithstanding this, there is also a repentance and a faith (taking the words in another sense; a sense not quite the same, nor yet entirely different) which are requisite after we have "believed the gospel"; yea, and in every subsequent stage of our Christian course, or we cannot "run the race which is set before us." And this repentance and faith are full as necessary, in order to our *continuance* and *growth* in grace, as the former faith and repentance were, in order to our *entering* into the kingdom of God.

But in what sense are we to repent and believe, after we are justified? . . .

Repentance frequently means an inward change, a change of mind from sin to holiness. But we now speak of it in a quite different sense, as it is one kind of self-knowledge, the knowing ourselves sinners, yea, guilty, helpless sinners, even though we know we are children of God.

Indeed when we first know this; when we first find redemption in the blood of Jesus; when the love of God is first shed abroad in our hearts, and His kingdom set up therein; it is natural to suppose that we are no longer sinners, that all our sins are not only covered but destroyed.

As we do not then feel any evil in our hearts, we readily imagine none is there. Nay, some well-meaning men have imagined this not only at that time, but ever after; having persuaded themselves, that when they were justified, they were entirely sanctified: yea, they have laid it down as a general rule, in spite of Scripture, reason, and experience. These sincerely believe, and earnestly maintain, that all sin is destroyed when we are justified; and that there is no sin in the heart of a believer; but that it is altogether clean from that moment. But though we readily acknowledge, "he that believeth is born of God," and "he that is born of God doth not commit sin"; yet we cannot allow that he does not *feel* it within: it does not *reign*, but it does remain. And a conviction of the sin which *remains* in our heart, is one great branch of the repentance we are now speaking of.

For it is seldom long before he who imagined all sin was gone, feels there is still *pride* in his heart. He is convinced both that in many respects he has thought of himself more highly than he ought to think, and that he has taken to himself the praise of something he had received, and gloried in it as though he had not received it; and yet he knows he is in the favour of God. . . .

Nor is it long before he feels *self-will* in his heart; even a will contrary to the will of God. A will every man must inevitably have, as long as he has an understanding. This is an essential part of human nature, indeed of the nature of every intelligent being. Our blessed Lord Himself had a will as a man; otherwise He had not been a man. But His human will was invariably subject to the will of His Father. At all times, and on all occasions, even in the deepest affliction, He could say, "Not as I will, but as Thou wilt." But this is not the case at all times, even with a true believer in Christ. . . .

A conviction of their *guiltiness* is another branch of that repentance which belongs to the children of God. But this is cautiously to be understood, and in a peculiar sense. For it is certain, "there is no condemnation to them that are in Christ Jesus," that believe in Him, and, in the power of that faith, "walk not after the flesh, but after the Spirit."

Yet can they no more bear the *strict justice* of God now, than before they believed. This pronounces them to be still *worthy of death,* on all the preceding accounts. And it would absolutely condemn them thereto, were it not for the atoning blood. Therefore they are thoroughly convinced, that they still *deserve* punishment, although it is hereby turned aside from them. . . .

A conviction of their *utter helplessness* is yet another branch of this repentance. I mean hereby two things: first, that they are no more able now *of themselves* to think one good thought, to form one good desire, to speak one good word, or do one good work, than before they were justified; that they have still no kind or degree of strength *of their own;* no power either to do good, or resist evil; no ability to conquer or even withstand the world, the devil, or their own evil nature. They can, it is certain, do all these things; but it is not by their own strength. They have power to overcome all these enemies; for "sin hath no more dominion over them"; but it is not from nature, either in whole or in part; it is the *mere* gift of God: nor is it given all at once, as if they had a stock laid up for many years; but from moment to moment.

By this helplessness I mean, secondly, an absolute inability to deliver ourselves from that guiltiness or desert of punishment whereof we are still conscious; yea, and an inability to remove, by all the grace we have (to say nothing of our natural powers), either the pride, self-will, love of the world, anger, and general proneness to depart from God, which we experimentally know to *remain* in the heart, even of them that are regenerate; or the evil which, in spite of all our endeavours, cleaves to all our words and actions. Add to this, an utter inability wholly to avoid uncharitable, and, much more, unprofitable, conversation: and an inability to avoid sins of omission, or to supply the numberless defects we are convinced of; especially the want of love, and other right tempers both to God and man.

Sermons: "The Repentance of Believers," Introduction, 2-I, 4, 16-18 (S, II, 379-81, 88-90).

JW

The repentance consequent upon justification is widely different from that which is antecedent to it. This implies no guilt, no sense of condemnation, no consciousness of the wrath of God. It does not suppose any doubt of the favour of God, or any "fear that hath torment." It is properly a conviction, wrought by the Holy Ghost, of the *sin* which still *remains* in our heart; of the φρόνημα σαρκός, *the carnal mind,* which "does still *remain*" (as our Church speaks) "even in them that are regenerate"; although it does no longer *reign;* it has not now dominion over them. It is a conviction of our proneness to evil, of an heart bent to backsliding, of the still continuing tendency of the flesh to lust against the spirit. . . .

With this conviction of the sin remaining in our hearts, there is joined a clear conviction of the sin remaining in our lives; still *cleaving* to all our words and actions. In the best of these we now discern a mixture of evil, either in the spirit, the matter, or the manner of them; something that could not endure the righteous judgement of God, were He extreme to mark what is done amiss. Where we least suspected it, we find a taint of pride or self-will, of unbelief or idolatry; so that we are now more ashamed of our best duties than formerly of our worst sins: and hence we cannot but feel that these are so far from having anything meritorious in them, yea, so far from being able to stand in sight of the divine justice, that for those also we should be guilty before God, were it not for the blood of the covenant.

Experience shows that, together with this conviction of sin *remaining* in our hearts, and *cleaving* to all our words and actions; as well as the guilt which on account thereof we should incur, were we not continually sprinkled with the atoning blood; one thing more is implied in this repentance; namely a conviction of our helplessness, of our utter inability to think one good thought, or to form one good desire; and much more to speak one word aright, or to perform one good action, but through His free, almighty grace, first preventing us, and then accompanying us every moment.

Sermons: "The Scripture Way of Salvation," III, 6-8 (S, II, 454-55).

10. Entire Sanctification

"Do you believe we are sanctified by faith? We know you believe that we are justified by faith; but do not you believe, and accordingly teach, that we are sanctified by our works?" So it has been roundly and vehemently affirmed for these five-and-twenty years: but I have constantly declared just the contrary; and that in all manner of ways. I have continually testified in private and in public, that we are sanctified as well as justified by faith. And indeed the one of those great truths does exceedingly illustrate the other. Exactly as we are justified by faith, so are we sanctified by faith. Faith is the condition, and the only condition, of sanctification, exactly as it is of justification. It is the *condition:* none is sanctified but he that believes; without faith no man is sanctified. And it is the *only condition:* this alone is sufficient for sanctification. Every one that believes is sanctified, whatever else he has or has not. In other words, no man is sanctified till he believes: every man when he believes is sanctified.

Sermons: "The Scripture Way of Salvation," III, 3 (S, II, 452-53).

JW

From the moment we are justified, there may be a gradual sanctification, a growing in grace, a daily advance in the knowledge and love of God. And if sin cease before death, there must, in the nature of the thing, be an instantaneous change; there must be a last moment wherein it does exist, and a first moment wherein it does not. "But should we in preaching insist both on one and the other?" Certainly we must insist on the gradual change; and that earnestly and continually. And are there not reasons why we should insist on the instantaneous also? If there be such a blessed change before death, should we not encourage all believers to expect it? and the rather, because constant experience shows, the more earnestly they expect this, the more swiftly and steadily does the gradual work of God go on in their soul; the more watchful they are against all sin, the more careful to grow in grace, the more zealous of good works, and the more punctual in their attendance on all the ordinances of God. Whereas, just the contrary effects are observed whenever this expectation ceases. They are "saved by hope," by this hope of a total change, with a gradually increasing salvation. Destroy this hope, and the salvation stands still, or, rather, decreases daily. Therefore whoever would advance the gradual change in believers should strongly insist on the instantaneous.

Works: "Minutes of Several Conversations" (VIII, 329).

Q. 1. How much is allowed by our brethren who differ from us, with regard to entire sanctification?

A. They grant, (1) That every one must be entirely sanctified in the article of death.

(2) That, till then, a believer daily grows in grace, comes nearer and nearer to perfection.

(3) That we ought to be continually pressing after this, and to exhort all others so to do.

Q. 2. What do we allow them?

A. We grant, (1) That many of those who have died in the faith, yea, the greater part of those we have known, were not sanctified throughout, not made perfect in love, till a little before death.

(2) That the term, "sanctified," is continually applied by St. Paul to all that were justified, were true believers.

(3) That by this term alone, he rarely, if ever, means saved from all sin.

(4) That, consequently, it is not proper to use it in this sense, without adding the word "wholly, entirely," or the like.

(5) That the inspired writers almost continually speak of or to

183

those who are justified; but very rarely, either of or to those who were wholly sanctified.

(6) That, consequently, it behoves us to speak in public almost continually of the state of justification; but, more rarely, in full and explicit terms, concerning entire sanctification.

Q. 3. What then is the point wherein we divide?

A. It is this: Whether we should expect to be saved from all sin before the article of death.

Q. 4. Is there any clear scripture promise of this; that God will save us from *all* sin?

A. There is: "He shall redeem Israel from *all* his sins." (Psalm cxxx. 8.) This is more largely expressed in the prophecy of Ezekiel: "Then will I sprinkle clean water upon you, and ye shall be clean: From *all* your filthiness, and from *all* your idols, will I cleanse you. I will also save you from *all* your uncleannesses." (xxxvi. 25, 29.) No promise can be more clear. And to this the Apostle plainly refers in that exhortation: "Having these promises, let us cleanse ourselves from all filthiness of flesh and spirit, perfecting holiness in the fear of God." (2. Cor. vii, 1.) Equally clear and express is that ancient promise: "The Lord thy God will circumcise thine heart, and the heart of thy seed, to love the Lord thy God with all thy heart and with all thy soul." (Deut. xxx, 6.)

Q. 5. But does any assertion answerable to this occur in the New Testament?

A. There does, and that laid down in the plainest terms. So St. John: "For this purpose the Son of God was manifested, that he might destroy the works of the devil"; (iii, 8;) the works of the devil, without any limitation or restriction: But all sin is the work of the devil. Parallel to which is that assertion of St. Paul: "Christ loved the Church, and gave himself for it; that he might present it to himself a glorious Church, not having spot, or wrinkle, or any such thing; but that it should be holy and without blemish." (Ephes. v, 25, 27.) And to the same effect is his assertion in the eighth of Romans: "God sent his Son—that the righteousness of the law might be fulfilled in us, walking not after the flesh, but after the Spirit." (verses 3, 4.)

Q. 6. Does the New Testament afford any farther ground for expecting to be saved from all sin?

A. Undoubtedly it does, both in those prayers and commands which are equivalent to the strongest assertions.

Q. 7. What prayers do you mean?

A. Prayers for entire sanctification; which, were there no such thing, would be mere mockery of God. Such, in particular, are, (1) "Deliver us from evil"; or rather, "from the evil one." Now, when this is done, when we are delivered from all evil, there can be no sin remaining. (2) "Neither pray I for these alone, but for them also which shall believe on me through their word; that they all may be one; as thou, Father, art in me, and I in thee, that they also may be one in us: I in them, and thou in me, that they may be made perfect in one." (John xvii. 20, 21, 23.) (3) "I bow my knees unto the Father of our Lord Jesus Christ—that he would grant you—that ye, being rooted and grounded in love, may be able to comprehend, with all saints, what is the breadth, and length, and depth, and height; and to know the love of Christ, which passeth knowledge, that ye might be filled with all the fulness of God." (Ephes. iii. 14, 16-9.) (4) "The very God of peace sanctify you wholly; and I pray God your whole spirit and soul and body be preserved blameless unto the coming of our Lord Jesus Christ." (1 Thess. v. 23.)

Q. 8. What command is there to the same effect?

A. (1) "Be ye perfect, even as your Father which is in heaven is perfect." (Matt. v. 48.) (2) "Thou shalt love the Lord thy God with all thy heart, and with all thy soul, and with all thy mind." (Matt. xxii. 37.) But if the love of God fill all the heart, there can be no sin there.

Works: "Minutes of Some Late Conversations," Wed. June 17, 1747 (VIII, 293-96).

JW

Those believers who are not convinced of the deep corruption of their hearts, or but slightly, and, as it were, notionally convinced, have little concern about *entire sanctification*. They may possibly hold the opinion, that such a thing is to be, either at death, or some time they know not when, before it. But they have no great uneasiness for the want of it, and no great hunger or thirst after it. They cannot, until they know themselves better, until they repent in the sense above described, until God unveils the inbred monster's face, and shows them the real state of their souls. Then only, when they feel the burden, will they groan for deliverance from it. Then, and not till then, will they cry out, in the agony of their soul,

> Break off the yoke of inbred sin,
> And fully set my spirit free!
> I cannot rest till pure within,
> Till I am wholly lost in Thee.

Sermons: "The Repentance of Believers," III, 2 (S, II, 395-96).

JW

First, we have known a large number of persons, of every age and sex, from early childhood to extreme old age, who have given all the proofs which the nature of the thing admits, that they were "sanctified throughout"; "cleansed from all pollution of the flesh and spirit"; that they "loved the Lord their God with all their heart, and mind, and soul, and strength"; that they continually "presented" their souls and bodies "a living sacrifice, holy, acceptable to God"; in consequence of which, they "rejoiced evermore, prayed without ceasing, and in everything gave thanks." And this, and no other, is what we believe to be true, scriptural sanctification.

Secondly. It is a common thing for those who are thus sanctified, to believe they cannot fall; to suppose themselves "pillars in the temple of God, that shall go out no more." Nevertheless, we have seen some of the strongest of them, after a time, moved from their steadfastness. Sometimes suddenly, but oftener by slow degrees, they have yielded to temptation; and pride, or anger, or foolish desires have again sprung up in their hearts. Nay, sometimes they have utterly lost the life of God, and sin hath regained dominion over them.

Yet, Thirdly, several of these, after being thoroughly sensible of their fall, and deeply ashamed before God, have been again filled with his love, and not only perfected therein, but established, strengthened, and settled. They have received the blessing they had before with abundant increase. Nay, it is remarkable, that many who had fallen either from justifying or from sanctifying grace, and so deeply fallen that they could hardly be ranked among the servants of God, have been restored, (but seldom till they had been shaken, as it were, over the mouth of hell,) and that very frequently in an instant, to all that they had lost. They have, at once, recovered both a consciousness of his favour, and the experience of the pure love of God. In one moment they received anew both remission of sins, and a lot among them that were sanctified.

But let not any man infer from this longsuffering of God, that he hath given any one a license to sin. Neither let any dare to continue in sin, because of these extraordinary instances of divine mercy. This is the most desperate, the most irrational presumption, and leads to utter, irrecoverable destruction. In all my experience, I have not known one who fortified himelf in sin by a presumption that God would save him at the last, that was not miserably disappointed, and suffered to die in his sins. To turn the grace of God into an encouragement to sin is the sure way to the nethermost hell!

Sermons: "A Call to Backsliders," V, 7-10 (J, VI, 525-26).

JW

If the Scriptures are true, those who are holy or righteous in the judgement of God himself; those who are endued with the faith that purifies the heart, that produces a good conscience; those who are grafted into the good olive tree, the spiritual, invisible Church; those who are branches of the true vine, of whom Christ says, "I am the vine, ye are the branches"; those who so effectually know Christ, as by that knowledge to have escaped the pollutions of the world; those who see the light of the glory of God in the face of Jesus Christ, and who have been made partakers of the Holy Ghost, of the witness and of the fruits of the Spirit; those who live by faith in the Son of

God; those who are sanctified by the blood of the covenant, may nevertheless so fall from God as to perish everlastingly.

Therefore, let him that standeth take heed lest he fall.

Works: "Serious Thoughts Upon the Perseverance of the Saints," 30 (X; 298).

JW

Come, let us join our friends above,
   The God of our salvation praise,
The God of everlasting love,
   The God of universal grace.

'Tis not by works that we have done,
   'Twas grace alone His heart inclined,
'Twas grace that gave His only Son
   To taste of death for all mankind.

For every man He tasted death;
   And hence we in His sight appear,
Not lifting up our eyes beneath,
   But publishing His mercy here.

This is the ground of all our hope,
   The fountain this of all our good,
Jesus for all was lifted up,
   And shed for all His precious blood.

His blood, for all a ransom given,
   Has wash'd away the general sin;
He closed His eyes to open heaven,
   And all, who will, may enter in.

He worketh once to will in all,
   Or mercy we could ne'er embrace;
He calls with an effectual call,
   And bids us all receive His grace.

Thou drawest all men unto Thee,
   Grace doth to every soul appear;
Preventing grace for all is free,
   And brings to all salvation near.

Had not Thy grace salvation brought,
   Thyself we never could desire;
Thy grace suggests our first good thought,
   Thy only grace doth all inspire.

By nature only free to ill,
   We never had one motion known
Of good, hadst Thou not given the will,
   And wrought it by Thy grace alone.

'Twas grace, when we in sin were dead,
   Us from the death of sin did raise;
Grace only hath the difference made;
   Whate'er we are, we are by grace.

When on Thy love we turn'd our back,
   Thou wouldst not shut Thy mercy's door,
The forfeiture Thou wouldst not take,
   Thy grace did still our souls restore.

When twice ten thousand times we fell,
   Thou gav'st us still a longer space,
Didst freely our backslidings heal,
   And show'dst Thy more abundant grace.

'Twas grace from hell that brought us up;
   Lo! to Thy sovereign grace we bow,
Through sovereign grace we still have hope,
   Thy sovereign grace supports us now.

Grace only doth from sin restrain,
   From which our nature cannot cease;

By grace we still Thy grace retain,
   And wait to feel Thy perfect peace.

Kept by the mercy of our God,
   Through faith, to full salvation's hour,
Jesu', we spread Thy name abroad,
   And glorify Thy gracious power.

The constant miracle we own
   By which we every moment live,
To grace, to Thy free grace alone,
   The whole of our salvation give.

Strongly upheld by Thy right hand,
   Thy all-redeeming love we praise;
The monuments of Thy grace we stand,
   Thy free, Thine universal grace.

By grace we draw our every breath;
   By grace we live, and move, and are;
By grace we 'scape the second death;
   By grace we now Thy grace declare.

From the first feeble thought of good
   To when the perfect grace is given,
'Tis all of grace; by grace renew'd,
   From hell we pass through earth to heaven.

We need no reprobates to prove
   That grace, free grace, is truly free;
Who cannot see that God is love,
   Open your eyes, and look on me,

On us, whom Jesus hath call'd forth
   To' assert that all His grace may have,
To vindicate His passion's worth
   Enough ten thousand worlds to save.

He made it possible for all
His gift of righteousness to' embrace;
We all may answer to His call,
May all be freely saved by grace.

He promised all mankind to draw;
We feel Him draw us from above,
And preach with Him the gracious law,
And publish the DECREE OF LOVE.

Behold the all-atoning Lamb;
Come, sinners, at the gospel call;
Look, and be saved through Jesu's name;
We witness He hath died for all.

We join with all our friends above,
The God of our salvation praise,
The God of everlasting love.
The God of universal grace.

Poetics: "Free Grace" (III, 93-96).

SUPPLEMENTARY REFERENCES

GENERAL NATURE OF SALVATION—*Sermons:* "Salvation by Faith," II, III (S, I, 41-52.); "The Scripture Way of Salvation" (S, II, 444 ff.). *Works:* "A Farther Appeal to Men of Reason and Religion" (VIII, 46 ff.). *Letters:* "To the Church at Herrnhut" (I, 344 ff.); "To Dr. Conyers Middleton" (II, 380 ff.); "To a Roman Catholic" (III, 7 ff.). *Journal:* "Thur. 3 Sept. 1741" (II, 490 ff.). *Notes:* "Acts 26:18."

SALVATION THROUGH GRACE—*Sermons:* "The Righteousness of Faith" (S, I, 132 ff.); "On Working Out Our Own Salvation" (J, VI, 506 ff.); "Free Grace," (J, VII, 373 ff.). *Works:* "The Doctrine of Original Sin" (IX, 302-3); "Predestination Calmly Considered," 46 (X, 230); "The Question 'What is an Arminian?' Answered by a Lover of Free Grace," 1-12 (X, 358-61). *Journal:* "Tues. 13 Feb. 1781" (VI, 304). *Notes:* "Ephesians 3:7."

PREVENIENT GRACE—*Sermons:* "Justification by Faith," IV, 9 (S, I, 130); "The Witness of Our Own Spirit," 4-5 (S, I, 222-24); "On Conscience," I, 1-13 (J, VII, 186-90). *Works:* "Predestination Calmly Considered," 1-18 (X, 204-10); "The Doctrine of Original Sin" (IX, 268). *Letters:* "To John Fletcher" (V, 231); "To John Mason"

(VI, 239-40); "To Arthur Keene" (VII, 222). *Journal:* "Tues. 13 July 1756" (IV, 174). *Notes:* "John 6:44;" "Romans 2:14."

REPENTANCE—*Sermons:* "The Righteousness of Faith," III, 1-5 (S, I, 143-46); "The Way to the Kingdom," II (S, I, 155-61); "The Spirit of Bondage and of Adoption," II (S, I, 185-91); "Upon Our Lord's Sermon on the Mount: I," I, II (S, I, 321-34). *Works:* "A Farther Appeal to Men of Reason and Religion" (VIII, 56-57); "The Principles of a Methodist Farther Explained," VI, 4 (VIII, 472-73). *Letters:* "To a Friend" (I, 245); "To Thomas Church" (II, 197); "To Thomas Davenport" (VII, 95); "To Jane Bisson" (VIII, 7-8). *Journal:* "Fri. 15 June 1739" (II, 221-22); "Thur. 4 June 1772" (V, 466-67). *Notes:* "Romans 7:9;" "II Corinthians 10:5;" "Acts 5:31."

FAITH—*Sermons:* "Salvation by Faith" (S, I, 37 ff.); "The Almost Christian," II, 3-11 (S, I, 62-67); "Justification by Faith" (S, I, 114 ff.); "On Faith" (J, VII, 195 ff.). *Works:* "An Earnest Appeal to Men of Reason and Religion," 6-11 (VIII, 4-6). *Letters:* "To 'John Smith'" (II, 45 ff.); "To His Brother Charles" (II, 108-9); "To Richard Tompson" (III, 161-62). *Journal:* "Thur. 1 Nov. 1739" (II, 304-5); "Sun. 22 June 1740" (II, 354-55); "Fri. 1 Sept. 1769" (V, 338). *Notes:* "Matthew 15:28;" "Ephesians 2:8."

JUSTIFICATION BY FAITH (PARDON AND ACCEPTANCE)—*Sermons:* "Justification by Faith" (S, I, 114 ff.); "On the Death of the Rev. Mr. George Whitefield" (S, II, 509 ff.); "The Reward of the Righteous" (J, VII, 127 ff.). *Works:* "Minutes of Several Conversations" (VIII, 275-76, 290-91). *Letters:* "To His Brother Samuel" (I, 262 ff.); "To Dr. Horne" (IV, 172 ff.); "To Ann Bolton" (V, 325). *Journal:* "Mon. 27 Aug. 1739" (II, 261 ff.); "Mon. 31 Dec. 1739" (II, 328 ff.). *Notes:* "Romans 4:5-6; 18;" "Hebrews 11:1-2."

NEW BIRTH (REGENERATION)—*Sermons:* "The First-Fruits of the Spirit" (S, I, 162 ff.); "The Spirit of Bondage and of Adoption," III-IV (S, I, 191-98); "The Marks of the New Birth" (S, I, 283 ff.); "The Great Privilege of Those that are Born of God," I (S, I, 298 ff.); "The Nature of Enthusiasm," 16 (S, II, 91-92); "The New Birth" (S, II, 226 ff.); "On God's Vineyard," I, 6-8 (J, VII, 205). *Works:* "Minutes of Some Late Conversations" (VIII, 279). *Letters:* "To Mr. Potter" (IV, 37 ff.); "To His Nephew Samuel Wesley" (VII, 230-31). *Notes:* "II Corinthians 5:17;" "Hebrews 9:14."

SIN IN BELIEVERS—*Sermons:* "The Wilderness State" (S, II, 245 ff.); "On Sin in Believers" (S, II, 361 ff.); "The Lord Our Righteousness" (S, II, 423 ff.); "On Temptation" (J, VI, 475 ff.). *Works:* "Serious Thoughts upon the Perseverance of the Saints" (X, 284 ff.). *Letters:* "To William Dodd" (III, 167 ff.); "To Peggy Dale" (V, 48-49); "To Mrs. Barton" (V, 185); "To Miss March" (V, 192). *Journal:* "Sun. 11-Mon. 12 Jan. 1741" (II, 415-16).

REPENTANCE OF BELIEVERS—*Sermons:* "Heaviness Through Manifold Temptations" (S, II, 264 ff.); "The Repentance of Believers" (S, II, 379 ff.); "A Call to Backsliders" (J, VI, 514 ff.). *Letters:* "To Miss March" (V, 256). *Notes:* "II Peter 3:18."

ENTIRE SANCTIFICATION—*Sermons:* "The Righteousness of Faith," I, 7-8 (S, I, 136-37); "Wandering Thoughts" (S, II, 179 ff.); "Satan's Devices" (S, II, 192 ff.); "On Patience" (J, VI, 484 ff.). *Works:* "Minutes of Some Late Conversations" (VIII, 285 ff.); "An Extract from 'A Short View of the Difference between the Moravian Brethren, (so called,) and the Rev. Mr. John and Charles Wesley'" (X, 201 ff.). *Letters:* "To Miss March" (IV, 313); "To his Brother Charles" (V, 40-41). *Journal:* "Fri. 22 May 1761" (IV, 460). *Notes:* "I Corinthians 1:30;" I Thessalonians 5:23;" "Hebrews 2:10."

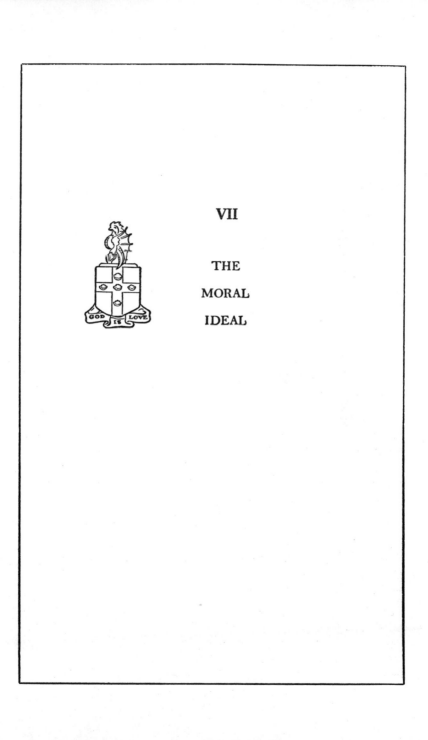

VII

THE

MORAL

IDEAL

VII. THE MORAL IDEAL

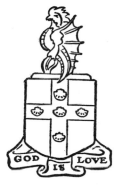

THIS CHAPTER *is concerned with the moral ideal of the Christian life, which is an object of continuous effort and prayerful expectancy for the man of faith. For Wesley entire sanctification is an event, a subjective act, wrought by God in the human soul on the condition of faith. Christian perfection is a process, the resulting objective life of holiness that is never completed but always subject to development. Christian perfection itself is defined in relation both to an obligatory standard, realizable by men under grace, and an absolute perfect moral law—Adamic perfection—which cannot be fulfilled. The atonement of Christ is necessary to both. The person made "perfect in love" does not commit sin, defined as a conscious violation of a known law, though he is subject to ignorance, mistakes and infirmities which result in involuntary transgressions of the law. The counsels of the law and the profound example of God's redeeming love are ever before the earnest Christian to guide him and help establish him on the way to perfection. The kingdom of God is generally defined by Wesley as the kingdom within, and as such it is closely related to his description of Christian perfection.*

1. The Law

Lay aside the terms "Adamic law," "gospel law," or any law. The thing is beyond dispute, and you may as well demand a scriptural proof that two and two make four. Adam in Paradise was able to apprehend *all* things distinctly, and to *judge truly* concerning them; therefore it was his duty so to do. But no man living *is* now *able* to do this; therefore neither is it the duty of any man now living. Neither is there any man now in the body who does or can walk in this instance by that rule which was bound upon Adam. Can anything be more plain than this—that Adam *could,* that I *cannot* avoid mistaking? Can anything be plainer than this—If he *could* avoid it, he *ought?* or than this—If I *cannot,* I *ought not?* I mean it is not my duty: for the clear reason that no one can do the impossible. Nothing in the Sermon or the Law contradicts this. If anything does, it is wrong.

Letters: "To Samuel Furly" (IV, 98).

JW

[The law] is, indeed, in the highest degree, pure, chaste, clean, holy. Otherwise it could not be the immediate offspring, and much less the express resemblance, of God, who is essential holiness. It is pure from all sin, clean and unspotted from any touch of evil. It is a chaste virgin, incapable of any defilement, of any mixture with that which is unclean or unholy. It has no fellowship with sin of any kind: for "what communion hath light with darkness?" As sin is, in its very nature, enmity to God, so His law is enmity to sin.

Therefore it is that the Apostle rejects with such abhorance that blasphemous supposition, that the law of God is either sin itself, or the cause of sin. God forbid that we should suppose it is the cause of sin, because it is the discoverer of it; because it detects the hidden things of darkness, and drags them out into open day. It is true, by this means (as the Apostle observes, Rom. vii. 13), "sin appears to be sin." All its disguises are torn away, and it appears in its native deformity. It is true likewise, that "sin, by the commandment, becomes exceeding sinful": being now committed against light and knowledge, being stripped even of the poor plea of ignorance, it loses its excuse, as well as disguise, and becomes far more odious both to God and man. Yea, and it is true, that "sin worketh death by that which is good"; which in itself is pure and holy. When it is dragged out to light, it rages the more: when it is restrained, it bursts out with greater violence. . . .

And it is, secondly, just. It renders to all their due. It prescribes exactly what is right, precisely what ought to be done, said, or thought, both with regard to the Author of our being, with regard to ourselves, and with regard to every creature which He has made. . . .

"But is the will of God the cause of His law? Is His will the original of right and wrong? Is a thing *therefore* right, because God wills it? or does He will it because it is right?"

I fear this celebrated question is more curious than useful. And perhaps in the manner it is usually treated of, it does not so well consist with the regard that is due from a creature to the Creator and Governor of all things. It is hardly decent for man to call the supreme God to give an account to him. Nevertheless, with awe and reverence we may speak a little. The Lord pardon us if we speak amiss!

It seems, then, that the whole difficulty arises from considering God's will as distinct from God: otherwise it vanishes away. For none can doubt but God is the cause of the law of God. But the will of God is God Himself. It is God considered as willing thus or thus. Consequently, to say that the will of God, or that God Himself, is the cause of the law, is one and the same thing. . . .

The law, then, is right and just concerning all things. And it is good as well as just. This we may easily infer from the fountain whence it flowed. For what was this, but the goodness of God? What but goodness alone inclined Him to impart that divine copy of Himself to the holy angels? To what else can we impute His bestowing upon man the same transcript of His own nature? And what but tender love constrained Him afresh to manifest His will to fallen man—either to Adam, or any of his seed, who like him were "come short of the glory of God"? Was it not mere love that moved Him to publish His law after the understandings of men were darkened? and to send His prophets to declare that law to the blind, thoughtless children of men? . . .

It remains only to show, in the fourth and last place, the uses of the law. And the first use of it, without question, is, to convince the world of sin. This is, indeed, the peculiar work of the Holy Ghost; who can work it without any means at all, or by whatever means it pleaseth Him, however insufficient in themselves, or even improper, to produce such an effect. And, accordingly, some there are whose hearts have been broken in pieces in a moment, either in sickness or in health, without any visible cause, or any outward means whatever; and others (one in an age) have been awakened to a sense of the "wrath of God abiding on them," by hearing that "God was in Christ, reconciling the world unto Himself." But it is the ordinary method of the Spirit of God to convict sinners by the law. It is this which, being set home on the conscience, generally breaketh the rocks in pieces. It is more especially this part of the word of God which is ζῶν καὶ ἐνεργής, —*quick and powerful,* full of life and energy, "and sharper than any two-edged sword." This, in the hand of God and of those whom He hath sent, pierces through all the folds of a deceitful heart, and "divides asunder even the soul and the spirit"; yea, as it were, the very "joints and marrow." By this is the sinner discovered to himself. All his fig-leaves are torn away, and he sees that he is "wretched, and poor, and miserable, and blind, and naked." The law flashes conviction on every side. He feels himself a mere sinner. He has nothing to pay. His "mouth is stopped," and he stands "guilty before God."

To slay the sinner is, then, the first use of the law; to destroy the life and strength wherein he trusts, and convince him that he is dead while he liveth; not only under the sentence of death, but actually dead unto God, void of all spiritual life, "dead in trespasses and sins." The second use of it is, to bring him unto life, unto Christ, that he may live. It is true, in performing both these offices, it acts the part of a severe schoolmaster. It drives us by force, rather than draws us by love. And yet love is the spring of all. It is the spirit of love which, by this painful means, tears away our confidence in the flesh, which leaves us no broken reed whereon to trust, and so constrains the sinner, stripped of all, to cry out in the bitterness of his soul, or groan in the depth of his heart,

> I give up every plea beside,—
> Lord, I am damn'd; but Thou hast died.

The third use of the law is, to keep us alive. It is the grand means whereby the blessed Spirit prepares the believer for larger communications of the life of God. . . .

Allowing then, that every believer has done with the law, as it means the Jewish ceremonial law, or the entire Mosaic dispensation (for these Christ hath taken out of the way); yea, allowing we have done with the moral law, as a means of procuring our justification (for we are "justified freely by His grace, through the redemption that is in Jesus"); yet, in another sense, we have not done with this law: for it is still of unspeakable use, first, in convincing us of the sin that yet remains both in our hearts and lives, and thereby keeping us close to Christ, that His blood may cleanse us every moment; secondly, in deriving strength from our Head into His living members, whereby He empowers them to do what His law commands; and, thirdly, in confirming our hope of whatsoever it commands and we have not yet attained,—of receiving grace upon grace, till we are in actual possession of the fullness of His promises. . . .

If thy Lord hath already fulfilled His word, if He hath already "written His law in thy heart," then "stand fast in the liberty wherewith Christ hath made thee free." Thou art not only made free from Jewish ceremonies, from the guilt of sin, and the fear of hell (these are so far from being the whole, that they are the least and lowest part of Christian liberty); but, what is infinitely more, from the power of sin, from serving the devil, from offending God. O stand fast in this liberty: in comparison of which, all the rest is not even worthy to be named! Stand fast in loving God with all thy heart, and serving Him with all thy strength! This is perfect freedom; thus to keep His law, and to walk in all His commandments blameless. "Be not entangled again with the yoke of bondage." I do not mean of Jewish bondage; nor yet of bondage to the fear of hell: these, I trust, are far from thee. But beware of being entangled again with the yoke of sin, of any inward or outward transgression of the law. Abhor sin far more than death or hell; abhor sin itself, far more than the punishment of it. Beware of the bondage of pride, of desire, of anger; of every evil temper, or word, or work. "Look unto Jesus"; and in order thereto, look more and more into the perfect law, "the law of liberty"; and "continue therein"; so shalt thou daily "grow in grace, and in the knowledge of our Lord Jesus Christ."

Sermons: "The Original, Nature, Property, and Use of the Law," III, 3-7, 10, IV, 1-4, 10 (S, II, 47-54, 56-57).

How may we establish the law in our own hearts, so that it may have its full influence on our lives? And this can only be done by faith.

Faith alone it is which effectually answers this end, as we learn from daily experience. For so long as we walk by faith, not by sight, we go swiftly on in the way of holiness. While we steadily look, not at the things which are seen, but at those which are not seen, we are more and more crucified to the world, and the world crucified to us. Let but the eye of the soul be constantly fixed, not on the things which are temporal, but on those which are eternal, and our affections are more and more loosened from earth, and fixed on things above. So that faith, in general, is the most direct and effectual means of promoting all righteousness and true holiness; of establishing the holy and spiritual law in the hearts of them that believe.

Sermons: "The Law Established Through Faith: II," III, 2 (S, II, 80-81).

JW

How blasphemously does [Luther] speak of good works and of the law of God—constantly coupling the law with sin, death, hell, or the devil; and teaching that Christ delivers us from them all alike. Whereas it can no more be proved by Scripture that Christ delivers us from the law of God than that He delivers us from holiness or from heaven. Here (I apprehend) is the real spring of the grand error of the Moravians. They follow Luther, for better, for worse. Hence their "No works; no law; no commandments." But who art thou that "speakest evil of the law, and judgest the law"?

Journal: "Mon. 15 June 1741" (II, 467).

JW

"You say, 'A mistake is not a sin, if love is the sole principle of action; yet it is a transgression of the perfect law'; therefore perfect love is not the perfect law"! Most sure; for by "the perfect law" I mean that given to Adam at his creation. But the loving God with all his heart was not the whole of that law: it implied abundantly more; even thinking, speaking, and acting right in every instance, which he was then able, and therefore obliged, to do. But none of his descendants are able to do this; therefore love is the fulfilling of their law.

Perhaps you had not adverted to this. The law of love, which is the whole law given to us, is only one branch of that perfect law which was given to Adam in the beginning. His law was far wider than ours, as his faculties were more extensive. Consequently many things might be transgressions of the latter which were not of the former.

"But if ignorance be a transgression of the perfect law." Whoever said or thought so? Ignorance is not, but mistake is. And this Adam was able to avoid; that kind of ignorance which was in him not constraining him to mistake, as ours frequently does.

"But is 'a voluntary transgression of a known law' a proper definition of sin?" I think it is of all such sin as is imputed to our condemnation. And it is a definition which has passed uncensured in the Church for at least fifteen hundred years. . . .

The thing is plain. All in the body are liable to mistakes, practical as well as speculative. Shall we call them sins or no? I answer again and again, Call them just what you please.

Letters: "To John Hosmer" (IV, 155).

2. *Christian Love*

"Beloved, if God so loved us, we ought also to love one another." If God *SO* loved us;—observe, the stress of the argument lies on this very point: *SO loved us,* as to deliver up his only Son to die a cursed death for our salvation. Beloved, what manner of love is this wherewith God hath loved us; so as to give his *only Son,* in glory equal with the Father, in majesty co-eternal? What manner of love is this wherewith the only-begotten Son of God hath loved us, as to *empty himself,* as far as possible, of his eternal Godhead; as to divest himself of that glory which he had with the Father before the world began; as to take upon him the form of a servant, being found in fashion as a man;

201

and then, to humble himself still further, "being obedient unto death, even the death of the cross!" If God *SO* loved us, how ought we to love one another!

Sermons: "God's Love to Fallen Man," 5 (J, VI, 235).

JW

We must love God, before we can be holy at all; this being the root of all holiness. Now we cannot love God, till we know He loves us. "We love Him, because He first loved us." And we cannot know His pardoning love to us, till His spirit witnesses it to our spirit. Since, therefore, this testimony of His spirit must precede the love of God and all holiness, of consequence it must precede our inward consciousness thereof, or the testimony of our spirit concerning them.

Then, and not till then—when the Spirit of God beareth that witness to our spirit, "God hath loved thee, and given His own Son to be the propitiation for thy sins; the Son of God hath loved thee, and hath washed thee from thy sins in His blood"—"we love God, because He first loved us"; and, for His sake, we love our brother also. And of this we cannot but be conscious to ourselves; we "know the things that are freely given to us of God." We know that we love God, and keep His commandments, and "hereby also we know that we are of God." This is that testimony of our own Spirit, which, so long as we continue to love God and keep His commandments, continues joined with the testimony of God's Spirit, "that we are the children of God."

Sermons: "The Witness of the Spirit: I," I, 8-9 (S, I, 208-09).

JW

There is no fear in love—No slavish fear can be where love reigns; *but perfect,* adult *love casteth out* slavish *fear; because* such *fear hath torment,* and so is inconsistent with the happiness of love. A natural man has neither fear, nor love; one that is awakened, fear without love; a babe in Christ, love and fear; a father in Christ, love without fear.

We love him, because he first loved us—This is the sum of all religion, the genuine model of Christianity. None can say more. Why
should any one say less? or less intelligibly?

Notes: "I John 4:18-19."

JW

Reason, however cultivated and improved, cannot produce the love
of God; which is plain from hence: It cannot produce either faith or
hope; from which alone this love can flow. It is then only, when we
"behold" by faith "what manner of love the Father hath bestowed
upon us," in giving his only Son, that we might not perish, but have
everlasting life, that "the love of God is shed abroad in our heart by
the Holy Ghost which is given unto us." It is only then, when we
"rejoice in hope of the glory of God," that "we love Him because he
first loved us." But what can cold reason do in this matter? It may
present us with fair ideas; it can draw a fine picture of love: But this
is only a painted fire. And farther than this reason cannot go. I made
the trial for many years. I collected the finest hymns, prayers, and
meditations which I could find in any language; and I said, sung, or
read them over and over, with all possible seriousness and attention.
But still I was like the bones in Ezekiel's vision: "The skin covered
them above: but there was no breath in them."

And as reason cannot produce the love of God, so neither can it
produce the love of our neighbour; a calm, generous, disinterested
benevolence to every child of man. This earnest, steady good-will to
our fellow-creatures never flowed from any fountain but gratitude
to our Creator.

Sermons: "The Case of Reason Impartially Considered," II, 8-9 (J, VI, 358-59).

JW

Having no knowledge, we can have no love of God: we cannot love
Him we know not. Most men *talk* indeed of loving God, and perhaps

imagine they do; at least, few will acknowledge they do not love Him: but the fact is too plain to be denied. No man loves God by nature, any more than he does a stone, or the earth he treads upon. What we love we delight in: but no man has naturally any delight in God. In our natural state we cannot conceive how any one should delight in Him. We take no pleasure in Him at all; he is utterly tasteless to us. To love God! it is far above, out of our sight. We cannot, naturally, attain unto it.

Sermons: "Original Sin," II, 5 (S, II, 217).

JW

As soon as he believes, he loves God. . . . "We love Him because he first loved us"; of which faith is the evidence. The love of a pardoning God is "shed abroad in our hearts, by the Holy Ghost which is given unto us." Indeed this love may admit of a thousand degrees: But still every one, as long as he believes, may truly declare before God, " 'Lord, thou knowest that I love thee.' Thou knowest that 'my desire is unto thee, and unto the remembrance of thy name.' "

Sermons: "On Family Religion," I, 2 (J, VII, 78).

JW

O let your heart be whole with God! Seek your happiness in him and him alone. Beware that you cleave not to the dust! "This earth is not your place." See that you use this world as not abusing it; *use* the world, and *enjoy* God. Sit as loose to all things here below, as if you were a poor beggar. Be a good steward of the manifold gifts of God; that when you are called to give an account of your stewardship, he may say, "Well done, good and faithful servant, enter thou into the joy of thy Lord!"

Sermons: "On Riches," II, 12 (J, VII, 221-22).

We ourselves could not love our brethren, unless we were passed from spiritual death to life: that is, born of God. . . . And he that is not born of God, cannot love his brother.

Notes: "I John 3:14."

Go and do thou in like manner—Let us *go and do likewise,* regarding every man as our neighbour who needs our assistance. Let us renounce that bigotry and party zeal which would contract our hearts, into an insensibility for all the human race, but a small number whose sentiments and practices are so much our own, that our love to them is but self-love reflected. With an honest openness of mind let us always remember that kindred between man and man, and cultivate that happy instinct whereby, in the original constitution of our nature, God has strongly bound us to each other.

Notes: "Luke 10:37."

[A Christian's love] is in itself generous and disinterested; springing from no view of advantage to himself, from no regard to profit or praise—no, nor even the pleasure of loving. This is the daughter, not the parent, of his affection. By experience he knows that social love, if it mean the love of our neighbour, is absolutely different from self-love, even of the most allowable kind—just as different as the objects at which they point. And yet it is sure that, if they are under due regulations, each will give additional force to the other till they mix together never to be divided.

Letters: "To Dr. Conyers Middleton" (II, 377).

3. Christian Perfection

Perhaps the general prejudice against Christian Perfection . . . may chiefly arise from a misapprehension of the nature of it. We willingly allow, and continually declare, there is no such perfection, in this life, as implies either a dispensation from doing good, and attending all the ordinances of God; or a freedom from ignorance, mistake, temptation, and a thousand infirmities necessarily connected with flesh and blood.

First. We not only allow, but *earnestly contend,* . . . that there is no perfection in this life which implies any dispensation from attending all the ordinances of God, or from *doing good unto all men, while we have time,* though *especially unto the household of faith.* . . . We believe that not only the babes in Christ who have newly found Redemption in His blood, but those also who are *grown up into perfect men,* . . . are indispensably obliged, as oft as they have opportunity, to eat bread and drink wine *in remembrance of Him,"* to *search the Scriptures;* by fasting (as well as temperance) to *keep their bodies under, and bring them into subjection;* and, above all, to pour out their souls in prayer, both *secretly,* and *in the great congregation.*

We, secondly, believe, . . . that there is no such perfection in this life as implies an entire deliverance, either from ignorance or mistake, in things not essential to salvation, or from manifold temptations, or from numberless infirmities, wherewith the corruptible body, more or less, presses down the soul. . . . We cannot find any ground in Scripture to suppose that any inhabitant of a house of clay is wholly exempt, either from bodily infirmities, or from ignorance of many things; or to imagine any is incapable of mistake, or falling into divers temptations. . . .

But what then, . . . do you mean by *one that is perfect . . .* ? We mean, one in whom is *the mind which was in Christ,* and who *so walketh as* [*Christ*] *walked;* a man that *hath clean hands and a pure heart;* or that is *cleansed from all filthiness of flesh and spirit;* one *in whom there is no occasion of stumbling,* and who, accordingly, *doth not commit sin.* To declare this a little more particularly: We understand by that scriptural expression, *a perfect man,* one in whom God hath fulfilled His faithful word, *From all your filthiness, and from all your idols, I will cleanse you. I will also save you from all your uncleannesses.* We understand hereby, one whom God hath sanctified throughout, *even in body, soul, and spirit;* one who *walketh in the light, as He is in the light,* in whom *is no darkness at all;* the blood of Jesus Christ His Son having *cleansed him from all sin.*

This man can now testify to all mankind, *I am crucified with Christ; nevertheless I live; yet I live not, but Christ liveth in me.* He is *holy, as God who called him is holy,* both in life and *in all manner of conversation.* He *loveth the Lord his God with all his heart,* and *serveth Him with all his strength.* He *loveth his neighbour* (every man) *as himself;* yea, *as Christ loveth us;* them in particular that *despitefully use him and persecute him,* because *they know not the Son, neither the Father.* Indeed his soul is all love, filled with *bowels of mercies, kindness, meekness, gentleness, longsuffering.* And his life agreeth thereto, full of *the work of faith, the patience of hope, the labour of love.* And *whatsoever he doth, either in word or deed,* he doth it *all in the name,* in the love and power, *of the Lord Jesus.* In a word, he doeth the will of God *on earth, as it is* done *in heaven.*

This is to be *a perfect man,* to be *sanctified throughout.* . . . Even "to have a heart so all-flaming with the love of God," (to use Archbishop Usher's words) "as continually to offer up every thought, word, and work, as a spiritual sacrifice, acceptable unto God through Christ." In every thought of our hearts, in every word of our tongues, in every work of our hands, *to show forth His praise who hath called us out of darkness into His marvellous light!* O that both we, and all who seek the Lord Jesus in sincerity, may thus be *made perfect in One!*

Poetics: "The Preface" (II, 45-48).

JW

"Ye shall therefore be perfect, as your Father who is in heaven is perfect." And who says, ye shall not; or, at least, not till your soul is separated from the body? It is the doctrine of St. Paul, the doctrine of St. James, of St. Peter, and St. John; and no otherwise Mr. Wesley's, than as it is the doctrine of every one who preaches the pure and the whole gospel. I tell you, as plain as I can speak, where and when I found this. I found it in the oracles of God, in the Old and New Testament; when I read them with no other view or desire but to save my own soul. But whosesoever this doctrine is, I pray you, what harm is there in it? Look at it again; survey it on every side, and that with the closest attention. In one view, it is purity of intention, dedicating all the life to God. It is the giving God all our heart; it is one desire and design ruling all our tempers. It is the devoting, not a part, but all, our soul, body, and substance to God. In another view, it is all the mind which was in Christ, enabling us to walk as Christ walked. It is the circumcision of the heart from all filthiness, all inward as well as outward pollution. It is a renewal of the heart in the whole image of God, the full likeness of Him that created it. In yet another, it is the loving God with all our heart, and our neighbour as ourselves. Now, take it in which of these views you please, (for there is no material difference), and this is the whole and sole perfection, as a train of writings prove to a demonstration, which I have believed and taught for these forty years, from the year 1725 to the year 1765.

Works: "A Plain Account of Christian Perfection," 27 (XI, 444).

JW

In the year 1764, upon a review of the whole subject, I wrote down the sum of what I had observed in the following short propositions:—

(1) There is such a thing as perfection; for it is again and again mentioned in Scripture.

(2) It is not so early as justification; for justified persons are to "go on unto perfection." (Heb. vi. 1.)

(3) It is not so late as death; for St. Paul speaks of living men that were perfect. (Philip. iii. 15.)

(4) It is not absolute. Absolute perfection belongs not to man, nor to angels, but to God alone.

(5) It does not make a man infallible: None is infallible, while he remains in the body.

(6) Is it sinless? It is not worth while to contend for a term. It is "salvation from sin."

(7) It is "perfect love." (I John iv. 18.) This is the essence of it; its properties, or inseparable fruits, are, rejoicing evermore, praying

without ceasing, and in everything giving thanks. (I Thess. v. 16 etc.)

(8) It is improvable. It is so far from lying in an indivisible point, from being incapable of increase, that one perfected in love may grow in grace far swifter than he did before.

(9) It is amissible, capable of being lost; of which we have numerous instances. But we were not thoroughly convinced of this, till five or six years ago.

(10) It is constantly both preceded and followed by a gradual work.

Works: "A Plain Account of Christian Perfection," 26 (XI, 441-42).

Thus much is certain: they that love God with all their heart and all men as themselves are scripturally perfect. And surely such there are; otherwise the promise of God would be a mere mockery of human weakness. Hold fast this. But then remember, on the other hand, you have this treasure in an earthen vessel; you dwell in a poor, shattered house of clay, which presses down the immortal spirit. Hence all your thoughts, words, and actions are so imperfect, so far from coming up to the standard (that law of love which, but for the corruptible body, your soul would answer in all instances), that you may well say till you go to Him you love:

> Every moment, Lord, I need
> The merit of Thy death.

Letters: "To Miss March" (IV, 208).

(1) Not only sin, properly so called, (that is, a voluntary transgression of a known law,) but sin, improperly so called, (that is, an involuntary transgression of a divine law, known or unknown,) needs the atoning blood. (2) I believe there is no such perfection in this life as excludes these involuntary transgressions which I apprehend to be naturally consequent on the ignorance and mistakes inseparable

from mortality. (3) Therefore *sinless perfection* is a phrase I never use, lest I should seem to contradict myself. (4) I believe, a person filled with the love of God is still liable to these involuntary transgressions. (5) Such transgressions you may call sins, if you please: I do not, for the reasons above-mentioned.

Works: "A Plain Account of Christian Perfection," 19 (XI, 396).

JW

I was with two persons who believe they are saved from all sin. Be it so, or not, why should we not rejoice in the work of God, so far as it is unquestionably wrought in them? For instance, I ask John C., "Do you pray always? Do you rejoice in God every moment? Do you in everything give thanks? In loss? In pain? In sickness, weariness, disappointments? Do you desire nothing? Do you fear nothing? Do you feel the love of God continually in your heart? Have you a witness, in whatever you speak or do, that it is pleasing to God?" If he can solemnly and deliberately answer in the affirmative, why do I not rejoice and praise God on his behalf? Perhaps because I have an exceeding complex idea of sanctification or a sanctified man. And so, for fear he should not have attained all I include in that idea, I cannot rejoice in what he has attained.

Journal: "Sun. 2 Dec. 1744" (III, 154).

JW

I do not conceive the perfection here spoken of, to be the perfection of angels. As those glorious beings never "left their first estate," never declined from their original perfection, all their native faculties are unimpaired: Their understanding, in particular, is still a lamp of light, their apprehension of all things clear and distinct, and their judgment always true. Hence, though their knowledge is limited, (for they are creatures,) though they are ignorant of innumerable things, yet they are not liable to mistake: Their knowledge is perfect in its kind. And as their affections are all constantly guided by their unerring understanding, so that all their actions are suitable thereto; so they do, every moment, not their own will, but the good and acceptable will of God. Therefore it is not possible for man, whose understanding is darkened, to whom mistake is as natural as ignorance; who cannot think at all, but by the mediation of organs which are weakened and depraved, like the other parts of his corruptible body; it is not possible, I say, for men always to think right, to apprehend things distinctly, and to judge truly of them. In consequence hereof, his affections, depending on his understanding, are variously disordered. And his words and actions are influenced, more or less, by the disorder both of his understanding and affections. It follows, that no man, while in the body, can possibly attain to angelic perfection.

Neither can any man, while he is in a corruptible body, attain to Adamic perfection. Adam, before his fall, was undoubtedly as pure, as free from sin, as even the holy angels. In like manner, his understanding was as clear as theirs, and his affections as regular. In virtue of this, as he always judged right, so he was able always to speak and act right. But since man rebelled against God, the case is widely different with him. He is no longer able to avoid falling into innumerable mistakes; consequently, he cannot always avoid wrong affections, neither can he always think, speak, and act right. Therefore man, in his present state, can no more attain Adamic than angelic perfection.

Sermons: "On Perfection," I, 1-2 (J, VI, 411-12).

JW

In the first place, I shall endeavour to show, in what sense Christians are *not perfect*. And both from experience and Scripture it appears, first, that they are not perfect in knowledge; they are not *so* perfect in this life as to be free from ignorance. They know, it may be, in common with other men, many things relating to the present world; and they know, with regard to the world to come, the general truths which God hath revealed. They know likewise (what the natural man receiveth not; for these things are spiritually discerned) "what manner of love" it is, wherewith "the Father" hath loved them, "that they should be called the sons of God." They know the mighty working of His Spirit in their hearts; and the wisdom of His providence, directing all their paths, and causing all things to work together for their good. Yea, they know in every circumstance of life what the Lord requireth of them, and how to keep a conscience void of offence both toward God and toward man. . . . .

No one, then, is so perfect in this life, as to be free from ignorance. Nor, secondly, from mistake; which indeed is almost an unavoidable consequence of it; seeing those who "know but in part" are ever liable to err touching the things which they know not. It is true, the children of God do not mistake as to the things essential to salvation: they do not "put darkness for light, or light for darkness"; neither "seek death in the error of their life." For they are "taught of God"; and the way which He teaches them, the way of holiness, is so plain, that "the wayfaring man, though a fool, need not err therein." But in things unessential to salvation they do err, and that frequently. The best and wisest of men are frequently mistaken even with regard to facts; believing those things not to have been which really were, or those to have been done which were not. Or, suppose they are not mistaken as to the fact itself, they may be with regard to its circumstances; believing them, or many of them, to have been quite different from what, in truth, they were. And hence cannot but arise many farther mistakes. Hence they may believe either past or present actions which were or are evil, to be good; and such as were or are good, to be evil. Hence also they may judge not according to truth with regard to the characters of men; and that, not only by supposing good men to be better, or wicked men to be worse, than they are; but by believing them to have been or to be good men, who were or are very wicked; or perhaps those to have been or to be wicked men, who were or are holy and unreprovable. . . . .

Even Christians, therefore, are not *so* perfect as to be free either from ignorance or error: we may, thirdly, add, nor from infirmities. Only let us take care to understand this word aright: only let us not give that soft title to known sins, as the manner of some is. So, one man tells us, "Every man has his infirmity, and mine is drunkenness"; another has the infirmity of uncleanness; another, that of taking God's holy name in vain; and yet another has the infirmity of calling his brother, "Thou fool," or returning "railing for railing." It is plain that all you who thus speak, if ye repent not, shall, with your infirmities, go quick into hell! But I mean hereby, not only those which are properly termed *bodily infirmities,* but all those inward or outward imperfections which are not of a moral nature. Such are the weakness or slowness of understanding, dullness or confusedness of apprehension, incoherency of thought, irregular quickness or heaviness of imagination. Such (to mention no more of this kind) is the want of a ready or retentive memory. Such, in another kind, are those which are commonly, in some measure, consequent upon these; namely, slowness of speech, impropriety of language, ungracefulness of pronunciation; to which one might add a thousand nameless defects, either in conversation or behaviour. These are the infirmities which are found in the best of men, in a larger or smaller proportion. And from these none can hope to be perfectly freed, till the spirit returns to God that gave it.

Nor can we expect, till then, to be wholly free from temptation. Such perfection belongeth not to this life. It is true, there are those who, being given up to work all uncleanness with greediness, scarce perceive the temptations which they resist not; and so seem to be without temptation. There are also many whom the wise enemy of souls seeing to be fast asleep in the dead form of godliness, will not tempt to gross sin, lest they should awake before they drop into everlasting burnings. I know there are also children of God who, being now justified freely, having found redemption in the blood of Christ, for the present feel no temptation. God hath said to their enemies, "Touch not Mine anointed, and do My children no harm." And for this season, it may be for weeks or months, He causeth them to ride on high places, He beareth them as on eagles' wings, above all the fiery darts of the wicked one. But this state will not last always; as we may learn from that single consideration, that the Son of God Himself, in the days of His flesh, was tempted even to the end of His life. Therefore, so let his servant expect to be; for "it is enough that he be as his Master."

Christian perfection, therefore, does not imply (as some men seem to have imagined) an exemption either from ignorance, or mistake, or infirmities, or temptations. Indeed, it is only another term for holiness. They are two names for the same thing. Thus, every one that is holy is, in the Scripture sense, perfect. Yet we may, lastly, observe, that neither in this respect is there any absolute perfection on earth. There is no *perfection of degrees*, as it is termed; none which does not admit of a continual increase. So that how much soever any man has attained, or in how high a degree soever he is perfect, he hath still need to "grow in grace," and daily to advance in the knowledge and love of God his Saviour. . . .

In conformity, therefore, both to the doctrine of St. John, and to the whole tenor of the New Testament, we fix this conclusion,—*a Christian is so far perfect, as not to commit sin.*

This is the glorious privilege of every Christian; yea, though he be but *a babe in Christ.* But it is only of those who *are strong* in the Lord, "and have overcome the wicked one," or rather of those who "have known Him that is from the beginning," that it can be affirmed they are in such a sense perfect, as, secondly, to be freed from evil thoughts and evil tempers. First, from evil or sinful thoughts. But here let it be observed, that thoughts concerning evil are not always evil thoughts; that a thought concerning sin, and a sinful thought, are widely different. A man, for instance, may think of a murder which another has committed; and yet this is no evil or sinful thought. So our blessed Lord Himself doubtless thought of, or understood, the thing spoken by the devil, when he said, "All these things will I give Thee, if Thou wilt fall down and worship me." Yet had He no evil or sinful thought; nor indeed was capable of having any. And even hence it follows, that neither have real Christians; for "every one that is perfect is as his Master" (Luke vi, 40). Therefore, if He was free from evil or sinful thoughts, so are they likewise. . . .

And as Christians indeed are freed from evil thoughts, so are they, secondly, from evil tempers. This is evident from the above-mentioned declaration of our Lord Himself: "The disciple is not above his Master: but every one that is perfect shall be as his Master." He had been delivering, just before, some of the sublimest doctrines of Christianity, and some of the most grievous to flesh and blood. "I say unto you,

Love your enemies, do good to them which hate you; . . . and unto him that smiteth thee on the one cheek, offer also the other." Now these He well knew the world would not receive; and therefore immediately adds, "Can the blind lead the blind? will they not both fall into the ditch?" As if He had said, "Do not confer with flesh and blood, touching these things—with men void of spiritual discernment, the eyes of whose understanding God hath not opened—lest they and you perish together." In the next verse He removes the two grand objections with which these wise fools meet us at every turn. "These things are too grievous to be borne"; or, "They are too high to be attained,"—saying, " 'The disciple is not above his Master'; therefore, if I have suffered, be content to tread in My steps. And doubt ye not then, but I will fulfil My word: 'For every one that is perfect shall be as his Master.' " But his Master was free from all sinful tempers. So, therefore, is His disciple, even every real Christian.

Sermons: "Christian Perfection," I, 1, 4, 7-9, 20-21, 24 (S, II, 152-56, 168-71).

[Satan] is sensible, how few are able to distinguish (and too many are not willing so to do) between the accidental abuse, and the natural tendency, of a doctrine. These, therefore, will he continually blend together, with regard to the doctrine of Christian perfection; in order to prejudice the minds of unwary men against the glorious promises of God. And how frequently, how generally, I had almost said how universally, has he prevailed herein! For who is there that observes any of these accidental ill effects of this doctrine, and does not immediately conclude, this is its natural tendency; and does not readily cry out, "See, these are the fruits (meaning the natural, necessary fruit) of such doctrine?" Not so: they are fruits which may accidentally spring from the abuse of a great and precious truth: but the abuse of this, or any other scriptural doctrine, does by no means destroy its use. Neither can the unfaithfulness of man, perverting his right way, make the promise of God of no effect. No: let God be true, and every man a liar.

The word of the Lord, it shall stand. "Faithful is He that hath promised: He also will do it."

Sermons: "Satan's Devices," I, 14 (S, II, 199-200).

4. Kingdom of God

The kingdom of heaven, and the kingdom of God, are but two phrases for the same thing. They mean, not barely a future happy state in heaven, but a state to be enjoyed on earth: the proper disposition for the glory of heaven, rather than the possession of it. *Is at hand* —As if he had said, God is about to erect that kingdom, spoken of by Daniel (ch. ii. 44. and vii, 13, 14.) the kingdom of the God of heaven. It properly signifies here, the gospel dispensation, in which subjects were to be gathered to God by his Son, and a society to be formed, which was to subsist first on earth, and afterward with God in glory. In some places of Scripture, the phrase more particularly denotes the state of it on earth: in others, it signifies only the state of glory: but it generally includes both. The Jews understood it of a temporal kingdom, the seat of which they supposed would be Jerusalem; and the expected sovereign of this kingdom they learned from Daniel to call the Son of Man.

Notes: "Matthew 3:2."

JW

The most prevailing fault among the Methodists is to be *too outward* in religion. We are continually forgetting that the kingdom of God is *within us,* and that our fundamental principle is, We are saved *by faith,* producing all *inward* holiness, not by works, by any externals whatever.

Letters: "To John Valton" (V, 289).

Holiness and happiness, joined in one, are sometimes styled, in the inspired writings, "the kingdom of God" (as by our Lord in the text), and sometimes, "the kingdom of heaven." It is termed, "the kingdom of God," because it is the immediate fruit of God's reigning in the soul. So soon as ever He takes unto Himself His mighty power, and sets up His throne in our hearts, they are instantly filled with this "righteousness, and peace, and joy in the Holy Ghost." It is called "the kingdom of heaven," because it is (in a degree) heaven opened in the soul. For whosoever they are that experience this, they can aver before angels and men,

> Everlasting life is won,
> Glory is on earth begun;

according to the constant tenor of Scripture, which everywhere bears record, God "hath given unto us eternal life, and this life is in His Son. He that hath the Son" (reigning in his heart) "hath life," even life everlasting (I John v. 11, 12). For "this is life eternal, to know Thee the only true God, and Jesus Christ, whom Thou hast sent." (John xvii. 3). And they to whom this is given may confidently address God, though they were in the midst of a fiery furnace,—

> Thee, Lord, safe-shielded by Thy power,
> Thee, Son of God, JEHOVAH, we adore;
> In form of man descending to appear:
> To Thee be ceaseless hallelujahs given,
> Praise, as in heaven Thy throne, we offer here;
> For where Thy presence is display'd, is heaven.

And this "kingdom of God," or of heaven, "is at hand." As these words were originally spoken, they implied that "the time" was then fulfilled, God being "made manifest in the flesh," when He would set up His kingdom among men, and reign in the hearts of His people. And is not the time now fulfilled? For, "Lo," (saith He), "I am with you always," you who preach remission of sins in My name, "even unto the end of the world" (Matt. xxviii. 20.) Wheresoever, therefore, the gospel of Christ is preached, this His "kingdom is nigh at hand." It is not far from every one of you. Ye may this hour enter thereinto, if so be ye hearken to His voice, "Repent ye, and believe the gospel."

Sermons: "The Way to the Kingdom," I, 12-13 (S, I, 154-55).

For the kingdom of God—That is, true religion, does not consist in external observances; but in righteousness, the image of God stamped on the heart, the love of God and man, accompanied with the peace that passeth all understanding, and joy in the Holy Ghost.

Notes: "Romans 14:17."

In order that the name of God may be hallowed, we pray that His kingdom, the kingdom of Christ, may come. This kingdom then comes to a particular person, when he "repents and believes the gospel"; when he is taught of God, not only to know himself, but to know Jesus Christ and Him crucified. As "this is life eternal, to know the only true God, and Jesus Christ whom He hath sent"; so it is the kingdom of God begun below, set up in the believer's heart; "the Lord God Omnipotent" then "reigneth," when He is known through Christ Jesus. He taketh unto Himself His mighty power, that He may subdue all things unto Himself. He goeth on in the soul conquering and to conquer, till He hath put all things under His feet, till "every thought is brought into captivity to the obedience of Christ."

When therefore God shall "give His Son the heathen for His inheritance, and the uttermost parts of the earth for His possession"; when "all kingdoms shall bow before Him, and all nations shall do Him service"; when "the mountain of the Lord's house," the church of Christ, "shall be established in the top of the mountains"; when "the fullness of the Gentiles shall come in, and all Israel shall be saved"; then shall it be seen, that "the Lord is King, and hath put on glorious apparel," appearing to every soul of man as King of kings and Lord of lords. And it is meet for all those who love His appearing, to pray that He would hasten the time; that this His kingdom, the kingdom of grace, may come quickly, and swallow up all the kingdoms of the earth; that all mankind, receiving Him for their King, truly believing in His name, may be filled with righteousness, and peace, and joy, with holiness and happiness; till they are removed hence into His heavenly kingdom, there to reign with Him for ever and ever.

For this also we pray in those words, "Thy kingdom come": we pray for the coming of His everlasting kingdom, the kingdom of glory in heaven, which is the continuation and perfection of the kingdom of grace on earth. Consequently this, as well as the preceding petition, is offered up for the whole intelligent creation, who are all interested in this grand event, the final renovation of all things, by God's putting an end to misery and sin, to infirmity and death, taking all things into His own hands, and setting up the kingdom which endureth throughout all ages.

Sermons: "Upon Our Lord's Sermon on the Mount: VI," III, 8 (S, I, 136-37).

Jesus, God of peace and love,
Send Thy blessing from above,
Take, and seal us for Thine own,
Touch our hearts, and make them one.

By the sense of sin forgiven
Purge out all the former leaven,
Malice, guile, and proud offence;
Take the stone of stumbling hence.

Root up every bitter root,
Multiply the Spirit's fruit,
Love, and joy, and quiet peace,
Meek, long-suffering gentleness;

Strict and general temperance,
Boundless, pure benevolence,
Cordial firm fidelity;
All the mind which was in Thee.

Poetics: "For the Fruits of the Spirit," Hymn XXV (IV, 194-95).

SUPPLEMENTARY REFERENCES

THE LAW—*Sermons:* "Upon Our Lord's Sermon on the Mount: V" (S, I, 398 ff.); "The Original, Nature, Property, and Use of the Law" (S, II, 38 ff.); "The Law Established Through Faith: I" (S, II, 58 ff.); "The Law Established Through Faith: II" (S, II, 72-83). *Works:* "A Second Dialogue Between an Antinomian and His Friend" (X, 276 ff.); "A Blow at the Root; or, Christ Stabbed in the House of His Friends," 1-11 (X, 364-69). *Letters:* "To Joseph Benson" (V, 211-12). *Journal:* "Mon. 23 June 1740" (II, 355-56); "Sun. 23 March 1746" (III, 237). *Notes:* "Matthew 5:17-18"; "Galatians 3:19."

CHRISTIAN LOVE—*Sermons:* "Upon Our Lord's Sermon on the Mount: II," III (S, I, 345-55); "Upon Our Lord's Sermon on the Mount: IV" (S, I, 379-97); "Upon Our Lord's Sermon on the Mount: IX" (S, I, 495-513); "Catholic Spirit" (S, II, 129 ff.); "On Charity" (J, VII, 45 ff.); "The Important Question," III (J, VI, 498); "An Israelite Indeed" (J, VII, 37 ff.). *Works:* "An Earnest Appeal to Men of Reason and Religion," 2-3 (VIII, 3). *Letters:* "To Dr. Conyers Middleton" (II, 375 ff.); "To Philothea Briggs" (V, 317-18); "To Penelope Newman" (V, 341-42); "To Dr. Rutherforth" (V, 363 ff.). *Journal:* "Wed. 24 April 1776" (VI, 102); "Thur. 4 July 1776" (VI, 114). *Notes:* "Luke 6:32"; "I Corinthians 13."

CHRISTIAN PERFECTION—*Sermons:* "The First-Fruits of the Spirit" (S, I, 162 ff.); "Upon Our Lord's Sermon on the Mount: VIII," Introduction, 1-4 (S, I, 473-76); "Christian Perfection" (S, II, 150 ff.); "On Perfection" (J, VI, 411 ff.); "On the Wedding Garment" (J, VII, 311 ff.). *Works:* "The Principles of a Methodist," 11-13 (VIII, 363-65); "A Plain Account of Christian Perfection" (XI, 366 ff.); "Brief Thoughts on Christian Perfection" (XI, 446). *Letters:* "To Elizabeth Hardy" (IV, 10-13); "To John Fletcher" (V, 3-4); "To his Brother Charles" (V, 38-39); "To Joseph Benson" (V, 203-4; 214-15). *Journal:* "Mon. 1 Nov. 1762" (IV, 535-38); "Tues. 15 Nov. 1763" (V, 40-41); "Tues. 27 June 1769" (V, 323-25). *Notes:* "Matthew 5:8"; "Philippians 3:12."

KINGDOM OF GOD—*Sermons:* "The Way to the Kingdom" (S, I, 148 ff.); "Upon Our Lord's Sermon on the Mount: I," I, 11-12 (S, I, 327-28); "Upon Our Lord's Sermon on the Mount: IX" Introduction 20-23 (S, I, 506-9); "The Signs of the Times," II (J, VI, 306-13). *Journal:* "Sun. 29 Oct. 1738" (II, 97); "Sat. 24 Nov. 1739" (II, 321 ff.). *Notes:* "Luke 11:52."

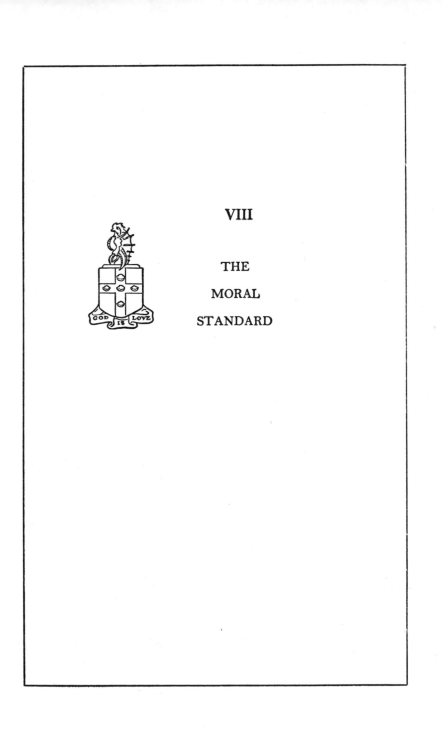

VIII

THE

MORAL

STANDARD

VIII. THE MORAL STANDARD

FOR THE regulation of the life of his societies Wesley frequently indicates various duties and traits of character for which the Christian is amenable. In doing so he often falls into detailed casuistry in his many letters, essays, and journal entries in which he is concerned with precise ethical prescriptions. Some of this today seems far removed from the vital theology which made the Revival live, though most of it is concerned with specific problems his people faced. Wesley's practical ethic is primarily individual; his social ethic is an extension of that applied to the individual. This, however, in no way restricted his active criticism, in the name of Christian love, of the many social evils that prevailed in eighteenth-century England. God's prior redeeming love, which places every Christian under obligation, led to the intense ethical interest of the Wesleyan movement and has had widespread social consequences not only in Wesley's day but throughout the history of Methodism.

1. Christian Character

It is impossible for any that have it, to conceal the religion of Jesus Christ. This our Lord makes plain beyond all contradiction, by a two-fold comparison: "Ye are the light of the world: a city set upon a hill cannot be hid." Ye Christians are "the light of the world," with regard both to your tempers and actions. Your holiness makes you as conspicuous as the sun in the midst of heaven. As ye cannot go out of the world, so neither can ye stay in it without appearing to all mankind. Ye may not flee from men; and while ye are among them, it is impossible to hide your lowliness and meekness, and those other dispositions whereby ye aspire to be perfect as your Father which is in heaven

223

is perfect. Love cannot be hid any more than light; and least of all, when it shines forth in action, when ye exercise yourselves in the labour of love, in beneficence of every kind. As well may men think to hide a city, as to hide a Christian; yea, as well may they conceal a city set upon a hill, as a holy, zealous, active lover of God and man. . . .

So impossible it is, to keep our religion from being seen, unless we cast it away; so vain is the thought of hiding the light, unless by putting it out! Sure it is, that a secret, unobserved religion cannot be the religion of Jesus Christ. Whatever religion can be concealed, is not Christianity. If a Christian could be hid, he could not be compared to a city set upon a hill; to the light of the world, the sun shining from heaven, and seen by all the world below. Never, therefore, let it enter into the heart of him whom God hath renewed in the spirit of his mind, to hide that light, to keep his religion to himself; especially considering it is not only impossible to conceal true Christianity, but likewise absolutely contrary to the design of the great Author of it.

Sermons: "Upon Our Lord's Sermon on the Mount: IV," II, 2, 4 (S, I, 388-89).

JW

Are there not many present here who . . . believe that a good moral man, and a good Christian, mean the same thing? that a man need not trouble himself any further, if he only practices as much Christianity as was written over the Heathen Emperor's gate,—"Do as thou wouldest be done unto"; especially if he be not an infidel, or an heretic, but believes all that the Bible and the Church say is true?

I would not be understood, as if I despised these things, as if I undervalued right opinions, true morality, or a zealous regard for the constitution we have received from our fathers. Yet what are these things, being alone? What will they profit us in that day? What will it avail to tell the Judge of all, "Lord, I was not as other men were; not unjust, not an adulterer, not a liar, not an immoral man?" Yea, what will it avail, if we have done all good, as well as done no harm,—if we have given all our goods to feed the poor,—and have not charity? How shall we then look on those who taught us to sleep on and take our rest, though "the love of the Father was not in us?" or who, teaching us to seek salvation by works, cut us off from receiving that faith freely, whereby alone the love of God could have been shed abroad in our hearts?

Sermons: "True Christianity Defended," I, 9-10 (J, VII, 456-57).

JW

Hence we learn, that the first and great end of God's permitting the temptations which bring heaviness on His children, is the trial of their faith, which is tried by these, even as gold by the fire. Now we know, gold tried in the fire is purified thereby; is separated from its dross. And so is faith in the fire of temptation; the more it is tried, the more it is purified; yea, and not only purified, but also strengthened, confirmed, increased abundantly, by so many more proofs of the wisdom and power, the love and faithfulness of God. This, then—to increase our faith—is one gracious end of God's permitting those manifold temptations.

They serve to try, to purify, to confirm, and increase that living hope also, whereunto "the God and Father of our Lord Jesus Christ hath begotten us again of His abundant mercy." Indeed our hope cannot but increase in the same proportion with our faith. On this foundation it stands: believing in His name, living by faith in the Son of God, we hope for, we have a confident expectation of, the glory which shall be revealed; and, consequently, whatever strengthens our faith, increases our hope also. At the same time it increases our joy in the Lord, which cannot but attend an hope full of immortality. In this view the Apostle exhorts believers in the other chapter: "Rejoice that ye are partakers of the sufferings of Christ." On this very account, "happy are you; for the Spirit of glory and of God resteth upon you": and hereby ye are enabled, even in the midst of sufferings, to "rejoice with joy unspeakable and full of glory."

They rejoice the more, because the trials which increase their faith and hope increase their love also; both their gratitude to God for all His mercies, and their good-will to all mankind. Accordingly, the more deeply sensible they are of the loving-kindness of God their Saviour, the more is their heart inflamed with love to Him who "first loved us." The clearer and stronger evidence they have of the glory that shall be revealed, the more do they love Him who hath purchased it for them, and "given them the earnest" thereof "in their hearts." And this, the increase of their love, is another end of the temptations permitted to come upon them.

Yet another is their advance in holiness; holiness of heart, and holiness of conversation,—the latter naturally resulting from the former; for a good tree will bring forth good fruit. And all inward holiness is the immediate fruit of the faith that worketh by love. By this the blessed Spirit purifies the heart from pride, self-will, passion; from love of the world, from foolish and hurtful desires, from vile and vain affections. Beside that, sanctified afflictions have, through the grace of God, an immediate and direct tendency to holiness. Through the operation of His Spirit, they humble, more and more, and abase the soul before God. They calm and meeken our turbulent spirit, tame the fierceness of our nature, soften our obstinacy and self-will, crucify us to the world, and bring us to expect all our strength from, and to seek all our happiness in, God.

And all these terminate in that great end, that our faith, hope, love, and holiness "may be found," if it doth not yet appear, "unto praise" from God Himself, "and honour" from men and angels, "and glory," assigned by the great Judge to all that have endured unto the end.

Sermons: "Heaviness Through Manifold Temptations," IV, 2-6 (S, II, 275-76).

JW

[Christian meekness] keeps clear of every extreme, whether in excess or defect. It does not destroy but balance the affections, which the God of nature never designed should be rooted out by grace, but only brought and kept under due regulations. It poises the mind aright. It holds an even scale, with regard to anger, and sorrow, and fear; preserving the mean in every circumstance of life, and not declining either to the right hand or the left.

Meekness, therefore, seems properly to relate to ourselves: but it may be referred either to God or our neighbour. When this due composure of mind has reference to God, it is usually termed "resignation"; a calm acquiescence in whatsoever is His will concerning us, even though it may not be pleasing to nature; saying continually, "It is the Lord; let Him do what seemeth Him good." When we consider it more strictly with regard to ourselves, we style it "patience" or "contentedness." When it is exerted toward other men, then it is "mildness" to the good, and "gentleness" to the evil.

Sermons: "Upon Our Lord's Sermon on the Mount: II," I, 3-4 (S, I, 336-37).

Christian joy is joy in obedience; joy in loving God, and keeping His commandments: and yet not in keeping them as if we were thereby to fulfill the terms of the covenant of works; as if by any works or righteousness of ours we were to procure pardon and acceptance with God. Not so: we are already pardoned and accepted through the mercy of God in Christ Jesus. Not as if we were by our own obedience to procure life, life from the death of sin: this also we have already through the grace of God. Us "hath He quickened, who were dead in sins"; and now we are "alive to God, through Jesus Christ our Lord." But we rejoice in walking according to the covenant of grace, in holy love and happy obedience. We rejoice in knowing that, "being justified through His grace," we have "not received that grace of God in vain"; that God having freely (not for the sake of our willing or running, but through the blood of the Lamb) reconciled us to Himself, we run, in the strength which He hath given us, the way of His commandments. He hath "girded us with strength unto the war," and we gladly "fight the good fight of faith." We rejoice, through Him who liveth in our hearts by faith, to "lay hold of eternal life."

Sermons: "The Witness of Our Own Spirit," 20 (S, I, 236).

From Matt. xviii, 3 I endeavoured to show those who use the word without understanding it what Christian simplicity properly is, and what it is not. It is not ignorance or folly; it is not enthusiasm or credulity. It is faith, humility, willingness to be taught, and freedom from evil reasonings.

Journal: "Sun. 19 Dec. 1762" (IV, 541).

The truth is, neither this opinion nor that, but the love of God, humbles man, and that only. Let but this be shed abroad in his heart, and he abhors himself in dust and ashes. As soon as this enters into his soul, lowly shame covers his face. That thought, "What is God? What hath he done for me?" is immediately followed by, "What am I?" And he knoweth not what to do, or where to hide, or how to abase himself enough, before the great God of love, of whom he now knoweth, that as his majesty is, so is his mercy. Let him who has felt this (whatever be his opinion) say, whether he could then take glory to himself; whether he could ascribe to himself any part of his salvation, or the glory of any good word or thought. Lean, then, who will, on that broken reed for humility; but let the love of God humble my soul!

Works: "Predestination Calmly Considered," 84 (X, 256).

2. Christian Duties

We may clearly perceive the wide difference there is between Christianity and morality. Indeed nothing can be more sure, than that true Christianity cannot exist without both the inward experience and outward practice of justice, mercy and truth; and this alone is genuine morality. But it is equally certain, that all morality, all the justice, mercy, and truth which can possibly exist without Christianity, profiteth nothing at all; is of no value, in the sight of God, to those that are under the Christian dispensation. Let it be observed, I purposely add, to those that are under the Christian dispensation; because I have no authority from the word of God "to judge those that are without"; nor do I conceive that any man living has a right to sentence all the heathen and Mahometan world to damnation. It is far better to leave them to Him that made them, and who is "the Father of the spirits of all flesh"; who is the God of the Heathens as well as the Christians, and who hateth nothing that he hath made. But, meantime, this is nothing to those that name the name of Christ;—all those, being under the law, the Christian law, shall undoubtedly be judged thereby; and, of consequence, unless those be so changed . . . , unless they have new senses, ideas, passions, tempers, they are no Christians. However just, true, or merciful they may be, they are but Atheists still!

Perhaps there may be some well-meaning persons who carry this farther still; who aver, whatever change is wrought in men, whether in their hearts or lives, yet if they have not clear views of those capital doctrines, the fall of man, justification by faith, and of the atonement made by the death of Christ, and of his righteousness transferred to them, they can have no benefit from his death. I dare in nowise affirm this. Indeed I do not believe it. I believe the merciful God regards the lives and tempers of men more than their ideas. I believe he respects the goodness of the heart, rather than the clearness of the head; and that if the heart of a man be filled (by the grace of God, and the power of his Spirit) with the humble, gentle, patient love of God and man, God will not cast him into everlasting fire, prepared for the devil and his angels, because his ideas are not clear, or because his conceptions are confused. "Without holiness," I own, "no man shall see the Lord"; but I dare not add, "or clear ideas."

Sermons: "On Living Without God," 14-15 (J, VII, 353-54).

JW

[The Means of Grace] are either Instituted or Prudential:—
I. The INSTITUTED are,
(1) Prayer; private, family, public; consisting of deprecation, petition, intercession, and thanksgiving. Do you use each of these? Do you

use private prayer every morning and evening? If you can, at five in the evening; and the hour before or after morning preaching? Do you forecast daily, wherever you are, how to secure these hours? Do you avow it everywhere? Do you ask everywhere, "Have you family prayer?" Do you retire at five o'clock?

(2) Searching the Scriptures by,

(i) Reading: Constantly, some part of every day; regularly, all the Bible in order; carefully, with the Notes; seriously, with prayer before and after; fruitfully, immediately practising what you learn there?

(ii) Meditating: At set times? by any rule?

(iii) Hearing: Every morning? carefully; with prayer before, at, after; immediately putting in practice? Have you a New Testament always about you?

(3) The Lord's supper: Do you use this at every opportunity? with solemn prayer before; with earnest and deliberate self-devotion?

(4) Fasting: How do you fast every Friday?

(5) Christian conference: Are you convinced how important and how difficult it is to "order your conversation right?" Is it "always in grace? seasoned with salt? meet to minister grace to the hearers? Do not you converse too long at a time? Is not an hour commonly enough? Would it not be well always to have a determinate end in view; and to pray before and after it?

II. PRUDENTIAL MEANS we may use either as common Christians, as Methodists, as Preachers, or as Assistants.

(1) As common Christians. What particular rules have you in order to grow in grace? What arts of holy living?

(2) As Methodists. Do you never miss your class, or Band?

(3) As Preachers. Do you meet every society; also the Leaders and Bands, if any?

(4) As Assistants. Have you thoroughly considered your office; and do you make a conscience of executing every part of it?

These means may be used without fruit: But there are some means which cannot; namely, watching, denying ourselves, taking up our cross, exercise of the presence of God.

Works: "Minutes of Several Conversations" (VIII, 322).

To the public, constantly add the private means of grace, particularly prayer and reading. Most of you have been greatly wanting in this; and without this you can never grow in grace. You may as well expect a child to grow without food as a soul without private prayer; and reading is an excellent help to this.

Letters: "To the Societies at Bristol" (IV, 272).

JW

First, all who desire the grace of God are to wait for it in the way of prayer. This is the express direction of our Lord Himself. In His Sermon upon the Mount, after explaining at large wherein religion consists, and describing the main branches of it, He adds, "Ask, and it shall be given you; seek, and ye shall find; knock, and it shall be opened unto you: for every one that asketh receiveth; and he that seeketh findeth; and to him that knocketh it shall be opened" (Matt. vii, 7, 8). Here we are in the plainest manner directed to ask, in order to, or as a means of, receiving; to seek, in order to find, the grace of God, the pearl of great price; and to knock, to continue asking and seeking, if we would enter into His kingdom.

That no doubt might remain, our Lord labours this point in a more peculiar manner. He appeals to every man's own heart: "What man is there of you, who, if his son ask bread, will he give him a stone? or, if he ask a fish, will he give him a serpent? If ye then, being evil, know how to give good gifts unto your children, how much more shall your Father which is in heaven," the Father of angels and men, the Father of the spirits of all flesh, "give good things to them that ask Him"? (verses 9-11). Or, as He expresses Himself on another occasion, including all good things in one, "How much more shall your heavenly Father give the Holy Spirit to them that ask Him?" (Luke xi. 13). It should be particularly observed here, that the persons directed to ask had not then received the Holy Spirit: nevertheless our Lord directs them to use this means, and promises that it should be effectual; that upon asking they should receive the Holy Spirit, from Him whose mercy is over all His works. . . .

Secondly. All who desire the grace of God are to wait for it in searching the Scriptures.

Our Lord's direction, with regard to the use of this means, is likewise plain and clear. "Search the Scriptures," saith He to the unbelieving Jews, "for they testify of Me" (John v. 39). And for this very end did He direct them to search the Scriptures, that they might believe in Him.

The objection, that "this is not a command, but only an assertion, that they did search the Scriptures," is shamelessly false. I desire those who urge it, to let us know how a command can be more clearly expressed, than in those terms, Ἐρευνᾶτε τὰς γραφάς. It is as peremptory as so many words can make it. . . .

Thirdly. All who desire an increase of the grace of God are to wait for it in partaking of the Lord's supper; for this also is a direction Himself hath given: "The same night in which He was betrayed He took bread, and brake it, and said, Take, eat: this is My Body"; that is, the sacred sign of My body: "this do in remembrance of Me." Likewise "He took the cup, saying, This cup is the new testament," or covenant, "in My blood"; the sacred sign of that covenant: "this do ye in remembrance of Me. For as often as ye eat this bread, and drink this cup, ye do show forth the Lord's death till He come" (I Cor. xi. 23, &c.): ye openly exhibit the same, by these visible signs, before God, and angels, and men; ye manifest your solemn remembrance of His death, till He cometh in the clouds of heaven.

Sermons: "The Means of Grace," III, 1-2, 7, 11 (S, I, 245-46, 248-49, 251-52).

JW

The cure of spiritual, as of bodily, diseases must be as various as are the causes of them. The first thing, therefore, is, to find out the cause; and this will naturally point out the cure.

For instance: is it sin which occasions darkness? What sin? Is it outward sin of any kind? Does your conscience accuse you of committing any sin, whereby you grieve the Holy Spirit of God? Is it on this account that He is departed from you, and that joy and peace are departed with Him? And how can you expect they should return, till you put away the accursed thing? "Let the wicked forsake his way"; "cleanse your hands, ye sinners"; "put away the evil of your doings"; so shall your "light break out of obscurity"; the Lord will return and "abundantly pardon."

If, upon the closest search, you can find no sin of commission which causes the cloud upon your soul, inquire next, if there be not some sin of omission which separates between God and you. . . . Till the sin, whether of omission or commission, be removed, all comfort is false and deceitful. It is only skinning the wound over, which still festers and rankles beneath. Look for no peace within, till you are at peace with God; which cannot be without "fruits meet for repentance."

Sermons: "The Wilderness State," III, 1-3 (S, II, 256-57).

JW

But what is self-denial? Wherein are we to deny ourselves? And whence does the necessity of this arise? I answer, the will of God is the supreme, unalterable rule for every intelligent creature; equally binding every angel in heaven, and every man upon earth. Nor can it be otherwise: this is the natural, necessary result of the relation between creatures and their Creator. But if the will of God be our one rule of action in everything, great and small, it follows, by undeniable consequence, that we are not to do our own will in anything. Here, therefore, we see at once the nature, with the ground and reason, of self-denial. We see the nature of self-denial: it is the denying or refusing to follow our own will, from a conviction that the will of God is the only rule of action to us. And we see the reason thereof, because we are creatures; because "it is He that hath made us, and not we ourselves."

Sermons: "Self-Denial," I, 2 (S, II, 285-86).

JW

There is no employment of our time, no action or conversation, that is purely indifferent. All is good or bad, because all our time, as every thing we have, is not our own. All these are, as our Lord speaks, τὰ ἀλλότρια—*the property of another;* of God our Creator. Now, these either are or are not employed according to His will. If they are so employed, all is good; if they are not, all is evil. Again: it is His will, that we should continually grow in grace, and in the living knowledge of our Lord Jesus Christ. Consequently, every thought, word, and work, whereby this knowledge is increased, whereby we grow in grace, is good; and every one whereby this knowledge is not increased, is truly and properly evil.

Sermons: "The Good Steward," IV, 2 (S, II, 478-79).

JW

"Take heed," saith He, "that ye do not your alms before men, to be seen of them: otherwise ye have no reward of your Father which is in heaven." "That ye do not your alms": although this only is named, yet is every work of charity included, everything which we give, or speak, or do, whereby our neighbour may be profited; whereby another man may receive any advantage, either in his body or soul. The feeding the hungry, the clothing the naked, the entertaining or assisting the stranger, the visiting those that are sick or in prison, the comforting the afflicted, the instructing the ignorant, the reproving the wicked, the exhorting and encouraging the well-doer; and if there be any other work of mercy, it is equally included in this direction.

Sermons: "Upon Our Lord's Sermon on the Mount: VI," I 1 (S, I, 426).

JW

Let us take care to afflict our souls as well as our bodies. Let every season, either of public or private fasting, be a season of exercising all those holy affections which are implied in a broken and contrite heart. Let it be a season of devout mourning, of godly sorrow for sin; such a sorrow as that of the Corinthians, concerning which the Apostle saith, "I rejoice, not that ye were made sorry, but that ye sorrowed to repentance. For ye were made sorry after a godly manner, that ye might receive damage by us in nothing. For godly sorrow," ἡ κατὰ Θεὸν λύπη—the sorrow which is according to God, which is a precious gift of His Spirit, lifting the soul to God from whom it flows—"worketh repentance to salvation, not to be repented of."

Sermons: "Upon Our Lord's Sermon on the Mount: VII," IV, 5 (S, I, 468).

JW

"Therefore take no thought for the morrow." Not only, take ye no thought how to lay up treasures on earth, how to increase in worldly substance; take no thought how to procure more food than you can eat, or more raiment than you can put on, or more money than is required from day to day, for the plain, reasonable purposes of life;—but take no uneasy thought, even concerning those things which are absolutely needful for the body. Do not trouble yourself now, with thinking what you shall do at a season which is yet afar off. Perhaps that season will never come; or it will be no concern of yours; before then you will have passed through all the waves, and be landed in eternity. All those distant views do not belong to you, who are but a creature of a day. Nay, what have you to do with the morrow, more strictly speaking? Why should you perplex yourself without need? God provides for you to-day what is needful to sustain the life which He hath given you. It is enough: give yourself up into His hands. If you live another day, He will provide for that also.

Sermons: "Upon Our Lord's Sermon on the Mount: IX," 24 (S, I, 509).

JW

If [a Christian] sees anything which he approves not, it goes not out of his lips, unless to the person concerned, if haply he may gain his brother. So far is he from making the faults or failings of others the matter of his conversation, that of the absent he never does speak at all, unless he can speak well. . . .

He makes one only exception. Sometimes he is convinced that it is for the glory of God, or (which come to the same) the good of his neighbour, that an evil should not be covered. In this case, for the benefit of the innocent, he is constrained to declare the guilty. But even here, (1) He will not speak at all, till love, superior love, constrains him. (2) He cannot do it from a general confused view of doing good, or promoting the glory of God, but from a clear sight of some particular end, some determinate good, which he pursues. (3) Still he cannot speak, unless he be fully convinced that this very means is necessary to that end; that the end cannot be answered, at least not so effectually, by any other way. (4) He then doeth it with the utmost sorrow and reluctance; using it as the last and worst medicine, a desperate remedy in a desperate case, a kind of poison never to be used but to expel poison. Consequently, (5) He uses it as sparingly as possible. And this he does with fear and trembling, lest he should transgress the law of love by speaking too much, more than he would have done by not speaking at all.

Sermons: "Upon Our Lord's Sermon on the Mount: II," III, 14 (S, I, 352).

JW

It is certain, so long as we know but *in part,* that all men will not see all things alike. It is an unavoidable consequence of the present weakness and shortness of human understanding, that several men will be of several minds in religion as well as in common life. So it has been from the beginning of the world, and so it will be "till the restitution of all things."

Nay, farther: although every man necessarily believes that every particular opinion which he holds is true (for to believe any opinion is not true, is the same thing as not to hold it); yet can no man be assured that all his own opinions, taken together, are true. Nay, every thinking man is assured they are not; seeing *humanum est errare et nescire:* "to be ignorant of many things, and to mistake in some, is the necessary condition of humanity." This, therefore, he is sensible, is his own case. He knows, in the general, that he himself is mistaken;

236

although in what particulars he mistakes, he does not, perhaps he cannot, know.

I say, "perhaps he cannot know"; for who can tell how far invincible ignorance may extend? or (that comes to the same thing) invincible prejudice?—which is often so fixed in tender minds, that it is afterwards impossible to tear up what has taken so deep a root. And who can say, unless he knew every circumstance attending it, how far any mistake is culpable? seeing all guilt must suppose some concurrence of the will; of which He only can judge who searcheth the heart.

Every wise man, therefore, will allow others the same liberty of thinking which he desires they should allow him; and will no more insist on their embracing his opinions, than he would have them to insist on his embracing theirs. He bears with those who differ from him, and only asks him with whom he desires to unite in love that single question, "Is thy heart right, as my heart is with thy heart?"

Sermons: "Catholic Spirit," I, 3-6 (S, II, 131-33).

3. The Family

I strongly inculcated family religion, the grand desideratum among the Methodists. Many were ashamed before God, and at length adopted Joshua's resolution, "As for me and my house, we will serve the Lord."

Journal: "Sun. 16 Dec. 1766" (V, 193).

Let no man deceive you with vain words; riches and happiness seldom dwell together. Therefore, if you are wise, you will not seek riches for your children by their marriage. See that your eye be single in this also: Aim simply at the glory of God, and the real happiness of your children, both in time and eternity.

Sermons: "On Family Religion," III, 17 (J, VII, 85).

Have you both the consent of your parents? Without this there is seldom a blessing. Secondly, Is he able to keep you? I mean in such a manner as you have lived hitherto. Otherwise, remember! When poverty comes in at the door, love flies out at the window.

Letters: "To Jane Hilton" (V, 109).

JW

Nor may marriage itself, holy and honourable as it is, be used as a pretence for giving a loose to our desires. Indeed, "it hath been said, Whosoever will put away his wife, let him give her a writing of divorcement": and then all was well; though he alleged no cause, but that he did not like her, or liked another better. "But I say unto you, That whosoever shall put away his wife, save for the cause of fornication" (that is, adultery; the word πορνεία signifying unchastity in general, either in the married or unmarried state), "causeth her to commit adultery," if she marry again: "and whosoever shall marry her that is put away committeth adultery" (verses 31, 32).

All polygamy is clearly forbidden in these words, wherein our Lord expressly declares, that for any woman who has a husband alive, to marry again is adultery. By parity of reason, it is adultery for any man to marry again, so long as he has a wife alive, yea, although they were divorced; unless that divorce had been for the cause of adultery: in that only case there is no scripture which forbids [the innocent person] to marry again.

Sermons: "Upon Our Lord's Sermon on the Mount: III," I, 5 (S, I, 359-60).

JW

The person in your house that claims your first and nearest attention, is, undoubtedly, your wife; seeing you are to love her, even as Christ hath loved the Church, when he laid down his life for it, that he might "purify it unto himself, not having spot, or wrinkle, or any such thing." The same end is every husband to pursue, in all his intercourse with his wife; to use every possible means, that she may be freed from every spot, and may walk unblamable in love.

Next to your wife are your children; immortal spirits whom God hath, for a time, entrusted to your care, that you may train them up in all holiness, and fit them for the enjoyment of God in eternity. This is a glorious and important trust; seeing one soul is of more value than all the world beside. Every child, therefore, you are to watch over with the utmost care, that when you are called to give an account of each to the Father of Spirits, you may give your accounts with joy and not with grief. . . .

It is undoubtedly true, that if you are steadily determined to walk in this path; to endeavour by every possible means, that you and your house may thus serve the Lord; that every member of your family may worship him, not only in form, but in spirit and in truth; you will have need to use all the grace, all the courage, all the wisdom which God has given you; for you will find such hinderances in the way, as only the mighty power of God can enable you to break through.

Sermons: "On Family Religion," II, 1-2; III, 18 (J, VII, 78-79, 85).

JW

There are two ways of writing or speaking to children: the one is, to let ourselves down to them; the other, to lift them up to us. Dr. Watts has wrote on the former way, and has succeeded admirably well, speaking to children as children, and leaving them as he found them. The following Hymns are written on the other plan: they contain strong and manly sense, yet expressed in such plain and easy language as even children may understand. But when they do understand them, they will be children no longer, only in years and in stature.

Poetics: "Preface to the Abridged Edition of 'Hymns for Children' " (VI, 369).

JW

Although it is rather to be desired than expected that the general plan of modern education may be amended, yet a treatise on that subject, which was printed in England some years since, has not been without success. A few have dared to go out of the common road and to educate their children in a Christian manner; and some tutors of the University have trained up them under their care in a manner not unworthy of the primitive Christians.

Letters: "To the Society Pro Fide et Christianismo" (VI, 196-97).

4. *The Economic Order*

Has poverty nothing worse in it than this, that it *makes men liable to be laughed at?* ... Is not want of food something worse than this? God pronounced it as a curse upon man, that he should earn it "by the sweat of his brow." But how many are there in this Christian country, that toil, and labour, and sweat, and have it not at last, but struggle with weariness and hunger together? Is it not worse for one, after a hard day's labour, to come back to a poor, cold, dirty, uncomfortable lodging, and to find there not even the food which is needful to repair his wasted strength? You that live at ease in the earth, that want nothing but eyes to see, ears to hear, and hearts to understand how well God hath dealt with you, is it not worse to seek bread day by day, and find none? perhaps to find the comfort also of five or six children crying for what he has not to give! Were it not that he is restrained by an unseen hand, would he not soon "curse God and die"? O want of bread! want of bread! Who can tell what this means, unless he hath felt it himself? I am astonished it occasions no more than heaviness even in them that believe.

Sermons: "Heaviness Through Manifold Temptations," III, 3 (S, II, 270-71).

JW

"Gain all you can." Here we may speak like the children of the world: we meet them on their own ground. And it is our bounden duty to do this: we ought to gain all we can gain, without buying gold too dear, without paying more for it than it is worth. But this it is certain we ought not to do; we ought not to gain money at the expense of life, nor (which is in effect the same thing) at the expense of our health. Therefore, no gain whatsoever should induce us to enter into, or to continue in, any employ, which is of such a kind, or is attended with so hard or so long labour, as to impair our constitution. Neither should we begin or continue in any business which necessarily deprives us of proper seasons for food and sleep, in such a proportion as our nature requires. Indeed, there is a great difference here. Some employments are absolutely and totally unhealthy; as those which imply the dealing much with arsenic, or other equally hurtful minerals, or the breathing an air tainted with streams of melting lead, which must at length destroy the firmest constitution. Others may not be absolutely unhealthy, but only to persons of a weak constitution. Such are those which require many hours to be spent in writing; especially if a person write sitting, and lean upon his stomach, or remain long in an uneasy posture. But whatever it is which reason or experience shows to be destructive of health or strength, that we may not submit to; seeing "the life is more" valuable "than meat, and the body than raiment": and, if we are already engaged in such an employ, we should exchange it, as soon as possible, for some which, if it lessen our gain, will, however, not lessen our health.

We are, secondly, to gain all we can without hurting our mind, any more than our body. For neither may we hurt this: we must preserve, at all events, the spirit of an healthful mind. Therefore, we may not engage or continue in any sinful trade; any that is contrary to the law of God, or of our country. . . .

We are, thirdly, to gain all we can, without hurting our neighbour. But this we may not, cannot do, if we love our neighbour as ourselves. We cannot, if we love every one as ourselves, hurt any one *in his substance*. We cannot devour the increase of his lands, and perhaps the lands and houses themselves, by gaming, by overgrown bills (whether on account of physic, or law, or anything else), or by requiring or taking such interest as even the laws of our country forbid. Hereby all pawnbroking is excluded: seeing, whatever good we might do thereby, all unprejudiced men see with grief to be abundantly overbalanced by the evil. And if it were otherwise, yet we are not allowed to "do evil that good may come." We cannot, consistent with brotherly love, sell our goods below the market price; we cannot study to ruin our neighbor's trade, in order to advance our own; much less can we entice away, or receive, any of his servants or workmen whom he has need of. None can gain by swallowing up his neighbour's substance, without gaining the damnation of hell!

Neither may we gain by hurting our neighbour *in his body.* Therefore we may not sell anything which tends to impair health. Such is, eminently, all that liquid fire, commonly called drams, or spiritous liquors. It is true, these may have a place in medicine; they may be of use in some bodily disorders; although there would rarely be occasion for them, were it not for the unskilfulness of the practitioner. Therefore, such as prepare and sell them only for this end may keep their conscience clear. But who are they? Who prepare them only for this end? Do you know ten such distillers in England? Then excuse these. But all who sell them in the common way, to any that will buy, are poisoners general. They murder His Majesty's subjects by wholesale, neither does their eye pity or spare. They drive them to hell, like sheep. And what is their gain? Is it not the blood of these men? Who then would envy their large estates and sumptuous palaces? A curse is in the midst of them: the curse of God cleaves to the stones, the timber, the furniture of them! The curse of God is in their gardens, their walks, their groves; a fire that burns to the nethermost hell! Blood, blood is there: the foundation, the floor, the walls, the roof, are stained with blood! And canst thou hope, O thou man of blood, though thou art "clothed in scarlet and fine linen, and farest sumptuously every day"; canst thou hope to deliver down thy *fields of blood* to the third generation? Not so; for there is a God in heaven: therefore, thy name shall soon be rooted out. Like as those whom thou hast destroyed, body and soul, "thy memorial shall perish with thee!"

And are not they partakers of the same guilt, though in a lower degree, whether surgeons, apothecaries, or physicians, who play with the lives or health of men, to enlarge their own gain? who purposely lengthen the pain or disease, which they are able to remove speedily? who protract the cure of their patient's body, in order to plunder his substance? Can any man be clear before God, who does not shorten every disorder "as much as he can," and remove all sickness and pain "as soon as he can"? He cannot: for nothing can be more clear, than that he does not ["love his neighbour as himself"; than that he does not] "do unto others, as he would they should do unto himself."

This is dear-bought gain. And so is whatever is procured by hurting our neighbour *in his soul;* by ministering, suppose, either directly or indirectly, to his unchastity or intemperance; which certainly none can do who has any fear of God, or any real desire of pleasing Him. It nearly concerns all those to consider this, who have anything to do with taverns, victualling-houses, opera-houses, play-houses, or any other places of public, fashionable diversion. If these profit the souls of men, you are clear; your employment is good, and your gain innocent; but if they are either sinful in themselves, or natural inlets to sin of various kinds, then, it is to be feared, you have a sad account to make. O beware, lest God say in that day, "These have perished in their iniquity, but their blood do I require at thy hands!" . . .

Having gained all you can, by honest wisdom, and unwearied diligence, the second rule of Christian prudence is, "Save all you can." Do not throw the precious talent into the sea: leave that folly to heathen philosophers. Do not throw it away in idle expenses, which is just the same as throwing it into the sea. Expend no part of it merely to gratify the desire of the flesh, the desire of the eye, or the pride of life. . . .

And why should you throw away money upon your children, any more than upon yourself, in delicate food, in gay or costly apparel, in superfluities of any kind? Why should you purchase for them more pride or lust, more vanity, or foolish and hurtful desires? They do not want any more; they have enough already; nature has made ample provision for them: why should you be at farther expense to increase their temptations and snares, and to pierce them through with many sorrows?

Do not leave it to them to throw away. If you have good reason to believe they would waste what is now in your possession, in gratifying, and thereby increasing, the desire of the flesh, the desire of the eye, or the pride of life; at the peril of theirs and your own soul, do not set these traps in their way. . . .

But let not any man imagine that he has done anything, barely by going thus far, by "gaining and saving all he can," if he were to stop here. All this is nothing, if a man go not forward, if he does not point all this at a farther end. Nor, indeed, can a man properly be said to save anything, if he only lays it up. You may as well throw your money into the sea, as bury it in the earth. And you may as well bury it in the earth, as in your chest, or in the Bank of England. Not to use, is effectually to throw it away. If, therefore, you would indeed "make yourselves friends of the mammon of unrighteousness," add the third rule to the two preceding. Having, first, gained all you can, and, secondly, saved all you can, then "give all you can.". . .

If, then, a doubt should at any time arise in your mind concerning what you are going to expend, either on yourself or any part of your family, you have an easy way to remove it. Calmly and seriously inquire, "(1) In expending this, am I acting according to my character? Am I acting herein, not as a proprietor, but as a steward of my Lord's goods? (2) Am I doing this in obedience to His Words? In what scripture does He require me so to do? (3) Can I offer up this action, this expense, as a sacrifice to God through Jesus Christ? (4) Have I reason to believe, that for this very work I shall have a reward at the resurrection of the just?" You will seldom need anything more to remove any doubt which arises on this head; but, by this four-fold consideration, you will receive clear light as to the way wherein you should go.

If any doubt still remain, you may farther examine yourself by prayer, according to those heads of inquiry. Try whether you can say to the Searcher of hearts, your conscience not condemning you, "Lord, Thou seest I am going to expend this sum on that food, apparel, furniture. And Thou knowest, I act therein with a single eye, as a steward of Thy goods, expending this portion of them thus, in pursuance of the design Thou hadst in entrusting me with them. Thou knowest I do this in obedience to Thy Word, as Thou commandest, and because Thou commandest it. Let this, I beseech Thee, be an holy sacrifice, acceptable through Jesus Christ! And give me a witness in myself, that for this labour of love I shall have a recompense when Thou rewardest every man according to his works." Now, if your conscience bear you witness in the Holy Ghost, that this prayer is well-pleasing to

God, then have you no reason to doubt but that expense is right and good, and such as will never make you ashamed.

Sermons: "The Use of Money," I, 1-6, II, 1, 6-7, III, 1, 4-5 (S, II, 314-20, 322-25).

JW

I gave all our brethren a solemn warning not to love the world or the things of the world. This is one way whereby Satan will surely endeavour to overthrow the present work of God. Riches swiftly increase on many Methodists, so called. What but the mighty power of God can hinder their setting their hearts upon them? And if so, the life of God vanishes away.

Journal: "Wed. 11 July 1764" (V, 82-83).

JW

Reflecting to-day on the case of a poor woman who had continual pain in her stomach, I could not but remark the inexcusable negligence of most physicians in cases of this nature. They prescribe drug upon drug, without knowing a jot of the matter concerning the root of the disorder. And without knowing this they cannot cure, though they can murder, the patient. Whence came this woman's pain (which she would never have told had she never been questioned about it)? From fretting for the death of her son. And what availed medicines while that fretting continued? Why, then, do not all physicians consider how far bodily disorders are caused or influenced by the mind, and in those cases which are utterly out of their sphere call in the assistance of a minister; as ministers, when they find the mind disordered by the body, call in the assistance of a physician? But why are these cases out of their sphere? Because they know not God. It follows, no man can be a thorough physician without being an experienced Christian.

Journal: "Sat. 12 May 1759" (IV, 313).

5. The Political Order

Now, I cannot but acknowledge, I believe an old book, commonly called the Bible, to be true. Therefore I believe, "there is no power but from God: The powers that be are ordained of God." (Rom. xiii. 1.) There is no subordinate power in any nation, but what is derived from the supreme power therein. So in England the King, in the United Provinces the States are the fountain of all power. And there is no supreme power, no power of the sword, of life and death, but what is derived from God, the Sovereign of all. . . .

The supposition, then, that the people are the origin of power, is every way indefensible. It is absolutely overturned by the very principle on which it is supposed to stand; namely, that a right of choosing his Governors belongs to every partaker of human nature. If this be so, then it belongs to every individual of the human species; consequently, not to freeholders alone, but to all men; not to men only, but to women also; not only to adult men and women, to those who have lived one-and-twenty years, but to those who have lived eighteen or twenty, as well as those who have lived threescore. But none did ever maintain this, nor probably ever will. Therefore this boasted principle falls to the ground, and the whole superstructure with it. So common sense brings us back to the grand truth, "There is no power but of God."

Works: "Thoughts Concerning the Origin of Power," 7, 21 (XI, 47-48; 52-53).

JW

You see whence arose this outcry for liberty, and these dismal complaints that we are robbed of our liberty echoing through the land. It is plain to every unprejudiced man, they have not the least foundation. We enjoy at this day throughout these kingdoms such liberty, civil and religious, as no other kingdom or commonwealth in Europe, or in the world, enjoys; and such as our ancestors never enjoyed from the Conquest to the Revolution. Let us be thankful for it to God and the King! Let us not, by our vile unthankfulness, yea, our denial that we enjoy it at all, provoke the King of kings to take it away. By one stroke, by taking to himself that Prince whom we know not how to value, He might change the scene, and put an end to our civil as well as religious liberty.

Works: "Thoughts Upon Liberty," 28 (XI, 45-46).

JW

Last Sunday, when one of our preachers was beginning to speak to a quiet congregation, a neighbouring Justice sent a constable to seize him, though he was licensed, and would not release him till he had paid twenty pounds, telling him his license was good for nothing because he was a Churchman.

Now, sir, what can the Methodists do? They are liable to be ruined by the Conventicle Act, and they have no relief from the Act of Toleration! If this is not oppression, what is? Where, then, is English liberty? the liberty of Christians? yea, of every rational creature, who as such has a right to worship God according to his own conscience?

Letters: "To William Wilberforce" (VIII, 231).

JW

There is a still more horrid reproach to the Christian name, yea, to the name of man, to all reason and humanity. There is war in the world! war between men! war between Christians! I mean, between those that bear the name of Christ, and profess to "walk as he also walked." Now, who can reconcile war, I will not say to religion, but to any degree of reason or common sense? . . .

Whatever be the cause, let us calmly and impartially consider the thing itself. Here are forty thousand men gathered together on this plain. What are they going to do? See, there are thirty or forty thousand more at a little distance. And these are going to shoot them through the head or body, to stab them, or split their skulls, and send most of their souls into everlasting fire, as fast as possibly they can. Why so? What harm have they done to them. O, none at all! They do not so much as know them. But a man, who is King of France, has a quarrel with another man, who is King of England. So these Frenchmen are to kill as many of these Englishmen as they can, to prove the King of France is in the right. Now, what an argument is this! What a method of proof! What an amazing way of deciding controversies! What must mankind be, before such a thing as war could ever be known or thought of upon earth? How shocking, how inconceivable a want must there have been of common understanding, as well as common humanity, before any two Governors, or any two nations in the universe, could once think of such a method of decision!

Works: "The Doctrine of Original Sin: I," II, 10 (IX, 221-22).

JW

Many thousands there are civilized by smuggling. The numbers concerned herein, upon all our coasts, are far greater than can be imagined. But what reason, and what religion, have these that trample on all laws, divine and human, by a course of thieving, or receiving stolen goods, of plundering their King and country? I say King and country; seeing, whatever is taken from the King, is in effect taken from the country, who are obliged to make up all deficiences in the royal revenue. These are, therefore, general robbers. They rob you and me, and every one of their countrymen; seeing, had the king his due customs, a great part of our taxes might be spared. A smuggler, then (and, in proportion, every seller or buyer of uncustomed goods,) is a thief of the first order, a highwayman or pickpocket of the worst sort. Let not any of those prate about reason or religion. It is an amazing instance of human folly, that every government in Europe does not drive these vermin away into lands not inhabited.

Works: "The Doctrine of Original Sin: I," II, 11 (IX, 225-26).

JW

I see not how you can go through your glorious enterprise in opposing that execrable villany [slavery], which is the scandal of religion, of England, and of human nature. Unless God has raised you up for this very thing, you will be worn out by the opposition of men and devils. But if God be for you, who can be against you? Are all of them together stronger than God? O be not weary of well doing! Go on, in the name of God and in the power of His might, till even American slavery (the vilest that ever saw the sun) shall vanish away before it.

Letters: "To William Wilberforce" (VIII, 265).

JW

> The flower now blooms, now hangs its head;
>   So fleets my short-lived day!
> O, may my useful fragrance spread
>   Before I fade away!
>
> What though the throne I then should fill
>   At the great day, were mine?
> The sweetness, which Thy gracious skill
>   Diffused, its praise were Thine.
>
> Let me not languish, then, and spend
>   A life dead to thy praise,
> As is the dust to which I tend
>   By sure though slow decays!
>
> All things are busy round but I;
>   Nor honey with the bees,
> Nor scent with flowers, nor husbandry
>   Have I to water these.
>
> I am no link of Thy great chain,
>   A cumbrous, fruitless weed:
> O, mend my music! Give one strain
>   Even to my useless reed!

Poetics: "Employment" (From George Herbert) (I, 30).

CHRISTIAN CHARACTER—*Sermons:* "The Almost Christian" (S, I, 54 ff.); "Scriptural Christianity," IV, 6-10 (S, I, 106-10); "Upon Our Lord's Sermon on the Mount: II; III; X; XI" (S, I, 335-77, 517-42); "A Caution Against Bigotry" (S, II, 104 ff.); "Self-Denial" (S, II, 281 ff.); "On Dissipation" (J, VI, 444 ff.). *Works:* "The Nature Design, and General Rules of the United Societies" (VIII, 270-71); "The Character of a Methodist," 1-18 (VIII, 340-47); "An Estimate of the Manners of the Present Times" (XI, 156 ff.). *Letters:* "To the Author of 'A Letter, &c.'" (III, 4-5); "To Lady Maxwell" (IV, 260-61); "To Ann Bolton" (V, 286-87).

CHRISTIAN DUTIES—*Sermons:* "The Means of Grace" (S, I, 238 ff.); "Upon Our Lord's Sermon on the Mount: VI; VII" (S, I, 423-70); "The Cure of Evil-Speaking" (S, II, 296 ff.); "The Duty of Reproving Our Neighbour" (J, VI, 296 ff.); "On Dress" (J, VII, 15 ff.); "The More Excellent Way" (J, VII, 26 ff.); "On Redeeming the Time" (J, VII, 67 ff.); "On a Single Eye" (J, VII, 297 ff.). *Works:* "Advice to the People Called Methodists" (VIII, 351 ff.); "A Word to a Sabbath-Breaker" (XI, 164 ff.). *Letters:* "To Miss Johnson" (IV, 59-60); "To Mrs. Barton" (V, 206); "To Martha Chapman" (VI, 7). *Journal:* "Wed. 25-Sun. 29 June 1740" (II, 359-62); "Wed. 2 Sept. 1767" (V, 229-30). *Notes:* "Matthew 16:24"; "Philippians 4:3"; "Hebrews 13:17."

THE FAMILY—*Sermons:* "On Family Religion" (J, VII, 76 ff.); "On the Education of Children" (J, VII, 86 ff.); "On Obedience to Parents" (J, VII, 98 ff.). *Works:* "List of Works Revised and Abridged from Various Authors" (XIV, 232-33; 237-38). *Letters:* "To Mary Bishop" (VI, 258). *Journal:* "Tues. 27 Nov. 1739" (II, 322-23).

THE ECONOMIC ORDER—*Sermons:* "Upon Our Lord's Sermon on the Mount: VIII" (S, I, 473-94); "The Danger of Riches" (J, VII, 1 ff.); "On Riches" (J, VII, 213 ff.); "On the Danger of Increasing Riches" (J, VII, 355 ff.). *Works:* "Thoughts on the Present Scarcity of Provisions" (XI, 53 ff.). *Letters:* "To the Editor of 'Lloyd's Evening Post'" (V, 350 ff.); "To Certain Proprietors of East India Stock" (VI, 46-47); "To Granville Sharp" (VIII, 277). *Journal:* "Tues. 21 June 1743" (III, 79-80); "Fri. 3 July 1761" (IV, 467-68); "Sat. 17 Aug. 1776" (VI, 123).

THE POLITICAL ORDER—*Sermons:* "The Reformation of Manners" (S, II, 482 ff.). *Works:* "Free Thoughts on the Present State of Public Affairs" (XI, 14 ff.); "Thoughts Upon Liberty" (XI, 34 ff.); "Thoughts Concerning the Origin of Power" (XI, 46 ff.); "Thoughts Upon Slavery" (XI, 59 ff.); "A Calm Address to our American Colonies" (XI, 80 ff.) "Some Observations on Liberty" (XI, 90 ff.); "A Seasonable Address to the More Serious Part of the Inhabitants of Great Britain" (XI, 119 ff.). *Letters:* "To John Baily" (III, 272 ff.); "To the Editor of the 'London Chronicle'" (IV, 127-28); "To a Friend" (V, 370 ff.); "To the Earl of Dartmouth" (VI, 155 ff.). *Journal:* "Mon. 5 March 1744" (III, 123-24); "Thur. 6 Oct. 1774" (VI, 40).

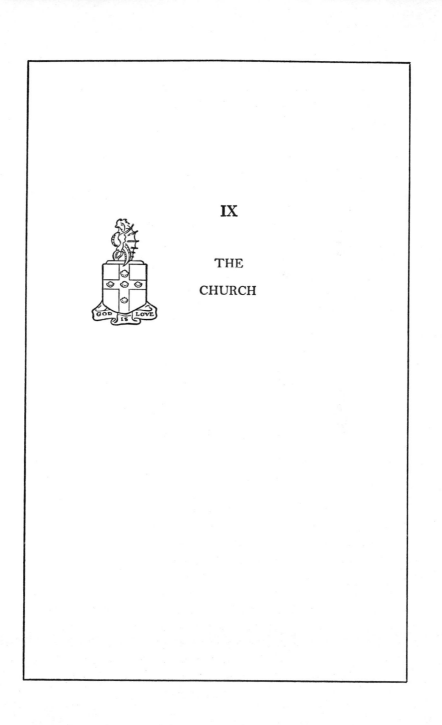

IX

THE

CHURCH

IX. THE CHURCH

NEVER RELINQUISHING his membership or ordination in the Church of England, Wesley was first and last a churchman. His religious societies were originally formed to buttress the work of the church and to meet needs of men not satisfied elsewhere. His primary contribution lies not in the creation of new techniques and types of organization, but rather in his selection and implementation of realistic goals. Although Wesley considered severing his societies from the mother church, the break did not become official until after his death. His use of lay preachers was the source of considerable controversy within and without the Methodist group. Late in his life, after much searching of heart and under the pressure of necessity, Wesley ordained some of his lay preachers so that they could administer the sacraments to the growing societies. For Wesley baptism is related to and requires the new birth for its reality. He insists on infant baptism, which he bases on prevenient grace—one of the universal benefits of the atonement. Wesley never ceases to stress the duty of frequent communion, desiring that his people partake of the sacrament at least once each week.

1. Nature of the Church

Let us consider, First, Who are properly the Church of God? What is the true meaning of that term? "The Church at Ephesus," as the Apostle himself explains it, means, "the saints," the holy persons, "that are in Ephesus," and there assemble themselves together to worship God the Father, and his Son Jesus Christ; whether they did this in one or (as we may probably suppose) in several places. But it is the Church in general, the catholic or universal Church, which the Apostle

here considers as one body: Comprehending not only the Christians ...
of one congregation, of one city, of one province, or nation; but all
the persons upon the face of the earth, who answer the character here
given. The several particulars contained therein, we may now more
distinctly consider.

"There is one Spirit" who animates all these, all the living members
of the Church of God. Some understand hereby the Holy Spirit himself,
the Fountain of all spiritual life; and it is certain, "if any man have not
the Spirit of Christ, he is none of his." Others understand it of those
spiritual gifts and holy dispositions which are afterwards mentioned.

"There is," in all those that have received this Spirit, "one hope"; a
hope full of immortality. They know, to die is not to be lost: Their
prospect extends beyond the grave. They can cheerfully say, "Blessed
be the God and Father of our Lord Jesus Christ, who, according to his
abundant mercy, hath begotten us again to a lively hope by the resurrection of Jesus Christ from the dead, to an inheritance incorruptible,
and undefiled, and that fadeth not away."

"There is one Lord," who has now dominion over them; who has
set up his kingdom in their hearts, and reigns over all those that are
partakers of this hope. To obey him, to run the way of his commandments, is their glory and joy. And while they are doing this with
a willing mind, they, as it were, "sit in heavenly places with Christ
Jesus."

"There is one faith"; which is the free gift of God, and is the
ground of their hope. This is not barely the faith of a Heathen:
Namely, a belief that "there is a God," and that he is gracious and
just, and, consequently, "a rewarder of them that diligently seek him."
Neither is it barely the faith of a devil; though this goes much farther
than the former: For the devil believes, and cannot but believe, all
that is written both in the Old and New Testament to be true. But it
is the faith of St. Thomas, teaching him to say with holy boldness, "My
Lord, and my God!" It is the faith which enables every true Christian
believer to testify with St. Paul, "The life which I now live, I live by
faith in the Son of God, who loved me, and gave himself for me."

"There is one baptism"; which is the outward sign our one Lord has been pleased to appoint, of all that inward and spiritual grace which he is continually bestowing upon his Church. It is likewise a precious means, whereby this faith and hope are given to those that diligently seek him. Some, indeed, have been inclined to interpret this in a figurative sense; as if it referred to that baptism of the Holy Ghost which the Apostles received at the day of Pentecost, and which, in a lower degree, is given to all believers: But it is a stated rule in interpreting Scripture, never to depart from the plain, literal sense, unless it implies an absurdity. And beside, if we thus understood it, it would be a needless repetition, as being included in, "There is one Spirit."

"There is one God and Father of all" that have the Spirit of adoption, which "crieth in their hearts, Abba, Father"; which "witnesseth" continually "with their spirits," that they are the children of God: "Who is above all,"—the Most High, the Creator, the Sustainer, the Governor of the whole universe: "And through all,"—pervading all space; filling heaven and earth . . . "And in you all,"—in a peculiar manner living in you, that are one body, by one Spirit:

Making your souls his loved abode,
The temples of indwelling God.

Here, then, is a clear unexceptionable answer to that question, "What is the Church?" The catholic or universal Church is, all the persons in the universe whom God hath so called out of the world as to entitle them to the preceding character; as to be "one body," united by "one Spirit"; having "one faith, one hope, one baptism; one God and Father of all, who is above all, and through all, and in them all."

Sermons: "Of the Church," 7-14 (J, VI, 394-96).

JW

Here is a native specimen of a New-Testament church; which is, a company of men, called by the Gospel, grafted into Christ by baptism, animated by love, united by all kind of fellowship, and disciplined by the death of Ananias and Sapphira.

Notes: "Acts 5:11."

As to my own judgement, I still believe "the Episcopal form of Church government to be both scriptural and apostolical": I mean, well agreeing with the practice and writings of the Apostles. But that it is prescribed in Scripture I do not believe. This opinion (which I once heartily espoused) I have been heartily ashamed of ever since I read Dr. Stillingfleet's *Irenicon*. I think he has unanswerably proved that neither Christ or His Apostles prescribed any particular form of Church government, and that the plea for the divine right of Episcopacy was never heard of in the primitive Church.

Letters: "To James Clark". (III, 182).

My conclusion (which I cannot yet give up), that it is lawful to continue in the Church, stands, I know not how, almost without any premises that are able to bear its weight.

My difficulty is very much increased by one of your observations. I know the original doctrines of the Church are sound; I know her worship is (in the main) pure and scriptural. But if "the essence of the Church of England, considered as such, consists in her orders and laws" (many of which I myself can say nothing for), "and not in her worship and doctrines," those who separate from her have a far stronger plea than I was ever sensible of.

At present I apprehend those, and those only, to separate from the Church who either renounce her fundamental doctrines or refuse to join in her public worship. As yet we have done neither; nor have we taken one step farther than we were convinced was our bounden duty. It is from a full conviction of this that we have (1) preached abroad, (2) prayed extempore, (3) formed Societies, and (4) permitted preachers who were not episcopally ordained. And were we pushed on this side, were there no alternative allowed, we should judge it our bounden duty rather wholly to separate from the Church than to give up any one of these points. Therefore, if we cannot stop a separation without stopping lay preachers, the case is clear—we cannot stop it at all. . . .

It is undoubtedly "needful," as you observe, "to come to some resolution in this point"; and the sooner the better. I therefore rejoice to hear that you think "this matter may be better and more inoffensively ordered; and that a method may be found which, conducted with prudence and patience, will reduce the constitution of Methodism to due order, and render the Methodists under God more instrumental to the ends of practical religion."

Letters: "To Samuel Walker," 3-5 (III, 145-46).

JW

Q. 10. Do you not entail a schism in the Church? that is, Is it not probable that your hearers, after your death, will be scattered into all sects and parties; or that they will form themselves into a distinct sect?

A. (1) We are persuaded the body of our hearers will even after our death remain in the Church, unless they be thrust out.

(2) We believe notwithstanding, either that they will be thrust out, or that they will leaven the whole Church.

(3) We do, and will do, all we can to prevent those consequences which are supposed likely to happen after our death.

(4) But we cannot with a good conscience neglect the present opportunity of saving souls while we live, for fear of consequences which may possibly or probably happen after we are dead.

Works: "Minutes of Some Late Conversations," Wed. June 27, 1744 (VIII, 281).

2. Band Societies

In the latter end of the year 1739, eight or ten persons came to me in London, who appeared to be deeply convinced of sin, and earnestly groaning for redemption. They desired (as did two or three more the next day) that I would spend some time with them in prayer, and advise them how to flee from the wrath to come; which they saw continually hanging over their heads. That we might have more time for this great work, I appointed a day when they might all come together, which from thenceforward they did every week, namely, on Thursday, in the evening. To these, and as many more as desired to join them, (for their number increased daily,) I gave those advices, from time to time, which I judged most needful for them; and we always concluded our meeting with prayer suited to their several necessities.

This was the rise of the United Society, first in London, and then in other places. Such a society is no other than "a company of men having the form and seeking the power of godliness, united in order to pray together, to receive the word of exhortation, and to watch over one another in love, that they may help each other to work out their salvation."

That it may the more easily be discerned, whether they are indeed working out their own salvation, each society is divided into smaller companies, called *classes,* according to their respective places of abode. There are about twelve persons in every class; one of whom is styled *the Leader.* It is his business, (1) To see each person in his class once a week at least, in order to inquire how their souls prosper; to advise, reprove, comfort, or exhort, as occasion may require; to receive what they are willing to give toward the relief of the poor. (2) To meet the Minister and the Stewards of the society once a week; in order to inform the Minister of any that are sick, or of any that walk disorderly, and will not be reproved; to pay to the Stewards what they have received of their several classes in the week preceding; and to show their account of what each person has contributed.

Works: "The Nature, Design, and General Rules of the United Societies," 1-3 (VIII, 269-70).

JW

You are supposed to have the faith that "overcometh the world." To you, therefore, it is not grievous,—

I. Carefully to abstain from doing evil; in particular,—

1. Neither to buy nor sell anything at all on the Lord's day.

2. To taste no spirituous liquor, no dram of any kind, unless prescribed by a Physician.

3. To be at a word both in buying and selling.

4. To pawn nothing, no, not to save life.

5. Not to mention the fault of any behind his back, and to stop those short that do.

6. To wear no needless ornaments, such as rings, ear-rings, necklaces, lace, ruffles.

7. To use no needless self-indulgence, such as taking snuff or tobacco, unless prescribed by a Physician.

II. Zealously to maintain good works; in particular,—

1. To give alms of such things as you possess, and that to the uttermost of your power.

2. To reprove all that sin in your sight, and that in love and meekness of wisdom.

3. To be patterns of diligence and frugality, of self-denial, and taking up the cross daily.

III. Constantly to attend on all the ordinances of God; in particular,—

1. To be at church and at the Lord's table every week, and at every public meeting of the Bands.

2. To attend the ministry of the word every morning, unless distance, business, or sickness prevent.

3. To use private prayer every day; and family prayer, if you are at the head of a family.

4. To read the Scriptures, and meditate therein, at every vacant hour. And,—

5. To observe, as days of fasting or abstinence, all Fridays in the year.

Works: "Directions Given to the Band Societies" (VIII, 273-74).

3. The Ministry

Ministers are still barely instruments in God's hand, and depend entirely as ever on his blessing, to give the increase to their labours.

Without this they are nothing; with it, their part is so small, that they hardly deserve to be mentioned. May their hearts and hands be more united! And retaining a due sense of the honour God doeth them in employing them, may they faithfully labour, not as for themselves, but for the great Proprietor of all, till the day come when he will reward them in full proportion to their fidelity and diligence.

Notes: "I Corinthians 3:8."

JW

[Ministers] are supposed to go before the flock, (as is the manner of the eastern shepherds to this day,) and to guide them in all the ways of truth and holiness; they are to "nourish them with the words of eternal life"; to feed them with the "pure milk of the word"; Applying it continually "for doctrine"; teaching them all the essential doctrines contained therein;—"for reproof"; warning them if they turn aside from the way, to the right hand or to the left;—"for correction"; showing them how to amend what is amiss, and guiding them back into the way of peace;—and "for instruction in righteousness"; training them up to outward holiness, "until they come to a perfect man, to the measure of the stature of the fulness of Christ."

They are supposed to "watch over your souls, as those that shall give account." "As those that shall give account!" How unspeakably solemn and awful are those words! May God write them upon the heart of every guide of souls!

Sermons: "On Obedience to Pastors," I, 4-5 (J, VII, 110).

JW

It is always difficult and frequently impossible for private men to judge of the measures taken by men in public offices. We do not see many of the grounds which determine them to act in this or the contrary manner. Generally, therefore, it behoves us to be silent, as we may suppose they know their own business best; but when they are censured without any colour of reason, and when an odium is cast on the King by that means, we ought to preach politics in this sense also; we ought publicly to confute those unjust censures: Only remembering still, that this is rarely to be done, and only when fit occasion offers; it being our main business to preach "repentance towards God, and faith in our Lord Jesus Christ."

Works: "How Far is it the Duty of a Christian Minister to Preach Politics?" 6 (XI, 155).

Man forbids me to do this in another's parish: that is, in effect, to do it at all; seeing I have now no parish of my own, nor probably ever shall. Whom, then, shall I hear, God or man? ...

Suffer me now to tell you my principles in this matter. I look upon all the world as my parish; thus far I mean, that in whatever part of it I am I judge it meet, right, and my bounden duty to declare, unto all that are willing to hear, the glad tidings of salvation. This is the work which I know God has called me to; and sure I am that His blessing attends it.

Letters: "To James Hervey" (I, 286).

I allow, that it is highly expedient, whoever preaches in His name should have an outward as well as an inward call; but that it is *absolutely necessary,* I deny.

Sermons: "A Caution Against Bigotry," III, 7 (S, II, 119).

Indeed, in the one thing which [lay ministers] profess to know, they are not ignorent men. I trust there is not one of them who is not able to go through such an examination, in substantial, practical, experimental Divinity, as few of our candidates for holy orders, even in the University, (I speak it with sorrow and shame, and in tender love,) are able to do. But, O! what manner of examination do most of those candidates go through! and what proof are the testimonials commonly brought, (as solemn as the form is wherein they run,) either of their piety or knowledge to whom are entrusted those sheep which God hath purchased with his own blood. . . .

If we come to later times: Was Mr. Calvin ordained? Was he either Priest or Deacon? And were not most of those whom it pleased God to employ in promoting the Reformation abroad, laymen also? Could that great work have been promoted at all in many places, if laymen had not preached? And yet how seldom do the very Papists urge this as an objection against the Reformation! Nay, as rigorous as they are in things of this kind, they themselves appoint, even in some of their strictest Orders, that "if any lay-brother believes himself called of God to preach as a Missionary, the Superior of the Order, being informed there of, shall immediately send him away."

Works: "A Farther Appeal to Men of Reason and Religion," III, 10, 12 (VIII, 221-22).

4. Sacrament of the Lord's Supper

Before you use any means [of grace], let it be deeply impressed on your soul,—there is no *power* in this. It is, in itself, a poor, dead, empty thing: separate from God, it is a dry leaf, a shadow. Neither is there any *merit* in my using this; nothing intrinsically pleasing to God; nothing whereby I deserve any favour at His hands, no, not a drop of water to cool my tongue. But, because God bids, therefore I do; because He directs me to wait in this way, therefore here I wait for His free mercy, whereof cometh my salvation.

Settle this in your heart, that the *opus operatum,* the mere *work done,* profiteth nothing; that there is no *power* to save but in the Spirit of God, no *merit* but in the blood of Christ; that, consequently, even what God ordains, conveys no grace to the soul, if you trust not in Him alone. On the other hand, he that does truly trust in Him cannot fall short of the grace of God, even though he were cut off from every outward ordinance, though he were shut up in the centre of the earth. . . .

In using all means, seek God alone. In and through every outward thing, look singly to the *power* of His Spirit, and the *merits* of His Son. Beware you do not stick in the *work* itself; if you do, it is all lost labour. Nothing short of God can satisfy your soul. Therefore, eye Him in all, through all, and above all.

Remember also, to use all means *as means;* as ordained, not for their own sake, but in order to the renewal of your soul in righteousness and true holiness. If, therefore, they actually tend to this, well; but, if not, they are dung and dross.

Sermons: "The Means of Grace," V, 4 (S, I, 259-60).

I am to show that it is the duty of every Christian to receive the Lord's Supper as often as he can.

The First reason why it is the duty of every Christian so to do is, because it is a plain command of Christ. That this is his command, appears from the words of the text, "Do this in remembrance of me": By which, as the Apostles were obliged to bless, break, and give the bread to all that joined with them in these holy things, so were all Christians obliged to receive those signs of Christ's body and blood. Here, therefore, the bread and wine are commanded to be received, in remembrance of his death, to the end of the world. Observe, too, that this command was given by our Lord when he was just laying down his life for our sakes. They are therefore, as it were, his dying words to all his followers.

A Second reason why every Christian should do this as often as he can, is, because the benefits of doing it are so great, to all that do it in obedience to him; viz., the forgiveness of our past sins, the present strengthening and refreshing of our souls. In this world we are never free from temptations. Whatever way of life we are in, whatever our condition be, whether we are sick or well, in trouble or at ease, the enemies of our souls are watching to lead us into sin. And too often they prevail over us. Now, when we are convinced of having sinned against God, what surer way have we of procuring pardon from him, than the "showing forth the Lord's death"; and beseeching him, for the sake of his Son's sufferings, to blot out all our sins?

The grace of God given herein confirms to us the pardon of our sins, and enables us to leave them. As our bodies are strengthened by bread and wine, so are our souls by these tokens of the body and the blood of Christ. This is the food of our souls: This gives strength to perform our duty, and leads us on to perfection. If, therefore, we have any regard for the plain command of Christ, if we desire the pardon of our sins, if we wish for strength to believe, to love and obey God, then we should neglect no opportunity of receiving the Lord's Supper; then we must never turn our backs on the feast which our Lord has prepared for us. We must neglect no occasion, which the good providence of God affords us, for this purpose. This is the true rule: So often are we to receive as God gives us opportunity. Whoever, therefore, does not receive, but goes from the holy table, when all things are prepared, either does not understand his duty, or does not care for the dying command of his Saviour, the forgiveness of his sins, the strengthening of his soul, and the refreshing it with the hope of glory.

Let every one, therefore, who has either any desire to please God, or any love of his own soul, obey God, and consult the good of his own soul, by communicating every time he can; like the first Christians, with whom the Christian Sacrifice was a constant part of the Lord's day service. And for several centuries they received it almost every day: Four times a week always, and every Saint's day beside. Accordingly, those that joined in the prayers of the faithful never failed to partake of the blessed sacrament. What opinion they had of any who turned his back upon it, we may learn from that ancient canon: "If any believer join in the prayers of the faithful, and go away without receiving the Lord's Supper, let him be excommunicated, as bringing confusion into the Church of God."

In order to understand the nature of the Lord's Supper, it would be useful carefully to read over those passages in the Gospel, and in the First Epistle to the Corinthians, which speak of the institution of it. Hence we learn that the design of this sacrament is, the continual remembrance of the death of Christ, by eating bread and drinking wine, which are the outward signs of the inward grace, the body and blood of Christ.

It is highly expedient for those who purpose to receive this, whenever their time will permit, to prepare themselves for this solemn ordinance by self-examination and prayer. But this is not absolutely necessary. And when we have not time for it, we should see that we have the habitual preparation which is absolutely necessary, and can never be dispensed with on any account or any occasion whatever. This is, First, a full *purpose* of heart to keep all the commandments of God; and, Secondly, a sincere *desire* to receive all his promises.

Sermons: "The Duty of Constant Communion," I, 1-6 (J, VII, 147-49).

I showed at large: (1) That the Lord's Supper was ordained by God to be a means of conveying to men either preventing, or justifying, or sanctifying grace, according to their several necessities. (2) That the persons for whom it was ordained are all those who know and feel that they want the grace of God, either to restrain them from sin, or to show their sins forgiven, or to renew their souls in the image of God. (3) That inasmuch as we come to His table, not to give Him anything, but to receive whatsoever He sees best for us, there is no previous preparation indispensably necessary, but a desire to receive whatsoever He pleases to give. And (4) That no fitness is required at the time of communicating, but a sense of our state, of our utter sinfulness and helplessness; every one who knows he is fit for hell being just fit to come to Christ in this as well as all other ways of His appointment.

Journal: "Sat. 28 June 1740" (II, 361-62).

5. *Sacrament of Baptism*

In baptism we, through faith, are ingrafted into Christ, and we draw new spiritual life from this new root, through his Spirit, who fashions us like unto him, and particularly with regard to his death and resurrection.

Notes: "Romans 6:3."

JW

What [is baptism?] It is the initiatory sacrament, which enters us into covenant with God. It was instituted by Christ, who alone has power to institute a proper sacrament, a sign, seal, pledge, and means of grace, perpetually obligatory on all Christians. We know not, indeed, the exact time of its institution; but we know it was long before our Lord's ascension. And it was instituted in the room of circumcision. For, as that was a sign and seal of God's Covenant, so is this.

The matter of this sacrament is water; which, as it has a natural power of cleansing, is the more fit for this symbolical use. Baptism is performed by washing, dipping, or sprinkling the person, in the name of the Father, Son, and Holy Ghost, who is hereby devoted to the ever-blessed Trinity. I say, *by washing, dipping, or sprinkling;* because it is not determined in Scripture in which of these ways it shall be done, neither by any express precept, nor by any such example as clearly proves it; nor by the force or meaning of the word *baptize....*

What are the benefits we receive by baptism, is the next point to be considered. And the first of these is, the washing away the guilt of original sin, by the application of the merits of Christ's death. That we are all born under the guilt of Adam's sin, and that all sin deserves eternal misery, was the unanimous sense of the ancient Church, as it is expressed in the Ninth Article of our own.... But "as by the offence of one, judgment came upon all men to condemnation; so by the righteousness of one, the free gift came upon all men, to justification of life." And the virtue of this free gift, the merits of Christ's life and death, are applied to us in baptism.... "It is certain, by God's word, that children who are baptized, dying before they commit actual sin are saved." And this is agreeable to the unanimous judgment of all the ancient Fathers.

By baptism we enter into covenant with God; into that everlasting covenant, which he hath commanded for ever; (Psalm cxi. 9;) that new covenant, which he promised to make with the spiritual Israel; even to "give them a new heart and a new spirit, to sprinkle clean water upon them," (of which the baptismal is only a figure,) "and to remember their sins and iniquities no more"; in a word, to be their God, as he promised to Abraham, in the evangelical covenant which he made with him and all his spiritual offspring. (Gen. xvii. 7, 8.) And as circumcision was then the way of entering into this covenant, so baptism is now; which is therefore styled by the Apostle, (so many good interpreters render his words), "the stipulation, contract, or covenant of a good conscience with God."

By baptism we are admitted into the Church, and consequently made members of Christ, its Head. The Jews were admitted into the Church by circumcision, so are the Christians by baptism. For "as many as are baptized into Christ," in his name, "have" thereby "put on Christ"; (Gal. iii. 27;) that is, are mystically united to Christ, and made one with him. For "by one Spirit we are all baptized into one body," (1 Cor. xii. 13,) namely, the Church, "the body of Christ." (Eph. iv. 12.) From which spiritual, vital union with him, proceeds the influence of his grace on those that are baptized; as from our union with the Church, a share in all its privileges, and in all the promises Christ has made to it.

By baptism, we who were "by nature children of wrath," are made the children of God. And this regeneration which our Church in so many places ascribes to baptism is more than barely being admitted into the Church, though commonly connected therewith; being "grafted into the body of Christ's Church, we are made the children of God by adoption and grace." This is grounded on the plain words of our Lord: "Except a man be born again of water and of the Spirit, he cannot enter into the kingdom of God." (John iii. 5.) By water then, as a means, the water of baptism, we are regenerated or born again; whence it is also called by the Apostle, "the washing of regeneration." Our Church therefore ascribes no greater virtue to baptism than Christ himself has done. Nor does she ascribe it to the outward washing, but to the inward grace, which, added thereto, makes it a sacrament. Herein a principle of grace is infused, which will not be wholly taken away, unless we quench the Holy Spirit of God by long continued wickedness.

In consequence of our being made children of God, we are heirs of the kingdom of heaven. "If children," (as the Apostle observes,) "then heirs, heirs of God, and joint-heirs with Christ." Herein we receive a title to, and an earnest of, "a kingdom which cannot be moved." Baptism doth now save us, if we live answerable thereto; if we repent, believe, and obey the gospel: Supposing this, as it admits us into the Church here, so into glory hereafter.

But did our Saviour design this should remain always in his Church? This is the Third thing we are to consider. And this may be dispatched in few words, since there can be no reasonable doubt, but it was intended to last as long as the Church into which it is the appointed means of entering. In the ordinary way, there is no other means of entering into the Church or into heaven. . . .

On the whole, therefore, it is not only lawful and innocent, but meet, right, and our bounden duty, in conformity to the uninterrupted practice of the whole Church of Christ from the earliest ages, to consecrate our children to God by baptism, as the Jewish Church were commanded to do by circumcision.

Works: "A Treatise on Baptism," I, *passim* (X, 188, 190-92, 201).

JW

Baptism is not the new birth: they are not one and the same thing. Many indeed seem to imagine that they are just the same: at least, they speak as if they thought so; but I do not know that this opinion is publicly avowed by any denomination of Christians whatever. . . .

What can be more plain, than that the one is an external, the other an internal, work; that the one is a visible, the other an invisible thing, and therefore wholly different from each other?—the one being an act of man, purifying the body; the other a change wrought by God in the soul: so that the former is just as distinguishable from the latter, as the soul from the body, or water from the Holy Ghost.

From the preceding reflections we may, secondly, observe, that as the new birth is not the same thing with baptism, so it does not always accompany baptism: they do not constantly go together. A man may possibly be "born of water," and yet not be "born of the Spirit." There may sometimes be the outward sign, where there is not the inward grace. I do not now speak with regard to infants: it is certain our Church supposes that all who are baptized in their infancy are at the same time born again; and it is allowed that the whole Office for the Baptism of Infants proceeds upon this supposition. Nor is it an objection of any weight against this, that we cannot comprehend how this work can be wrought in infants. For neither can we comprehend how it is wrought in a person of riper years. But whatever be the case with infants, it is sure all of riper years who are baptized are not at the same time born again. "The tree is known by its fruits." And hereby it appears too plain to be denied, that divers of those who were children of the devil before they were baptized continue the same after baptism; "for the works of their father they do": they continue servants of sin, without any pretence either to inward or outward holiness.

Sermons: "The New Birth," IV, 1-2 (S, II, 237-39).

JW

God, who wouldst a world forgive,
    Offerest all sufficient grace;
All *may* in Thy Son believe,
    Numbers *do* Thy Son embrace;
Numbers saved, from every sect,
Form the church of Thy elect.

Scatter'd o'er the earth they lie,
    Sheep with wolves encompass'd round,
Guided by their Shepherd's eye,
    Safe they in the fold are found:
Angels all their steps attend,
Serve, and keep them to the end.

When Thy judgments are abroad,
    Them Thou kindly dost conceal,

Hidden in the ark of God,
    Shelter'd, they in *Zoar* dwell;
Find a sanctuary prepared,
Find Omnipotence their guard.

Poor, and mean, whom all reject,
    Persecute or else despise,
They their enemies protect,
    Stay the vengeance of the skies:
Till Thou hast secured Thine own,
Stands the world for them alone.

States and empires rise, or fall,
    Stands the church till time shall end,
Waiting for the Bridegroom's call,
    Listening, longing to ascend,
Fair, and spotless, and complete,
Jesus in the clouds to meet.

Poetics: "Hymn XVI" (VIII, 305-06).

SUPPLEMENTARY REFERENCES

NATURE OF THE CHURCH—*Sermons:* "The Mystery of Iniquity" (J, VI, 253 ff.); "Of the Church" (J, VI, 392 ff.); "On Schism" (J, VI, 401 ff.). *Works:* "A Farther Appeal to Men of Reason and Religion," II, III (VIII, 180-200; 201-47); "Minutes of Several Conversations" (VIII, 321 ff.); "Popery Calmly Considered," I, III (X, 140-48). *Letters:* "To a Clerical Friend" (II, 29-32); "To Thomas Church" (II, 240-41); "To the Earl of Dartmouth" (IV, 147 ff.). *Journal:* "Sat. 16 June 1739" (II, 222-23); "Fri. 25 March 1743" (III, 72); "Mon. 20 Aug. 1764" (V, 92). *Notes:* "I Corinthians 11:18"; "Jude 19."

BAND SOCIETIES—*Sermons:* "On God's Vineyard," II-IV (J, VII, 206-10). *Works:* "A Plain Account of the People Called Methodists" (VIII, 248-49); "Minutes of Several Conversations" (VIII, 299 ff.); "A Short History of Methodism," 1-15 (VIII, 347-51). *Letters:* "To 'John Smith'" (II, 77-79); "To Samuel Walker" (III, 192 ff.); "To Henry Brooke" (VII, 331-34.). *Journal:* "Sun. 8 March 1747" (III, 284-85); "Sun. 31 April 1771" (V, 404-6).

THE MINISTRY—*Sermons:* "A Caution Against Bigotry," III (S, II, 117-23); "On

Obedience to Pastors" (J, VII, 108 ff.); "On Attending the Church Service" (J, VII, 174 ff.); "The Ministerial Office" (J, VII, 273 ff.). *Works:* "A Farther Appeal to Men of Reason and Religion," VI, 1; III, 3 (VIII, 111-20; 214-39); "Thoughts Concerning Gospel Ministers," 1-5 (X, 455-56); "An Address to the Clergy" (X, 480 ff.). *Letters:* "To George L. Fleury" (V, 249-50); "To Dr. Rutherforth" (V, 359 ff.). *Journal:* "Tues. 5 June 1739" (II, 211-12); "Fri. 27 Dec. 1745" (III, 229-31). *Notes:* "Ephesians 4:11-12."

SACRAMENT OF THE LORD'S SUPPER—*Sermons:* "The Means of Grace," III, 11-12 (S, I, 251-53); "The Duty of Constant Communion" (J, VII, 147 ff.). *Letters:* "To his Mother" (I, 118). *Journal:* "Thur. 20 Sept. 1739" (II, 279-80); "Wed. 7 Nov. 1739" (II, 314-15). *Notes:* "Mark 14:24, 25."

SACRAMENT OF BAPTISM—*Sermons:* "The New Birth," IV (S, II, 237 ff.). *Works:* "Popery Calmly Considered," IV (X, 149-58); "A Treatise on Baptism" (X, 188 ff.). *Notes:* "Colossians 2:12."

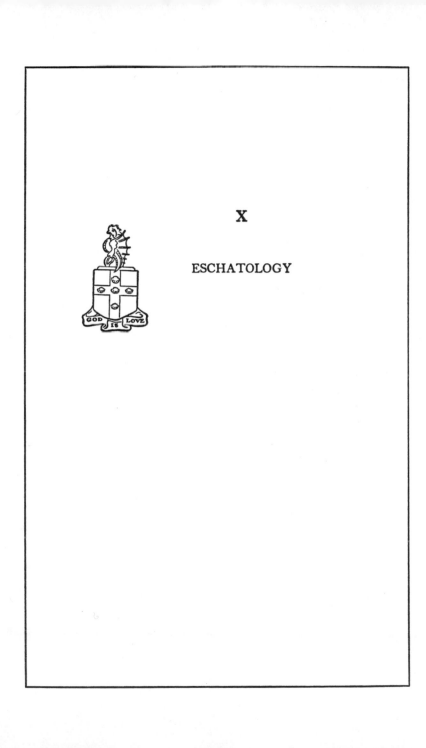

X

ESCHATOLOGY

X. ESCHATOLOGY

THE DOCTRINE of salvation has as its ultimate end the preparation of man for life with God. The faith and hope of the Christian life finally merge in perfect, God-given love—the goal of human life. The pure in heart shall see God; to the fulfillment of this redemptive purpose Wesley believes the whole pattern of salvation is oriented. The religious atmosphere of the time, for the most part, upheld belief in eternal life. Wesley never doubts its certainty and his writings reveal it as a constant theme. Because he sees God's judgment as an intrinsic, inescapable part of life after death, human existence has for Wesley an ever-present eternal dimension. There is an apocalyptic strain in his preaching, though it is not of primary concern. The same is true for his writings on the general resurrection. His work is singularly free from an attempt to win men to the Kingdom by inciting fear of the wrath to come. Since in Wesley's view the natural world and its creatures share in the effects of Adam's sin, they too will be redeemed on the last day, in which God's love for all his creation will be triumphant.

1. Human Destiny

For what end is life bestowed upon the children of men? Why were we sent into the world? For one sole end, and for no other, to prepare for eternity. For this alone we live. For this, and no other purpose, is our life either given or continued. It pleased the allwise God, at the season which he saw best, to arise in the greatness of his strength, and create the heavens and the earth, and all things that are therein. Having prepared all things for him, He "created man in his own image, after his own likeness." And what was the end of his creation? It was one, and no other—that he might know, and love, and enjoy, and serve his great Creator to all eternity. . . .

Remember! You were born for nothing else. You live for nothing else. Your life is continued to you upon earth, for no other purpose than this, that you may know, love, and serve God on earth, and enjoy him to all eternity. Consider! You were not created to please your senses, to gratify your imagination, to gain money, or the praise of men; to seek happiness in any created good, in anything under the sun. All this is "walking in a vain shadow"; it is leading a restless, miserable life, in order to a miserable eternity. On the contrary, you were created for this, and for no other purpose, by seeking and finding happiness in God on earth, to secure the glory of God in heaven. Therefore, let your heart continually say, "This one thing I do,"—having one thing in view, remembering why I was born, and why I am continued in life,—"I press on to the mark." I aim at the one end of my being, God; even at "God in Christ reconciling the world to himself." He shall be my God for ever and ever, and my guide even unto death!

Sermons: "What is Man?" 13, 15 (J, VII, 229-30).

JW

The one perfect Good shall be your one ultimate end. One thing shall ye desire for its own sake,—the fruition of Him that is All in all. One happiness shall ye propose to your souls, even an union with Him that made them; the having "fellowship with the Father and the Son"; the being joined to the Lord in one Spirit. One design you are to pursue to the end of time,—the enjoyment of God in time and in eternity. Desire other things, so far as they tend to this. Love the creature, as it leads to the Creator. But in every step you take, be this the glorious point that terminates your view. Let every affection, and thought, and word, and work, be subordinate to this. Whatever ye desire or fear, whatever ye seek or shun, whatever ye think, speak or do, be it in order to your happiness in God, the sole End, as well as Source, of your being.

Sermons: "The Circumcision of the Heart," I, 12 (S, I, 273-74).

How truly wise is [the Christian]! He knows himself: an everlasting spirit, which came forth from God, and was sent down into an house of clay, not to do his own will, but the will of Him that sent him. He knows the world: the place in which he is to pass a few days or years, not as an inhabitant, but as a stranger and sojourner, in his way to the everlasting habitations; and accordingly he uses the world as not abusing it, and as knowing the fashion of it passes away. He knows God: his Father and his Friend, the parent of all good, the centre of the spirits of all flesh, the sole happiness of all intelligent beings. He sees, clearer than the light of the noon-day sun, that this is the end of man, to glorify Him who made him for Himself, and to love and enjoy Him for ever. And with equal clearness he sees the means to that end, to the enjoyment of God in glory; even now to know, to love, to imitate God, and to believe in Jesus Christ whom He hath sent.

Sermons: "Upon Our Lord's Sermon on the Mount: XIII," II, 2 (S, II, 29-30).

J2W

Being persuaded—The grounds of which persuasion are set down in the following verse, *that he who hath begun a good work in you, will perfect it until the day of Christ*—That he who having justified, hath begun to sanctify you, will carry on this work till it issue in glory.

Notes: "Philippians 1:6."

J2W

Does not that expression, "The righteousness of the saints," point out what is the "wedding garment" in the parable? It is the "holiness without which no man shall see the Lord." The righteousness of Christ is doubtless necessary for any soul that enters into glory: But so is personal holiness too, for every child of man. But it is highly needful to be observed, that they are necessary in different respects. The former is necessary to *entitle* us to heaven; the latter, to *qualify* us for it. Without the righteousness of Christ we could have no *claim* to glory; without holiness we could have no *fitness* for it. By the former we become members of Christ, children of God, and heirs of the kingdom of heaven. By the latter "we are made meet to be partakers of inheritance of the saints in light."

Sermons: "On the Wedding Garment," 10 (J, VII, 314).

2. *Eternal Life*

"Without holiness no man shall see the Lord," shall see the face of God in glory. Nothing under heaven can be more sure than this; "for the mouth of the Lord hath spoken it. And though heaven and earth pass away, yet his word shall not pass away." As well therefore might God fall from heaven, as his word fall to the ground. No, it cannot be; none shall live with God, but he that now lives to God; none shall enjoy the glory of God in heaven, but he that bears the image of God on earth; none that is not saved from sin here can be saved from hell hereafter; none can see the kingdom of God above, unless the kingdom of God be in him below. Whosoever will reign with Christ in heaven, must have Christ reigning in him on earth. He must have "that mind in him which was in Christ," enabling him "to walk as Christ also walked."

Works: "A Blow at the Root; or Christ Stabbed in the House of His Friends," 1 (X, 364).

JW

When the Son of Man shall come in His glory and assign every man his own reward, that reward will undoubtedly be proportioned (1) to our inward holiness, our likeness to God; (2) to our works; and (3) to our sufferings. Therefore whatever you suffer in time you will be an unspeakable gainer in eternity. Many of your sufferings, perhaps the greatest part, are now past. But your joy is to come! Look up, my dear friend, look up! and see your crown before you! A little longer, and you shall drink of the rivers of pleasure that flow at God's right hand for evermore.

Letters: "To Ann Bolton" (VIII, 251).

JW

"He that hath the Son hath life,"—the eternal life here spoken of,—"and he that hath not the Son" of God "hath not" this "life." As if he had said, "This is the sum of the testimony which God hath testified of his Son, that God hath given us, not only a title to, but the real beginning of, eternal life: And this life is purchased by, and treasured up in his Son; who has all the springs and the fulness of it in himself, to communicate to his body, the Church.

This eternal life then commences, when it pleases the Father to reveal his Son in our hearts; when we first know Christ, being enabled to "call him Lord by the Holy Ghost"; when we can testify, our conscience bearing us witness in the Holy Ghost, "The life which I now live, I live by faith in the Son of God, who loved me, and gave himself for me." And then it is that happiness begins; happiness real, solid, substantial. Then it is that heaven is opened in the soul, that the proper, heavenly state commences, while the love of God, as loving us, is shed abroad in the heart, instantly producing love to all mankind; general, pure benevolence, together with its genuine fruits, lowliness, meekness, patience, contentedness in every state; an entire, clear, full acquiescence in the whole will of God; enabling us to "rejoice evermore, and in every thing to give thanks."

As our knowledge and our love of him increase, by the same degrees, and in the same proportion, the kingdom of an inward heaven must necessarily increase also; while we "grow up in all things into Him who is our Head." And when we are ἐν αὐτῷ πεπληρωμένοι, *complete in him,* as our translators render it; but more properly when we are *filled with him;* when "Christ in us, the hope of glory," is our God and our All; when he has taken the full possession of our heart; when he reigns therein without a rival, the Lord of every motion there; when we dwell in Christ, and Christ in us, we are one with Christ, and Christ with us; then we are completely happy; then we live "all the life that is hid with Christ in God"; then, and not till then, we properly experience what that word meaneth, "God is love; and whosoever dwelleth in love, dwelleth in God, and God in him."

Sermons: "Spiritual Worship," II, 4-6 (J, VI, 430-31).

JW

God hath joined from the beginning, pardon, holiness, heaven. And why should man put them asunder? O beware of this! Let not one link of the golden chain be broken. "God for Christ's sake hath forgiven me. He is now renewing me in His own image. Shortly He will make me meet for Himself, and take me to stand before His face. I, whom He hath justified through the blood of His Son, being thoroughly sanctified by His Spirit, shall quickly ascend to the 'New Jerusalem, the city of the living God.' Yet a little while and I shall 'come to the general assembly and church of the first-born, and to God the Judge of all, and to Jesus the Mediator of the new covenant.' How soon will these shadows flee away, and the day of eternity dawn upon me! How soon shall I drink of 'the river of the water of life, going out of the throne of God and of the Lamb! There all His servants shall praise Him, and shall see His face, and His name shall be upon their foreheads. And no night shall be there; and they have no need of a candle, or the light of the sun. For the Lord God enlighteneth them, and they shall reign for ever and ever.' "

Sermons: "Satan's Devices," II, 4 (S, II, 202-7).

JW

My Dear Brother,—St. Paul teaches that it is in heaven we are to be joined with "the spirits of just men made perfect," in such a sense as we cannot be on earth or even in paradise. In paradise the souls of good men rest from their labours and are with Christ from death to the resurrection. This bears no resemblance at all to the Popish purgatory, wherein wicked men are supposed to be tormented in purging fire till they are sufficiently purified to have a place in heaven. But we believe (as did the ancient Church) that none suffer after death but those who suffer eternally. We believe that we are to be *here* saved from sin and enabled to love God with all our heart.

Letters: "To George Blackall" (VII, 168).

The body that we shall have at the resurrection, shall be immortal and incorruptible: "For this corruptible must put on incorruption, and this mortal must put on immortality." Now these words, *immortal* and *incorruptible,* not only signify, that we shall die no more, (for in that sense the damned are immortal and incorruptible,) but that we shall be perfectly free from all the bodily evils which sin brought into the world; that our bodies shall not be subject to sickness, or pain, or any other inconveniences we are daily exposed to. This the Scripture calls "the redemption of our bodies,"—the freeing them from all their maladies. Were we to receive them again, subject to all their frailties and miseries which we are forced to wrestle with, I much doubt whether a wise man, were he left to his choice, would willingly take his again;— whether he would not choose to let his still lie rotting in the grave, rather than to be again chained to such a cumbersome clod of earth. Such a resurrection would be, as a wise Heathen calls it, "A resurrection to another sleep." It would look more like a redemption to death again, than a resurrection to life. . . .

Our bodies shall be raised in glory. "Then shall the righteous shine as the sun in the kingdom of their Father." A resemblance of this we have in the lustre of Moses's face, when he had conversed with God on the mount.

Sermons: "On the Resurrection of the Dead," II, 1-2 (J, VII, 479-80, 481).

3. Last Things

Surely ye are without excuse, all who do not yet know the day of your visitation! the day wherein the great God, who hath been forgotten among us days without number, is arising at once to be avenged of his adversaries, and to visit and redeem his people. Are not his judgments and mercies both abroad? and still will ye not learn righteousness? Is not the Lord passing by? Doth not a great and strong wind already begin "to rend the mountains and to break in pieces the rocks before the Lord?" Is not the earthquake also felt already? and a fire hath begun to burn in his anger. Who knoweth what will be the end thereof? But at the same time, he is speaking to many in "a still, small voice." He that hath ears to hear, let him hear, lest he be suddenly destroyed, and that without remedy!

What excuse can possibly be made for those who are regardless of such a season as this? who are, at such a crisis, stupid, senseless, unapprehensive? caring for none of these things; who do not give themselves the pains to think about them, but are still easy and unconcerned? What! can there ever be a point on which it more behoves you to think; and that with the coolest and deepest attention? As long as the heaven and earth remain, can there be anything of so vast importance, as God's last call to a guilty land, just perishing in its iniquity?

You, with those round about you, deserved long ago to have "drank the dregs of the cup of trembling"; yea, to have been "punished with everlasting destruction, from the presence of the Lord, and from the glory of his power." But he hath not dealt with you according to your sins, neither rewarded you after your iniquities. And once more he is mixing mercy with judgment. Once more he is crying aloud, "Turn ye, turn ye from your evil ways; for why will ye die, O house of Israel?" And will you not deign to give him the hearing? If you are not careful to answer him in this matter, do not still shut your eyes, and stop your ears, and harden your stubborn heart. O beware, lest God laugh at your calamity, and mock when your fear cometh!

Works: "A Farther Appeal to Men of Reason and Religion: III," iv, 1-2 (VIII, 239-40).

JW

Preaching in the evening at Spitalfields on "Prepare to meet thy God," I largely showed the utter absurdity of the supposition that the world was to end that night. But notwithstanding all I could say, many were afraid to go to bed, and some wandered about in the fields, being persuaded that, if the world did not end, at least London would be swallowed up by an earthquake. I went to bed at my usual time, and was fast asleep about ten o'clock.

Journal: "Mon. 28 Feb. 1763" (V, 9).

JW

And let not any who live and die in their sins vainly hope to escape His vengeance. "For if God spared not the angels that sinned, but cast them down to hell, and delivered them into chains of darkness, to be reserved unto judgement; the Lord knoweth how to reserve the unjust unto the day of judgement to be punished" (2 Pet. ii. 4-9). In that day, peculiarly styled "the day of the Lord," they "that sleep in the dust of the earth shall awake; some to everlasting life, and some to everlasting shame and contempt" (Dan. xii. 2). Among the latter will all those be found who are now by their obstinate impenitence "treasuring up to themselves wrath against the day of wrath and revelation of the righteous judgement of God; who will" then render "indignation and wrath, tribulation and anguish, upon every soul of man that doeth evil" (Rom. ii. 5, 8-9). He hath declared the very sentence which He will then pronounce on all the workers of iniquity: "Depart, ye cursed, into everlasting fire, prepared for the devil and his angels" (Matt. xxv. 41). And in that hour it will be executed: being "cast into outer darkness, where is wailing and gnashing of teeth" (verse 30) they "will be punished with everlasting destruction from the presence of the Lord, and from the glory of His power" (2 Thess. i. 9). A punishment not only without end, but likewise without intermission. For when once "they are cast into that furnace of fire," that "lake of fire burning with brimstone, the worm," gnawing their soul, "dieth not, and the fire," tormenting their body, "is not quenched." So that "they have no rest day or night; but the smoke of their torment ascendeth up for ever and ever."

Letters: "To William Law" (III, 369-70).

It now remains, that, being no longer stewards, we give an account of our stewardship. Some have imagined, this is to be done immediately after death, as soon as we enter into the world of spirits. Nay, the Church of Rome does absolutely assert this; yea, makes it an article of faith. And thus much we may allow, the moment a soul drops the body, and stands naked before God, it cannot but know what its portion will be to all eternity. It will have full in its view, either everlasting joy, or everlasting torment; as it is no longer possible for us to be deceived in the judgement which we pass upon ourselves. But the Scripture gives us no reason to believe, that God will then sit in judgement upon us. There is no passage in all the oracles of God which affirms any such thing. That which has been frequently alleged for this purpose seems rather to prove the contrary; namely (Heb. ix. 27), "It is appointed for men once to die, and after this the judgement": for, in all reason, the word "once" is here to be applied to judgement as well as death. So that the fair inference to be drawn from this very text is, not that there are two judgements, a particular and a general; but that we are to be judged, as well as to die, once only: not once immediately after death, and again after the general resurrection; but then only "when the Son of man shall come in His glory, and all His holy angels with Him." The imagination therefore of one judgement at death, and another at the end of the world, can have no place with those who make the written Word of God the whole and sole standard of their faith.

Sermons: "The Good Steward," III, 1 (S, II, 473-74).

JW

The most glorious of all will be the change which then will take place on the poor, sinful, miserable children of men. These had fallen in many respects, as from a greater height, so into a lower depth, than any other part of the creation. But they shall "hear a great voice out of heaven, saying, Behold the tabernacle of God is with men: And he will dwell with them; and they shall be his people; and God himself shall be their God." (Rev. xxi. 3, 4.) Hence will arise an unmixed state of holiness and happiness, far superior to that which Adam enjoyed in Paradise. In how beautiful a manner is this described by the Apostle: "God shall wipe away all tears from their eyes; and there shall be no more death, neither sorrow nor crying: neither shall there be any more pain; for the former things are done away." As there will be no more death, and no more pain or sickness preparatory thereto; as there will be no more grieving for, or parting with, friends; so there will be no more sorrow or crying. Nay, but there will be a greater deliverance than all this; for there will be no more sin. And, to crown all, there will be a deep, an intimate, an uninterrupted union with God; a constant communion with the Father and his Son Jesus Christ, through the Spirit; a continual enjoyment of the Three-One God, and of all the creatures in him!

Sermons: "The New Creation," 18 (J, VI, 295-96).

JW

But will "the creature," will even the brute creation, always remain in this deplorable condition? God forbid that we should affirm this; yea, or even entertain such a thought! While "the whole creation groaneth together," (whether men attend or not) their groans are not dispersed in idle air, but enter into the ears of Him that made them. While his creatures "travail together in pain," he knoweth all their pain, and is bringing them nearer and nearer to the birth, which shall be accomplished in its season. He seeth "the earnest expectation" wherewith the whole animated creation "waiteth for" that final "manifestation of the sons of God"; in which "they themselves also shall be delivered" (not by annihilation; annihilation is not deliverance) "from the" present "bondage of corruption, into" a measure of "the glorious liberty of the children of God."

Sermons: "The General Deliverance," III, 1 (J, VI, 248).

JW

The person by whom God will judge the world, is His only-begotten Son, whose "goings forth are from everlasting"; "who is God over all, blessed for ever." Unto Him, being "the outbeaming of His Father's glory, the express image of His person" (Heb. i. 3), the Father "hath committed all judgement, because He is the Son of Man" (John v. 22, 27); because, though He was "in the form of God, and thought it not robbery to be equal with God, yet He emptied Himself, taking upon Him the form of a servant, being made in the likeness of men" (Phil. ii, 6, 7); yea, because, "being found in fashion as a man, He humbled Himself" yet farther, "becoming obedient unto death, even the death of the cross. Wherefore God hath highly exalted Him," even in His human nature, and "ordained Him," as Man, to try the children of men, "to be the Judge both of the quick and the dead"; both of those who shall be found alive at His coming, and of those who were before gathered to their fathers.

The time, termed by the prophet, "the great and the terrible day," is usually, in Scripture, styled *the day of the Lord.* The space from the creation of man upon the earth, to the end of all things, is *the day of the sons of men;* the time that is now passing over us is properly *our day;* when this is ended, *the day of the Lord* will begin. But who can say how long it will continue? "With the Lord one day is as a thousand years, and a thousand years as one day" (2 Pet. iii. 8). And from this very expression, some of the ancient father's drew that inference, that, what is commonly called the day of judgement would be indeed a thousand years: and it seems they did not go beyond the truth; nay, probably they did not come up to it. For, if we consider the number of persons who are to be judged, and of actions which are to be inquired into, it does not appear that a thousand years will suffice for the transactions of that day; so that it may not improbably comprise several thousand years. But God shall reveal this also in its season. . . .

The persons to be judged, who can count, any more than the drops of rain, or the sands of the sea? "I beheld," saith St. John, "a great multitude which no man can number, clothed with white robes, and palms in their hands." How immense then must be the total multitude of all nations, and kindreds, and people, and tongues; of all that have sprung from the loins of Adam, since the world began, till time shall be no more! . . .

And in that day shall be discovered every inward working of every

286

human soul; every appetite, passion, inclination, affection, with the various combinations of them, with every temper and disposition that constitute the whole complex character of each individual. So shall it be clearly and infallibly seen, who was righteous, and who unrighteous; and in what degree every action, or person, or character was either good or evil. . . .

We may . . . consider a few of the circumstances which will follow the general judgement. And the first is the execution of the sentence pronounced on the evil and on the good: "These shall go away into eternal punishment, and the righteous into life eternal." It should be observed, it is the very same word which is used, both in the former and the latter clause. It follows, that either the punishment lasts for ever, or the reward too will come to an end:—no, never, unless God could come to an end, or His mercy and truth could fail. "Then shall the righteous shine forth as the sun in the kingdom of their Father," "and shall drink of those rivers of pleasure which are at God's right hand for evermore." But here all description falls short; all human language fails! Only one who is caught up into the third heaven can have a just conception of it. But even such a one cannot express what he hath seen: these things it is not possible for man to utter.

The wicked, meantime, shall be turned into hell, even all the people that forget God. They will be "punished with everlasting destruction from the presence of the Lord, and from the glory of His power." They will be "cast into the lake of fire burning with brimstone," originally "prepared for the devil and his angels"; where they will gnaw their tongues for anguish and pain; they will curse God and look upward. There the dogs of hell—pride, malice, revenge, rage, horror, despair—continually devour them. There "they have no rest, day or night, but the smoke of their torment ascendeth for ever and ever!" For "their worm dieth not, and the fire is not quenched."

Then the heavens will be shrivelled up as a parchment scroll, and pass away with a great noise: they will "flee from the face of Him that sitteth on the throne, and there will be found no place for them" (Rev. xx. 11). The very manner of their passing away is disclosed to us by the Apostle Peter: "In the day of God, the heavens, being on fire, shall be dissolved" (2 Pet. iii. 12). The whole beautiful fabric will be overthrown by that raging element, the connexion of all its parts destroyed, and every atom torn asunder from the others. By the same, "the earth also, and the works that are therein, shall be burned up" (verse 10). The enormous works of nature, the everlasting hills, mountains that have defied the rage of time, and stood unmoved so many thousand years, will sink down in fiery ruin. How much less will the works of art, though of the most durable kind, the utmost efforts of human industry—tombs, pillars, triumphal arches, castles, pyramids—be able to withstand the flaming conqueror! All, all will die, perish, vanish away, like a dream when one awaketh! . . .

There is one circumstance more which will follow the judgement, that deserves our serious consideration: "We look," says the Apostle, "according to His promise, for new heavens and a new earth, wherein dwelleth righteousness" (2 Pet. iii. 13). The promise stands in the prophecy of Isaiah: "Behold, I create new heavens and a new earth: and the former shall not be remembered" (Isa. lxv. 17), so great shall the glory of the latter be! These St. John did behold in the visions of God. "I saw," saith he, "a new heaven and a new earth; for the first heaven and the first earth were passed away" (Rev. xxi. 1). And only righteousness dwelt therein: accordingly, he adds, "And I heard a great voice from" the third "heaven, saying, Behold, the tabernacle of God is with men, and He will dwell with them, and they shall be His people, and God Himself shall be with them, and be their God" (xxi. 3). Of necessity, therefore, they will all be happy: "God shall wipe away all tears from their eyes; and there shall be no more death, neither sorrow, nor crying, neither shall there be any more pain" (xxi. 4). "There shall be no more curse; but they shall see His face" (xii. 3, 4),—shall have the nearest access to, and thence the highest, resemblance of, Him. This is the strongest expression in the language of Scripture, to denote the most perfect happiness. "And His name shall be on their foreheads"; they shall be openly acknowledged as God's own property, and His glorious nature shall most visibly shine forth in them. "And there shall be no night there; and they need no candle, neither light of the sun; for the Lord God giveth them light: and they shall reign for ever and ever."

Sermons: "The Great Assize," II, 1-2, 4, 7, III, 1-2, 5 (S, II, 405-9, 411-13, 415).

LAST THINGS

O HAPPY soul, thy work is done,
Thy fight is fought, thy course is run,
   And thou art now at rest:
Thou here wast perfected in love,
Thou now art join'd to those above,
   And number'd with the blest.

Thy sun no more goes down by night,
Thy moon no more withdraws its light;
   Those blessed mansions shine
Bright with an Uncreated Flame,
Full of the glories of the Lamb,
   The' eternal light Divine.

Our state if parted spirits know,
Thou pitiest now thy friends below
   In this dark vale of tears,
Who still beneath our burden groan
Or, grieved with sorrows not our own,
   Are living out our years.

Secure of the celestial prize,
Thou waitest now in paradise
   Till we are all convey'd
By angels to our endless rest,
Of thine and Jesu's joy possest,
   In Jesu's bosom laid.

Poetics: "After the Death of a Friend" (III, 156-57).

SUPPLEMENTARY REFERENCES

HUMAN DESTINY—*Sermons:* "Preface to the Sermons" (S, I, 29-34); "Upon Our Lord's Sermon on the Mount: XI," III, 6 (S, I, 542); "Catholic Spirit," I, 15-18 (S, II,

137-39); "The Good Steward" (S, II, 463 ff.); "What Is Man?" (J, VII, 225 ff.). *Works:* "An Earnest Appeal to Men of Reason and Religion" (VIII, 19); "Minutes of Some Late Conversations" (VIII, 289.). *Letters:* "To Sir James Lowther" (III, 120-22); "To Elizabeth Hardy" (IV, 10). *Journal:* "Wed. 25 Oct. 1752" (IV, 46); "Sun. 8 Aug. 1773" (V, 522). *Notes:* "John 8:12."

ETERNAL LIFE—*Sermons:* "The New Creation" (J, VI, 288 ff.); "The Rich Man and Lazarus," I (J, VII, 245-49); "On Faith" (J, VII, 326 ff.). *Journal:* "Thur. 22 April 1779" (VI, 230-31). *Notes:* "John 3:36."

LAST THINGS—*Sermons:* "Of Hell" (J, VI, 381 ff.); "The Important Question" II (J, VI, 495-98); "The Reward of the Righteous," Intro. (J, VII, 127-29). *Works:* "A Farther Appeal to Men of Reason and Religion" (VIII, 194-95). *Journal:* To the Reader, "Sat. 31 Jan. 1767" (V, 195); "Sat. 18 Aug. 1770" (V, 381). *Notes:* "Matthew 10:33 f; 25:30"; "Romans 2:10-12"; "I Corinthians 15:24."

BIBLIOGRAPHY

Wesley's Writings

Curnock, Nehemiah, ed. *The Journal of the Rev. John Wesley, A.M.; Enlarged from Original Mss., with Notes from Unpublished Diaries, Annotations, Maps, and Illustrations.* 8 vols.; London: The Epworth Press, 1909-16. The definitive edition of the *Journal* which contains a valuable sermon register and index.

Explanatory Notes upon the New Testament. London: William Bowyer, 1818. All editions are substantially the same. It contains Wesley's own translation of the New Testament, along with significant notes on the historical and spiritual meaning of books and passages. Wesley abridges and alters several commentaries but uses as his chief guide Bengel's *Gnomon Novi Testamenti.* With the *Standard Sermons* the *Notes* form the doctrinal guide set up by Wesley for the societies.

Jackson, Thomas, ed. *The Works of the Rev. John Wesley, A.M.; with the Last Corrections of the Author.* 3rd ed., 14 vols.; London: Wesleyan-Methodist Book-Room, 1829-31. This is the generally accepted edition of Wesley's works. Vols. I-IV contain the journal; V-VII the standards and the other collected sermons totaling 141. The first series of fifty-three sermons includes the standards and nine disputed as standards; the second series of fifty-five discourses appeared in 1788; the third, eighteen discourses, first appeared, like series two, in the *Arminian Magazine* but, unlike these earlier sermons, was not revised by Wesley for further publication. The fourth series consists of seven discourses published separately. The fifth series consists of eight sermons, the last seven of which antedate the conversion experience of 1738. Vol. VIII contains essays about Methodists and a few letters; IX, some letters and "The Doctrine of Original Sin"; X, essays on Catholicism, on Necessity; XI, essays, thoughts, and observations; XII, letters; XIII, letters, essays, and thoughts; XIV, letters, prefaces to various works, digested class texts, and an index.

Poetical Works of John and Charles Wesley, The. Collected and arranged by G. Osborn, 13 vols.; London: Wesleyan-Methodist Conference Office, 1868-72. Vols. I-IV, VI; and VIII contain both John and Charles's works. Vols. V and VII are Charles's as well as all the material in the last five, IX-XIII, which are entitled "Short Hymns on Select Passages of Holy Scriptures." Some of the introductions to various collections within the volumes are valuable.

Sugden, Edward H., ed. *Wesley's Standard Sermons.* 2 vols.; London: Epworth Press, 1921. This set contains the forty-four discourses selected by Wesley as doctrinal norms and nine additional sermons of the edition of 1771. Each sermon is introduced by historical and biographical material with some doctrinal development. Sermon III was written by Charles Wesley. For a history of the dispute over the inclusion of the additional nine sermons see Sugden's introduction and Vol. II (pp. 331-40).

Survey of the Wisdom of God in the Creation, A: or A Compendium of Natural Philosophy. Revised and enlarged with notes by B. Mayo. 3rd American ed., 2 vols.; New York: N. Bangs and T. Mason, 1823. The general outline and content of the work follows another author, Charles Bonnet of Geneva. It treats man and the natural world and has an appendix on human understanding. In introductions, transitions, and conclusions to the various parts Wesley's hand is discernible.

Telford, John, ed. *The Letters of the Rev. John Wesley, A.M.* 8 vols.; London: The Epworth Press, 1931. The standard edition of the letters, fully documented with entries placed in historical context. It contains many letters brought to light after Jackson and other early editions were published.

Wesleyana: A Complete System of Wesleyan Theology. New York: Lane and Scott, 1850. There is also an earlier English edition. It is a compend venture of the first quarter of the nineteenth century. Its representative value is decreased by its nearly exclusive quotation of sermonic material.

291

BIBLIOGRAPHY
Writings on Wesley's Theology

Anderson, William K., ed. *Methodism.* Nashville: The Methodist Publishing House, 1947. See especially Part II, articles by Ferré, Cushman, Rall, and Lee.

Bready, J. Wesley. *England: Before and After Wesley, the Evangelical Revival and Social Reform.* New York: Harper & Brothers, 1938. Careful treatment of the social and ethical implications of the Wesleyan theology and religious movement.

Cannon, William R. *The Theology of John Wesley, with Special Reference to the Doctrine of Justification.* New York and Nashville: Abingdon-Cokesbury Press, 1946. Fully documented study of justification and related doctrines; valuable bibliography.

Carter, Henry. *The Methodist Heritage.* New York and Nashville: Abingdon-Cokesbury Press, 1951. Perhaps the best single volume for a general picture of the Wesleyan theological heritage.

Cell, George C. *The Rediscovery of John Wesley.* New York: Henry Holt & Co., 1935. Pioneer work in the modern movement reappraising the value of Wesley's thought.

Faulkner, John A. *Wesley as Sociologist, Theologian, Churchman.* New York: The Methodist Book Concern, 1918. Brief, but suggestive, treatment.

Flew, R. Newton. *The Idea of Perfection in Christian Theology.* London: Oxford University Press, 1934. Important for general theme and chapter on Wesley.

Frost, Stanley B. *Die Autoritätslehre in den Werken John Wesleys.* München: Ernest Reinhardt, 1938. Considers the Bible, experience, and the church as authoritative in Wesley's thought.

Green, J. Brazier. *John Wesley and William Law.* London: The Epworth Press, 1945. Rewarding study of the influence of Law on Wesley and the differences between the two, particularly with reference to mysticism.

Green, Richard. *The Works of John and Charles Wesley.* London: C. H. Kelley, 1896. A bibliography containing an exact account of all the publications issued by the brothers Wesley arranged in chronological order, with a list of the early editions and descriptive and illustrative notes.

Lee, Umphrey. *John Wesley and Modern Religion.* Nashville: Cokesbury Press, 1936. Contributes to understanding of the relation of various aspects of Wesley's thought to present religious thinking.

Lerch, David. *Heil und Heiligung bei John Wesley, dargestellt unter besonderer Berücksichtigung seiner Anmerkungen sum Neuen Testament.* Zürich: Gedruckt bei der Christlichen Vereinsbuchhandlung, 1941. Helpful as an interpretation of the *Notes* and for its treatment of the subject under the heads of natural man, man under the law, and man under grace.

Lindström, Harald. *Wesley and Sanctification, a Study in the Doctrine of Salvation.* Stockholm: Nya Bokförlags Aktiebolaget, 1946. Together with Cannon's book this constitutes a complete treatment of theological doctrines. The chapter on love is significant; extensive bibliography with some foreign titles.

MacArthur, Kathleen W. *The Economic Ethics of John Wesley.* New York: The Abingdon Press, 1936. Well-documented treatment of some of Wesley's ethical interests.

McConnell, Francis J. *John Wesley.* New York and Nashville: Abingdon-Cokesbury Press, 1939. Contains a detailed chapter on Wesley's social ethics.

Nagler, Arthur W. *Pietism and Methodism.* Nashville: Smith and Lamar, 1918. Indicates the significance of German Pietism in the origin and early development of Methodism. Some consideration of mysticism; extensive bibliography.

Piette, Maximin. *John Wesley in the Evolution of Protestantism.* Trans. J. B. Howard; New York: Sheed & Ward, 1937. Written in French by a Catholic priest, appreciative of Wesley. It has stimulated some of the later work done by Protestant scholars.

Rattenbury, J. Ernest. *Wesley's Legacy to the World.* Nashville: Cokesbury Press, 1928. Some attention to the theology of Wesley.

Scott, Percy. *John Wesleys Lehre von der Heiligung verglichen mit einem lutherisch-pietistischen Beispiel.* Berlin: Alfred Töpelmann, 1939. Adds to the background and understanding of sanctification; there are some valuable Wesley-Luther contrasts.

Townsend, W. J., Workman, H. B., and Eayrs, George. *A New History of Methodism.* 2 vols.; London: Hodder & Stoughton, 1909. In Vol. I see Workman's article, "The Place of Methodism in the Life and Thought of the Christian Church," for distinctive emphases.

INDEX OF SOURCES

Below are listed those selections from Wesley's writings which appear in the *Compend*. Pages given are those on which selections begin.

Standard Sermons (Sugden)

Non-Standard Sermons (Jackson)

INDEX OF SOURCES

Works

Letters

Journal

INDEX OF SOURCES

Notes

Poetics

A Compendium of Natural Philosophy

INDEX OF SUBJECTS

INDEX OF SUBJECTS